Nature Walks in
Southern Florida

Nature Walks in Southern Florida

Alan McPherson

HUNTER
PUBLISHING, INC

Hunter Publishing, Inc.
300 Raritan Center Parkway
Edison NJ 08818
(908) 225 1900 Fax (908) 417 0482

ISBN 1-55650-604-X

© 1994 Hunter Publishing, Inc.

Cover photograph: *In the Everglades* (Eric Carle/Superstock)

Maps by Joyce Huber, PhotoGraphics

Contents

Discovering Southern Florida

Southern Florida's nature experiences are unique. Although many lament the destruction of the original landscape, residents and visitors are still fortunate in having an abundance and diversity of natural beauty to observe and enjoy. Despite the ongoing urbanization, industrialization, and agricultural development, any south Floridian will discover within a day's drive, isolated white sand beaches and dunes, wind-swept pine forests, wildlife, rich fresh and saltwater marshes, lakes and estuaries, vast and open wet and dry prairies, primitive rivers, towering bald cypress forests, verdant mangrove-lined shorelines, tropical and subtropical hammocks, seemingly endless Everglades, and remote keys or islands. To fully appreciate the special spirit of each place, you must head out on foot.

The main purpose of this book is to guide families, weekend naturalists, intrepid travellers and all lovers of the outdoors to a variety of these natural areas that are publicly accessible in southern Florida. Experiences described here range from a leisurely day outing at a nearby beach or botanic garden to an extended overnight in a wilderness area. Private groups, individuals, and public agencies have established a remarkable variety of parklands and institutions concerned with the natural areas of southern Florida. Exploring them on foot, you will discover the uniqueness of subtropical Florida.

Late fall to early spring is the most pleasant time of year for exploring southern Florida outdoors. Rainfall is scant, insects are at a low ebb, and the days are usually sunny and comfortable, though in some years it may be wet and cold.

The Florida peninsula is surrounded by the waters of the Atlantic Ocean, Florida Bay and the Gulf of Mexico. These large bodies of water provide a relatively cool summer and a moderate winter. Florida is located in the desert belt latitude of the world, but the offshore waters supply an abundant 53 inches of rainfall annually. The wettest months are from May to October. Hurricanes occur during late summer and fall.

Geologically, the Florida peninsula is young, having only in recent times risen above the receding seas. Today, the low flat terrain and the high amounts of rainfall combine to form a swampy or marshy landscape in some areas.

The majority of walks in this guide are short. A pleasant part of walking in southern Florida on day hikes is that little equipment is necessary. Of course, overnight trips require more supplies. Comfortable tennis shoes are adequate for most walks. Be prepared for getting your feet wet even in winter. It is a good idea to bring along an extra pair of cotton socks and even extra tennis shoes. To help ward off insects, as well as the hot sun or cool temperatures, bring long sleeve cotton shirts and pants. As a general rule, in all temperatures and conditions, layers of clothing are most practical. Although the angle of the winter sun is less intense than in summer, bring sunscreen, sunglasses and a hat for skin protection.

A day pack can carry your high energy food, water and other personal provisions, though you may find a flashlight, compass, or binoculars make the trip safer and more comfortable. Always be prepared for rain and seek low-lying areas during thunderstorms. Insects may be a problem even during winter. Chiggers, no-see-ums, ticks, sand fleas, fire ants, and especially mosquitoes can be troublesome. Be sure to bring insect repellent. Do watch for and avoid poison ivy and poison sumac. The manchineel and poison-wood are particularly common in the Everglades National Park and Florida Keys.

Poisonous reptiles of southern Florida include the coral snake, cottonmouth, pygmy and diamondback rattlesnakes. As a rule, snakes are shy, and will normally avoid any encounter with humans. More deaths have occurred from venomous insects than poisonous snakes during the last 25 years in Florida. Always allow plenty of room for alligators and wild feral pigs. You will probably never see a saltwater crocodile since they inhabit a small area of northeast Florida Bay in Everglades National Park. Learn to identify the variety of flora and fauna of the region, which will add greatly to the pleasure of your walks. Topographical maps are available from camping supply stores and the U.S. Geological Survey in Arlington, Virginia. Campgrounds are found throughout southern Florida and are administered by the various levels of government and private commercial parties.The author has personally visited every site. To ensure accuracy, all the following nature walks have been checked by the administering agency or property managers. Each write-up includes a capsule summary that features acreage, trail distance, activities, and fees. The main focus includes a description of the walk, its unique features, and how to arrive at the destination, The majority of walks are considered easy to moderate in difficulty.

Do explore the land, with its many moods and wonders, in your moments of freedom and make it a time of self-renewal and self-discovery.

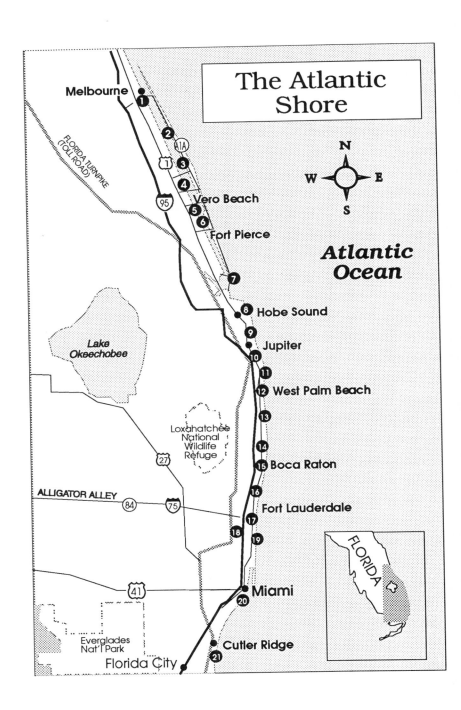

Along the Beach

"What dreams and speculative matter for thought arose as I stood on the strand, gazing out on the burnished treeless plain."

John Muir, *A Thousand Mile Walk to the Gulf*

The Atlantic Shore

The shining white beaches of southern Florida are internationally renowned and offer year-round recreation. With the exception of the mangrove-forested coast from the Florida Keys northwest to Cape Romano, all of southern Florida is fringed by white-powdered, sugar sand beaches. Millions of visitors arrive each year, primarily to enjoy the various types of beaches that range from those of the highly developed Miami Beach and Pinellas County Suncoast beaches, to the more remote "paradise" beaches such as Caspersens or Bowmans. Both beach types are described, but the main focus is on the more natural beaches of the Atlantic Ocean

1 Indiatlantic Boardwalk/Melbourne Beach/Spessard Holland Beach
2 Sebastian Inlet State Recreation Area
3 Treasure Shores/Golden Sands Beaches
4 Wabasso Beach/Sea Grape Trail/Turtle Trail
5 Vero Beach Area Beaches
6 Ft. Pierce Inlet SRA/Pepper Park/Jack Island/Bryn Mawr Beach/Avalon Beach/Round Island
7 South Hutchinson Island Beaches
8 Hobe Sound Beach & National Wildlife Refuge/St. Lucie Inlet State Park/Pecks Lake
9 Blowing Rocks Preserve
10 Dubois Park/Jupiter Beach/Carlin Park
11 Juno Beach/Loggerhead Park
12 John D. MacArthur Beach State Park
13 Atlantic Dunes Park
14 Spanish River Park
15 Gumbo Limbo Nature Center/Red Reef/South Beach
16 Hugh Taylor Birch SRA
17 Port Everglades Ocean Life Viewing Area
18 John U. Lloyd Beach SRA
19 Hollywood North Beach
20 Bill Baggs Cape Florida SRA/Crandon Park/Virginia Key Beach
21 Biscayne National Park

Royal palm

from Melbourne Beach south to Key West, and the Gulf of Mexico from Tarpon Springs to Marco Island.

The southern Florida beaches are not so dramatic and spectacular as the west Pacific coast beaches of California, Oregon, and Hawaii or as rugged as the New England shore. But the level to gently sloping shore makes for leisurely walking. Nothing is so tranquil and therapeutic as a seaside walk that stretches for miles.

Sculptured by the elements, the beaches have much broken shell mixed with silica sand. Wave action and a southward-moving, long-shore current moves the silica sand and restless waves create sandbars. The irregular Gulf coast beaches consist of the same white quartz silica sand as the Atlantic coastal beaches, but the more gentle wave action yields more unbroken shells. Due to their remoteness, a few of the barrier islands of the Gulf coast, such as Caladesi and LaCosta, have been saved from development. There are few sandy beaches south of Key Biscayne or Cape Romano. The Keys have their share of naturally developed sandy "pocket beaches" such as Bahia Honda. Sea oats, sea grape, sabal palm, Australian pine, and a myriad of coastal flora are rooted along the strand and dunes. Shore birds abound and sea creatures like the bottle-nose dolphin frolic in the surf. Numerous species of sharks also cruise the off-shore waters. An occasional manatee may be spotted surfacing for a breath of air. Sea turtles come ashore to lay their precious eggs in the warm summer sands.

For the majority of beaches, you must simply locate a point of access where parking is permitted and walk to the shore. Then you are on your own. Beachside trails, like the ones found at Blowing Rocks Preserve, MacArthur State Park, and Long Key, are rare. Public access may be limited in urban and suburban areas, but is improving with demand for such facilities. Normally the beaches are not as crowded during the weekdays, but each beach varies with season and locality.

To make the sandy trek as pleasant as possible, the beach walker should take certain precautions. Tennis shoes or other light footwear will prevent cuts and blisters. Sun screen lotion, a hat, wind breaker, and light clothing should be in your day pack to protect against sunburn and chill. Winter can be downright cold at the beach – it is always cooler near the shore. Be sure to bring insect repellent, especially in summer when the sand flies and mosquitoes are out in greater numbers.

Shorebirds

Sunglasses will come in handy to counter the intense light reflecting off the sand and sea. Always carry your own water. Take occasional breaks and sit in the shade of a palm or pine to avoid sun burn, dehydration, sun exhaustion or stroke. Humidity can be taxing in the warmer months. Do not tramp the protected sea oats and other beach vegetation. There are no truly private beaches. Shoreline rights at the high tide line give walkers the right to walk on all beaches.

People not only come to the beach to walk and explore the natural surroundings, but to engage in a wide variety of pursuits such as swimming, sunbathing, shell collecting, surf fishing, scuba diving, snorkeling, surfing, volleyball, picnicking, camping and more. Try as many activities as you can.

If you do go into the water, know how to swim. Be aware of the dangers. Shark attacks are rare, but do happen. Watch where you place your feet when wading offshore. Jellyfish and Portuguese-Man-of-War do sting. Red tide outbreaks can bring discomfort along the Gulf beaches, with sneezing, coughing, and choking.

The biggest threat to south Florida's beaches is reckless, uncontrolled real estate development. Few examples of remaining sea-

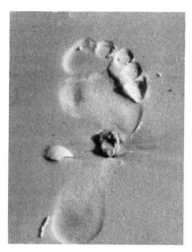

Leave only footprints

side wilderness exist today due to the zealous overexploitation by greedy developers. High rises built by the shore's edge have literally blocked out the sun. Preservation and maintainence of the beaches should be a top priority at all levels of government and enforeed by strict zoning laws. The recent adoption of construction setback lines in Florida's coastal areas will help alleviate future encroachment. But recent efforts may be too little, too late.

Those who have built by the sea's edge have discovered that beaches are not permanent, but are in a state of constant change. The "high energy" beaches are slowly and sometimes rapidly, being reclaimed by the sea. Nearly one third of all Florida's beaches are eroded and their temporary "renourishment" is expensive. The walker will see many areas where the tide now comes up to the sea walls and the former beach is no more. Groins, the short-term "beach builders," have limited application. Jetties destroy beaches by actually preventing the natural flow of sand. The rising seas, one foot per century, and man's attempts to block the shifting south-bound "river of sand," may possibly create a different future for south Florida's beaches.

The thin ribbon of white sands is a unique corridor between the watery seas and the earthy mainland. Do experience these delightful walks along the strand where rhythmic waves create sounds that heal and inspire.

Indiatlantic Boardwalk/Melbourne Beach/ Spessard Holland Beach
Indiatlantic & Melbourne/Brevard County
Beach Frontage: 2 miles total
Highlights: nature study, swimming, lifeguards, showers, picnicking, fishing, ballfields, golf course, restrooms
Fee(s): parking, golf course, group facilities rental

The developed urban beaches of the south Melbourne area are rather tame and ordinary compared to the wild primitive beaches in the north Brevard County areas of Cape Canaveral National Seashore and Merritt Island National Wildlife Refuge.

The Indiatlantic Boardwalk Municipal Park is purely city beach. The highly eroded narrow strand is bordered by hundreds of metered parking slots, fast food restaurants and a 100-yard-long boardwalk, Dune vegetation is sparse, although mass plantings of sea oats have been established.

Royal palm shore

Swimming, fishing and sunning are the main beach activities. The Indiatlantic beach draws many locals as well as visitors. It is a fine place to girl/boy or people watch. Limited parking and dune crossovers are also located at Watson Avenue in north Indiatlantic and Tampa Avenue at the south end of town. This municipal beach may be reached by driving oceanward from U.S. I in central Melbourne across the Melbourne Causeway and along AIA. When the waves are up this is an "in" surf spot.

Directly south of Indiatlantic Boardwalk, the city beach of Melbourne Beach lies along the corporate edge of the oceanside community and is somewhat less developed. Fee parking is at a premium at the crowded accesses. Access parking is located from B Street south to 6th Avenue alongside A1A. Ocean Avenue has the most parking spaces and includes a. historical marker that describes the beach town's past. Dune crossovers have been provided along the residential shores. Swimming and fishing are the main activities.

Approximately half a mile further south along AlA is the county beach known as Spessard Holland, named after the governor of Florida during World War II. Parking is plentiful and payment is due upon entering. Everything is more developed, including the dune vegetation of sea oats, sea grape, Spanish bayonet, railroad vine, and an occasional sabal palm, the Florida State Tree. Swimming, lifeguards, fishing, showers, and restrooms are available. The 1,200-foot boardwalk is handicapped-accessible and there is a first aid station. The golf course and ballfields are found across the west side of A1A. Patrick Air Force Base tracking station divides the north and south beach park on the shoreside and is slated to be removed in the future. The wooden park facility buildings blend well with the coastal surroundings but are not so inconspicuous you won't notice and drive on past.

Recent new beaches acquired from Save Our Coast funding include Coconut Point and Bonsteel, located south of Spessard Holland Park. These south Brevard County beach parks are minimally developed with parking and dune crossovers. Both beach parks are planned for inclusion in the proposed Archie Carr National Wildlife Refuge. The beaches from Melbourne south to Vero Beach are prime sea turtle nesting sites.

Sebastian Inlet State Recreation Area
Sebastian/Brevard and Indian River Counties
Beach Frontage: 3 miles
Area: 576 acres
Highlights: nature study, nature trails, swimming, surfing, showers, bathhouse, lifeguards, fishing, picnicking shelters, boat launch, visitor center, ranger programs, camping, concessions
Fee(s): entrance, visitors center, camping

One of the most popular and scenic state beach recreation areas in southern Florida, Sebastian Inlet attracts large numbers of visitors: beachcombers, surfers, fishermen, bird watchers, picnickers, campers and just plain nature lovers.

Located on North Hutchinson Island between the waters of the Atlantic Ocean and the Indian River, the barrier isle park is cut in half by the man-created inlet designed for boat passage. North of the inlet visitors will find the entrance station, nature trail, north jetty fishing, concessions, bathhouse, surfing and swimming areas. South of the inlet the facilities include the south jetty fishing, swimming, bathhouse, McCarty Visitor Center, boat ramp, dock and campground. The area has a diversity of aquatic habitats that maintain wildlife, especially waterfowl, with lagoons, coastal hammocks, mangrove forests, dunes and coastal strand. The Pelican Island National Wildlife Refuge, approximately four miles south of Sebastian inlet and within Indian River, has the distinction of being the country's first national refuge. Off limits to visitors, it was established in 1903 by Theodore Roosevelt, an avid conservationist.

Nature walkers will enjoy the vast expanse of beach in either direction and the backside of the park along Indian River. But Sebastian Inlet ranks even higher with surfers and fishermen. The surfing is widely considered the finest in southern Florida, thanks to the jetties that create frequent six-foot waves. Fishermen nearly outnumber surfers along the jetties, where they try to hook the big ones from the northbound Gulf Stream, which comes very close to shore here. Another distinct feature of the beach is the fact that over 1,000 loggerhead, leatherback, and green sea turtles annually nest along the miles of shoreline sand within the recreation area.

Situated at the south boundary of the state beach about two miles south of the inlet is the unique McCarty Visitors Center. Built upon the site of a former Spanish encampment, the two-acre, star-shaped archaeological museum features displays and dioramas of a 1715 hurricane-stricken Spanish treasure fleet. The many exhibits, obtained just offshore by a team of marine archaeologists, include a 12-pound cannon, gold and silver coins, and other salvaged artifacts. Also on display are a sea shell collection, trade items and a trade route-map, Ais Indian history and a diorama model of the survivors' salvage camp. A 15-minute slide presentation describes the natural and social history of the barrier island. The McCarty Visitor Center is open Wednesday through Sunday from 9 a.m. to 5 p.m. There is a small entrance fee.

If you seek a less active beach to swim and fish you may find the Ambersand Beach a good spot. The Indian River County beach access is located two miles south of the McCarty Visitors Center along A1A. This undeveloped beach has a parking lot limited to about 10 cars. The dune crossover boardwalk leads to the quiet sandy strand where you may pursue your own activities. If the Sebastian Inlet SRA campground is full, there may be a possibility of finding a site at Long Point Park Campground.

This Brevard County park is 1.5 miles north of Sebastian Inlet and one mile west of A1A towards Indian River. Long Point is a small camper's island and contains a convenient store, swimming lake, playground, ballfield, picnic pavilion, boat ramp, paddleboat and canoe rentals, and electric and non-electric campsites. Nearby Scout Island is reserved for large group campers and is boat accessible only. Be advised that this campground is usually busy and very crowded during the winter months.

To reach Sebastian Inlet State Recreation Area and other nearby facilities from U.S. 1, turn east in central Melbourne and proceed to Indiatlantic on the Melbourne Causeway. Head south approximately 20 miles on A1A to the park entrance. South access from U.S. 1 is at Wabasso. Turn east on S.R- 510 and drive to the junction with A1A and turn north and drive approximately seven miles to the park. Sebastian Inlet straddles the county line between Brevard and Indian River Counties.

Treasure Shores/Golden Sands Beaches
Wabasso/Indian River County
Beach Frontage: 4,533 ft. TS/959 ft. GS
Area: 77 acres TS/13.84 acres GS
Highlights: beach walk, nature study, swimming, surfing, showers, lifeguards, picnicking, shelters, playgrounds, surf fishing, handicapped access

These two Indian River County parks with romantic names are within beach walking distance from each other (1.5 miles) and occupy the most undeveloped shoreline in the area. Both are within the proposed boundary of the Archie Carr National Wildlife Refuge.

The golden shores are treasured by the loggerheads, leatherbacks and green sea turtles that lay their eggs in the fine coquina and shell sands found at these beaches and other locations between Melbourne Beach and Wabasso Beach. The area is the largest sea turtle nesting site in the United States and second in the world, surpassed only by Masirah Island, Oman in the Persian Gulf. The female lays eggs from May 1 until August and hatchlings can be spotted struggling back to the ocean until November.

The southeastern beach mouse, a threatened species, is also a resident here. Any future development must be coordinated with the U.S. Fish and Wildlife Service.

Families will enjoy picnicking in the shade of the wind-sculptured maritime hammock of Treasure Shores. Children can use a unique playground that features a pirate ship.

Treasure Shores Beach is 3.75 miles south of Sebastian Inlet at 11300 Highway AIA; telephone (407) 589-6441. Golden Sands is located 1.4 miles north of Wabasso Beach at 10350 Highway AlA; telephone (407) 388-5483.

Wabasso Beach/Sea Grape Trail/Turtle Trail
Orchid/Indian River County
Beach Frontage:1,000 ft. total
Highlights: nature study, swimming, lifeguards, scuba, picknicking, shelters, boat ramp, showers, restrooms, concessions

Currently these three north Indian River County beaches enjoy the placid natural surroundings of a near condo-free coast. Wabasso Reach has the atmosphere of a cozy small beach town. The no-fee parking lot is usually crowded during the winter months with out-of-staters although local natives and semi-natives manage to squeeze in. This beach even has its own shopping mall, that will supply all your beach needs and then some.

As you enter the parking lot, you will notice the sheltered picnic area and boardwalk are readily at hand and foot. Restrooms and showers are provided. Lifeguards watch out for the safety of swimmers. Surf fishing is a popular activity. Tanning, of course, is a major beach pursuit. In case you are wondering where the name Wabasso comes from, it is said settlers from Ossabaw, Georgia in 1898 decided to call their new home by the same name but spelled backwards. Strike out on your own and explore the seemingly endless shoreline in either direction. If you feel ambitious consider hiking two miles south to the Sea Grape Trail Acess or north four-plus miles to Ambersand Beach or, further yet, to Sebastian Inlet.

The trail at Sea Grape is a dune crossover of a few yards from the highway to the beach. Parking is limited. Fishing, swimming and scuba diving are popular pursuits at this undeveloped beach. Condos are being built adjacent to the access boundary and coastal property is for sale directly to the south. In a few years Sea Grape Trail will just be an alleyway to the shore. Turtle Trail Beach is located one mile south of Sea Grape and three miles south of Wabasso Beach. This access point offers the same kind of beach as Sea Grape Trail.

To reach these beaches from I-95 take Sebastian exit east onto Fellsmere Road/S.R.512 and drive 2.2 miles. Turn right/south on Wabasso Road/S.R.510 and proceed to U.S. 1. Continue across U.S. 1 on 510/Wabasso Beach Road at A1A. To reach Sea Grape Trail and Turtle Trail Beach access points, turn south on A1A two and three miles from Wabasso Beach, or from Vero Beach north three and four miles.

Vero Beach Area Beaches
Vero Beach/Indian River County
Beach Frontage: 2 miles total
Highlights: nature study, swimming, surfing, lifeguards, bathhouse, showers, picnicking, shelters, playground, nature trail, restrooms

Like most southern Florida seaside communities, Vero Beach has its fair share of sandy beach parks. The city and county park departments have been successful in their efforts to preserve shorefront properties for leisurely pursuits. Each beach experience varies, but basically all are developed urbanized beaches.

Tracking Station Park is two miles north of Beachland Boulevard/S.R. 60. This former U.S. Government military radar installation was in active service during World War II, but was dismantled in recent years for lack of mission. The Indian River County Parks Department now maintains the 9.5-acre site for recreational purposes. There is spacious free paved parking. The two beach crossovers give access to a sandy wide shore where swimming, surfing, surf fishing, picnicking, and sunbathing are the main activities. There are modern, though rustic-designed, restrooms equipped with showers. Lifeguards are on duty 9 a. m. to 5 p. m. as they are at Jaycee, Humiston and South Beach Parks further south. Facilities are available for the handicapped.

Jaycee Park or North Beach is a city-owned 8.3-acre seaside park partially developed by the local social organization, the Jaycees. The park site was formerly occupied by one of the established 10 federally funded Houses of Refuge that rescued and sheltered sailors from shipwrecks. The largest picnic grounds in Vero Beach

are here along with two play-
grands, a boardwalk, lifeguards,
bathhouse, showers, and
restrooms. Swimming and lazing
in the sun are a favorite pasttime
along the 2,000-foot shore. There
is plenty of free parking. Jaycee
Park is at 4200 North Ocean
Drive, 1.5 miles north of Beachland Boulevard/S.R. 60.

Conn Park is named in honor of
the real estate developer who donated the shorefront property to
the city of Vero Beach. This municipal beach is popular with surfers and some 300 feet of shore has
in fact been zoned for surfing.
There is free parking. The unde-

Morning jogger, Vero Beach

veloped beach may be found along North Ocean Drive at Gray
Twig Road, Conn Way and Lilac Road, one mile north of Beachland
Boulevard/S.R. 60.

Midway along the Vero Beach ocean strip is Sexton Plaza. Picnicking and swimming are the main pursuits at this small 150-foot
"pocket" beach located at the eastern terminus of Beachland Boule-
vard/S.R. 60.

Humiston Beach or Central Beach is an active 4.3-acre city park
with 500 feet of sandy white shore just .5 mile south of Beachland
Boulevard/S.R. 60 along South Ocean Drive. The congestion and
concrete boardwalk lend a citified "wharf-like" atmosphere. Street
parking is available. The park offers picnicking, with covered
pavilions, swimming, lifeguards, playground, showers, bathhouse, and restrooms. This park is named in honor of Dr. William
Humiston, a Cleveland, Ohio surgeon who was a co-founder of the
local Riomar resort in 1919. Immediately south at the end of Easter
Lily Lane is where Easter sunrise services are annually held.

South Beach is an exceptional city beach park in that it has a
mile-long self-guided plant identification walk. The wood chipped
loop trail has 16 numbered posts that correspond with a trail guide

provided by the Florida Division of Forestry. Plants of the pioneer and scrub zones are identified by their common and scientific names. Additional information includes description, ecological significance, folklore and usages as food and medicine. The path is immediately north of the paved parking lot. The park's other activities include sheltered picnicking, strolling the boardwalk, and swimming, with lifeguards observing the 300-foot beach. There are showers, bathhouse, and restrooms available. South Beach is three miles south of Beachland Boulevard/S.R. 60 and half a mile east at 17th Street/Causeway Boulevard and South Ocean Drive, east of A1A.

Additional beach access within the Vero Beach area is at the east end of Flame Vine Lane, Gayfeather Lane, Riomar Drive, Lady Bug Lane, Jasmine Lane, Coquina Lane, Pirate Cove Lane and Hibiscus Lane. Riomar Reef and Seashore Beach are excellent surf spots for experienced surfers.

Ft. Pierce Inlet State Recreation Area/ Pepper Park/Jack Island State Preserve/Bryn Mawr Beach/ Avalon Beach/Round Island Park

Ft. Pierce/St. Lucie County
Beach Frontage: 1.3 miles total
Area: 1,500 acres total
Trail Distance: 5 miles total
Highlights: nature study, hiking, picnicking, shelters, swimming, scuba, surfing, lifeguards, boardwalk, fishing, boat launch, observation tower, bathhouse, restrooms
Fee(s): entrance to Ft. Pierce Inlet SRA and UDT museum

Several public accessible state and county beach and bayside parks are situated in the area from the St. Lucie-Indian River County line south 6.5 miles to Ft. Pierce Inlet. It is possible to visit all of the parks along the south tip of North Hutchinson barrier island in one day, but it is easier to relax and take them one at a time.

The 340-acre Ft. Pierce Inlet State Recreation Area is a smaller urban counterpart of Sebastian Inlet State Recreation Area. The man-made north jetty not only provides boat passage to the sea, but has enhanced the fishing and surfing here. Land-bound fishermen can extend their lines further out for a more bountiful saltwater catch along the rocky extension. Surfers are "stoked" by the "gnarly" waves the jetty producess. Surf conditions are posted at the entrance station.

Four beach boardwalk crossovers lead past abundant natural dune flora of sea oats, sea grape, beach sunflower, railroad vine, inkberry and Spanish bayonet. The wide beach is ideal for jogging, swimming, sunbathing, shelling, or watching a sunrise. Picnicking is a scenic and shade-endowed experience underneath the Australian pines beside the inlet. Birdwatchers will discover the backwaters of Tucker Cove and Dynamite Point is a choice place to observe gulls, terns, sandpipers, plovers, ducks, herons, loons, and other wildlife. No camping is available in this day-use state facility.

A 1/8-mile loop Coastal Hammock Trail has been developed for the more terrestrial visitor. The posted trailhead begins at the northwest end of the parking area directly opposite the bathhouse. The beach hammock resembles the coastal forests of Cuba, the Bahamas, and Jamaica. The short path is self-guiding and a booklet is available at the trailhead. The well-defined trail leads past 16 numbered stations that correspond with the booklet. Gumbo limbo, red bay, and wild lime are but a few of the trees and plantlife noted. Raccoons, squirrels, bluejays, and cardinals are some of the wildlife residents commonly spotted. Ecology of the hammock is the major theme of the walk. Ft. Pierce Inlet State Recreation Area is open daily from 8 a.m. to sunset.

The 39-acre St. Lucie County-owned and maintained Pepper Park is 11 miles north of Ft. Pierce Inlet State Recreation Area on A1A. The 2,000-foot beachside features plenty of free paved parking, boardwalk, and three dune crossovers. Swimming, lifeguards, fishing, sheltered picnicking, bathhouse, showers, restrooms, and handicapped facilities are provided. The Indian River side of the divided park has several sheltered picnic sites and a boat launch ramp on the mangrove forested Wildcat Cove.

Pepper Park has the distinction of being part of the original training site of navy frogmen, the Underwater Demolition Team (UDT), in the 1940's at the beginning of World War II. Currently these servicemen are called SEALS, an acronym for Sea, Air, and Land Teams. A museum honoring this dedicated military elite has been established. Military exhibits, documents, photos, and a memorial reflecting pool are some of the displays. The UDT museum is open Wednesday through Sunday, 10 a.m. to 4 p.m. There is an entrance fee. Pepper Park is open to the public from sunrise to sunset.

The entrance road to Jack Island State Preserve is 1/4 mile north of Pepper County Park on the Indian River side of A1A and another 1/4 mile west to the paved parking lot and footbridge over the Ft. Pierce Cut. Over five miles (26,870 feet) of truck-wide sandy trails encircle the 631-acre island which is impounded, diked and flooded for mosquito control from April to October. The Mangrove and Marsh Trail loops around the island's water edge and there are few "window" openings through the dense mangroves for viewing the impoundment and river. There is a 25-foot observation tower halfway along the trail located at the middle of the island's Indian River shoreline. You can cut the hike short by following the Marsh Rabbit Run Trail east at the observation tower and return to the foot bridge starting point. This linear trail runs through the middle of the island and has several elevated wooden "lookovers" to observe the nursery mudflats and abundant birdlife. Bird observation is excellent early in the morning, especially in winter, with nearly 200 common to rare bird species identified in a bird list available at the footbridge. Marsh Rabbit Run Trail is self-guiding and a trail booklet is also available at the interpretive board at the footbridge parking area. It identifies 22 points of interest. Not far from the footbridge, near the trailhead of Marsh Rabbit Run Trail, a third trail identified as the Buttonwood Trail leads through 1/8 mile of tropical beach hammock.

Bryn Mawr Beach access is situated about 1.8 miles north of Jack Island or 3.5 miles north of Ft. Pierce Inlet State Recreation Area. This open and shadeless undeveloped access has unpaved parking and day visitors may swim and fish along the 300-foot beach.

Further north of the Bryn Mawr Beach is the Avalon Beach access. Also undeveloped, here the comforting shade of the tall Australian pines that have crowded out the native flora make this tract more pleasant, though they do not provide the visitor with a picture of natural Florida. The 60-foot beach is a fine place to swim and fish. Recently, St. Lucie County and the State of Florida under the Save Our Coast Program have purchased an additional 200 acres in this semi-natural area.

Round Island Park lies half a mile north of the St. Lucie County line in Indian River County. This large county beach and riverside park is divided in half by A1A. The beach side has extensive canopy-covered picnic facilities under the shade of sabal palms and the privacy and protection of dunes. The 400-foot white sandy beach is the scene for swimming, sunbathing, and surf fishing. The riverfront side is in a more natural state. A boat ramp accesses Round Island Creek and nearby Round Island.

To reach Ft. Pierce Inlet State Recreation Area and other recreational sites from I-95, exit east at Orange Avenue/S.R. 68 in Ft. Pierce and drive due east to the junction with U.S. 1. Follow U.S. 1 north through downtown to the North Beach Causeway/A1A and proceed across the Indian River to Atlantic Beach Boulevard/A1A. Turn south/right on Atlantic Boulevard and drive to the entrance of Ft. Pierce Inlet State Recreation Area. All other beach and riverside areas are found north along A1A.

Hutchinson Island Beaches (Northern)
Pt. Pierce/St. Lucie County
Beach Frontage: 2 miles total
Highlights: nature study, swimming, surfing, scuba, lifeguards, surf fishing, picnicking, shelters, boardwalk, boat launch, athletic courts, playfields, bathhouse, showers, restrooms, concessions

A variety of beaches ranging from active urban strands to remote stretches range along the northern half of South Hutchinson Island. From the south jetty of the Ft. Pierce Inlet to the St. Lucie-Martin County line, there is nearly 14 miles of low and narrow barrier island. At the center of this sandy expanse, is a 20th century landmark that is visible for several miles: the St. Lucie Nuclear Power Plant, which may be the only nuclear power plant in the world located on a barrier island.

Beginning from the Ft. Pierce Inlet is the city's busy South Jetty Park. A boardwalk provides beach access to the sandy shore. Picnickers underneath shady shelters watch boats of all sizes pass through the inlet. Pelicans become the fisherman's close companion, especially when there are fish to be cleaned. Parking space in the paved lot is usually limited because the beach is popular with people of all ages. Sea-oriented restaurants and other beachfront stores ring the beach park. This is one of Florida's longest jetties, and fishermen prefer to cast from the rock and concrete peninsula in their insatiable quest for snook, sea trout, and other ocean edibles. The jetty at low tide is a fine place to observe marine life such as crabs warming in the sun. South Jetty Park may be reached from U.S. 1 in downtown Ft. Pierce by crossing over South Bridge Causeway/A1A and driving directly east to the beach end at Seaway Drive.

The walkable public beach extends south for about a mile to the county-owned South Beach or Boardwalk Beach. Parking is limited to the mid-beach points at the ocean end of Gulfstream and Porpoise Avenues. This sandy section is endowed with amenities such as picnic shelters, lifeguards, showers, restrooms, concessions, boardwalk, and parking. There is an offshore reef with a variety of rock formations and ledges popular with scuba divers.

Driving or walking another half-mile south will bring you to the city beach of Surfside. This strand offers attractions similar to those at South Beach: swimming, lifeguards, showers, restrooms, and concessions. Directly across South Ocean Drive/A1A is the newly built Jaycee Park, a city-owned Ft. Pierce park that faces Jennings Cove and Indian River Lagoon. Plenty of free parking is available along with plenty of activity: two tennis courts, two handball courts, shuffleboard, horseshoe pits, three large picnic shelters to accommodate groups, numerous smaller picnic shelters, a playground and a boat launch ramp into Indian River.

One mile south of Surfside and Jaycee Parks on South Ocean Drive/A1A is Blue Heron Park or Exchange Park. Turn east on Blue Heron Boulevard and drive 1/4 mile down the long unpaved road to the oceanfront. Development is at a minimum here. Swimming and surf fishing are the main activities. There has been an effort to re-establish the denuded dunes. The semi-natural area has many sunny openings intermingled with Australian pines.

About two miles further south of Blue Heron or Exchange Park Beach (four miles south of the Ft. Pierce Inlet) on A1A is the Frederick Douglass Memorial Park. The entrance drive is a 1/4-mile shell gravel road to a remote open 1,000-foot beach studded with Australian pines. Swimming, surf fishing and picnic shelters are provided. The large pavilion, restrooms, and showers are in need of repair.

Hoping for a meal, South Hutchinson Island

The next public access point is Middle Cove County Beach, one mile south of Frederick Douglass Memorial Park and five miles south of the Ft. Pierce Inlet on A1A. Free parking is available. Swimming and fishing are the main activities at this undeveloped strand that is far from any maddening crowds.

Beyond Middle Cove Beach access, about two miles south, or seven miles south of the inlet, is the St. Lucie Nuclear Power Plant and Blind Creek Beach access. The Florida Power and Light Company has developed Walton Rocks Beach south of the power plant. The beach includes turtle nesting sites, picnicking, surfing, and swimming (with lifeguards), and restrooms. A living wormrock reef is just offshore from the 3,368-ft. beach. Herman's Bay access is one mile south of St. Lucie Nuclear Power Plant or about four miles from the St. Lucie-Martin County line. Normandy Bay access is two miles south of the plant and three miles from the county line. Both of these somewhat remote natural beaches are very popular with surf fishermen. Parking is limited and there are beach cross-overs.

To reach South Hutchinson Island beaches in south St. Lucie County from 1-95 in Ft. Pierce, exit Okeechobee Road/S.R. 70 or Orange Avenue/S.R. 68 and proceed west to U.S. 1. Turn north on

Shoreline fishing, Bob Graham Beach

U.S. 1 through downtown and turn east on South Bridge Causeway, which becomes Seaway Drive/AIA, and proceed to South Jetty Park. Continue south on AlA/Ocean Drive to the other beach parks. From the south, exit east from U.S. 1 in Jensen Beach on S.R.707/Commercial Street and proceed to Indian River Drive north to Jensen Beach Causeway and AlA/Ocean Drive. Or in Stuart go east from U.S. 1 on Ocean Boulevard/AlA across the Stuart Causway to South Hutchinson Island, then north.

Hutchinson Island Beaches (Southern)
Stuart/Martin County
Beach Frontage: 2 miles total
Highlights: nature study, swimming, surfing, scuba, lifeguards, picnicking, shelters, playground, museums, showers, restrooms, concessions
Fee(s): museum entrance

Within Martin County, South Hutchinson Island is highly urbanized with high rise condo rows facing the shore. There are 12 beach access points and parks, however, located along the nearly nine miles of strand.

Starting at the St. Lucie-Martin County line there is the North County Access Strip, sometimes called the Glasscock Strip. To the immediate south is 3,000-foot **Jensen Beach**. Plenty of unpaved, free sandy parking is conveniently located off Ocean Boulevard/A1A and at the North County Access Strip for a few cars. This lively county-owned public beach includes dune crossovers, sheltered picnic tables, concessions, showers and restrooms. There is a handicapped-access crossover at the south end. Lifeguards supervise the swimming area and surf fishing is popular.

Between Jensen Beach and **Stuart Beach**, nearly four miles to the south on Ocean Boulevard/A1A, there are five public county beach access strips that include free parking and dune crossovers: **Bob Graham Beach**, **Alex's** and **Stokes Access**, **Virginia Forrest** and **Tiger Shores**. All of these beaches are highly in demand with the wintertime surf fishermen who at times line up along the shore leaving little room for swimmers.

Stuart Beach is a five-acre south beach counterpart to Jensen Beach in the sense that it is county-owned, developed, and has the oceanfront atmosphere of a cozy city beach. Paved parking is shady and plentiful. The facilities include picnicking with shelters, a 250-foot boardwalk, dune crossovers, playground, swimming, lifeguards, concessions, surf fishing, showers, restrooms, and handicapped access. The entrance road is directly north of the Elliot American History Museum just off Ocean Boulevard/A1A.

Continuing southbound on Ocean Boulevard/A1A, the road curves westward as it proceeds toward the Stuart Causeway. Turn left/south on MacArthur Boulevard about 1.2 miles along the "condo route" to where the road skirts the beach. **Fletcher Strip Beach** access with limited parking and dune crossover is found here, but you have to look closely for it.

From Fletcher Strip it is another half-mile to the **Gilbert's Bar House of Refuge Museum** and beach maintained by the Historical Society of Martin County. The House of Refuge, built in 1875, is the oldest building in Martin County and the only existing refuge house of the 10 originally erected. It was a temporary haven for the shipwrecked until the end of World War II. The House is located on Gilbert's Bar, a part of the ocean reef that extends southwards across St. Lucie Inlet to Hobe Sound National Wildlife Refuge. The spectacular Anastasia "rock" formation in front of the house along the beach is composed of shell and sand.

A reef-building worm contributes to the formation. The House and Museum contains nautical and maritime exhibits, an observation lighthouse tower, furnishings from the Victorian Period and a gift shop. The grounds have several holding tanks of sea turtles being raised for scientific study and eventual release. The House of Refuge and Museum are open 1 p.m. to 5 p.m. Tuesday to Sunday with no admission after 4:45 p.m. There is a minimal entrance fee. The limited parking is restricted for visitors to the House of Refuge during their hours of operation; otherwise beach parking is allowed at all other times. South of the House of Refuge, along the mile to the security entrance of Sailfish Point, is the Chastain Access, another Martin County Beach access point with parking, a dune crossover, shower, and restroom.

At the extreme southern "publicly accessible" point of Hutchinson Island is Martin County's **Bathtub Reef Park**. Bathtub Reef Park is currently in the development stages, with proposed enlargement of parking areas, a proposed nature complex with restrooms and combination deck/dune walkover in the works. Existing elements of the park include the existing **Sailfish Point Access Strip** with parking, shower, restrooms, dune crossover, a river boardwalk, and a ramped dune walkover structure with two viewing or seating areas. The structure has handicapped access to the viewing or seating areas. The surf fishing and swimming are fine and the offshore ocean reef makes for good snorkeling and scuba diving. Martin County's South Hutchinson Island beaches are accessible from U.S.1 in Jensen Beach and Stuart. In Jensen Beach turn east on C.R.752/Commercial Street, drive 3.5 miles to Indian River Drive and turn north. Proceed about half a mile to Jensen Beach Causeway and turn east across the causeway to Ocean Boulevard/A1A and Jensen Beach. From Stuart, head west on Ocean Boulevard from U.S. 1 at Confusion Corners and proceed to the beaches. Watch for directional signs.

Hobe Sound Beach/Hobe Sound National Wildlife Refuge/St. Lucie Inlet State Park/Pecks Lake Park

Hobe Sound/Martin County
Beach Frontage: 6.6 miles total
Area: 1,765 acres
Highlights: nature study, swimming, fishing, picnicking, shelters, lifeguards, showers, restrooms
Fee(s): entrance for Hobe Sound National Wildlife Refuge

Consider a walk on the "wild side." The northern half of Jupiter Island east of Hobe Sound is in sharp contrast to the plush condo row high rises and private residences on the island's southern half. All development is left behind and a tranquil near-natural coastal sanctuary extends for miles to the St. Lucie-Inlet.

Driving east from U.S. 1 at Hobe Sound on S.R. 708/Bridge Road, the 1.5-mile drive ends at **Hobe Sound public beach** parking area. This Martin County beach has free asphalted and landscaped parking, along with sheltered picnic tables, lifeguards, showers and restrooms. Swimming, some surfing, surf fishing, and sunbathing are the standard beach activities. Extensive erosion in recent years is a major problem along the shores. There is nothing here too different from other developed beaches in the area. It is when you turn north from Bridge Road onto Beach Road/Jupiter Island Road and drive to the road's end that **Hobe Sound National Wildlife Refuge** begins. The extensive undisturbed four-mile beach provides a suitable habitat for the nearly 100,000 loggerhead and leatherback sea turtle's summertime hatchlings, thus making the refuge one of the most successful nesting beaches in the United States. In wintertime up to 50 manatees are found in adjoining waters. Usually less than five feet in elevation, the 736-acre refuge

Hobe Sound National Wildlife Refuge

is comprised of Atlantic coastal sand dunes and red, black, and white mangrove forest. A mangrove interpretive boardwalk trail is planned for the future. Pelicans, white ibis, snowy egrets, sandpipers, blue herons, raccoons, opossums and grey fox are some of the inhabitants of the tract. Prehistoric and historic Indians occupied the north portion of the refuge and evidence of their former occupation appears as shell mounds. The shipwrecked Quaker Jonathan Dickinson and his surviving party walked these shores in the beginning of their 200-mile trek northward to St. Augustine in 1696.

Further north of Pecks Lake and the North Jupiter Narrows is **South Point** at the St. Lucie Inlet. This area was recently acquired by the Florida Department of Natural Resources and is now known as **St. Lucie State Park**. Walking north to the inlet is possible but discouraged by the National Wildlife authorities. Day hikers would have to endure a 12-mile round trip consisting of several miles of mangrove forest, which are an obstacle during high tides. Approved access is by boat. The Florida Department of Natural Resources plans to establish ferry service to the park in the future.

While in the area you may want to visit **Pecks Lake Park**, a recent addition to the Martin County park system. Nature walkers will enjoy the 2,000-foot boardwalk that leads from pinelands through coastal hammock and mangrove forest to the Intracoastal Waterway or Indian River. The natural park is also a fine place to picnic, with shelters. Pecks Lake Park is located just off AIA north of Hobe Sound at 8108 Gomez Avenue. Follow the directional signs to this day-use park.

Blowing Rocks Preserve
Jupiter Island/Martin County
Beach Frontage: 2 miles
Area: 113 acres
Trail Distance: 2 miles
Highlights: nature study, hiking

Visiting Nature Conservancy-owned properties is always a special experience and the scenic Blowing Rocks Preserve is no exception. The preserve derives its name from the forceful pounding waves that break along the largest Anastasia limestone outcrop on the Atlantic coast, spewing spray several feet high through the eroded blowholes.

Blowing Rocks Preserve

Green, leatherback, and loggerhead sea turtles come ashore north of the rock formations to lay their eggs in summer. The visitor will pass through four separate natural communities that harbor over 120 plant species: dune, coastal strand, intracoastal mangrove forest, and a segment of tropical hardwood hammock. Aquatic waterfowl and shorebirds may be seen feeding or flying overhead. Adjacent to the sandy beach there is a foredune bluff trail called the **Main Trail** which follows the vegetated strand ridge. A short trail across S.R.707/Beach Road leads to the mangrove-lined bank of Hobe Sound Intracoastal Waterway, where occasional manatees are sighted.

Blowing Rocks Preserve lies one mile north of the Martin-Palm Beach County line on S.R.707/Beach Road. The parking lot is limited to 10 or 15 vehicles for daytime use only. A Nature Conservancy guide is on duty to explain the natural history of the preserve. For further information on The Nature Conservancy or the preserve, write Blowing Rocks Preserve, P.O. Box 3795, Tequesta, Florida 33458.

South of the preserve about two miles, or one mile south of the county line, is **Coral Cove Beach Park**, a Palm Beach County developed facility. From the paved free parking area there are dune crossovers that lead to the sandy beach. The rocky outcrops found here are not as spectacular as Blowing Rocks but are none-theless scenic. Lifeguards are on duty for swimmers and surfers. Surf fishing is popular, along with picnicking beneath shelters, and there is a fitness trail. Showers and restrooms are centrally situated and are handicapped-accessible.

To reach the area from U.S. 1 near Hobe Sound turn east on S.R. 707/Bridge Road and drive to Jupiter Island, then turn south on S.R.707/Beach Road. Blowing Rocks Preserve is located six miles south and Coral Cove Beach eight miles south. South access from U.S.1 to Jupiter Island and S.R. 707 is at Tequesta and Jupiter Inlet Colony, north of the Jupiter Inlet and the Loxahatchee River.

Dubois Park/Jupiter Beach/Carlin Park

Jupiter Beach/Palm Beach County
Beach Frontage: 5,400 ft. total
Area: 186 acres total
Highlights: nature study, swimming, snorkeling, scuba, lifeguards, surf-ing, jetty, pier, fishing, dock slips, boat launch, picnicking, shelters, play-ground, museum, exercise trail, tennis, baseball fields, volleyball, showers, restrooms, concessions

These three north Palm Beach County beaches merge into one big beach and the walker may access and explore all on foot without leaving the sandy shore. Compared to the more urbanized south Palm Beach County beaches, the pace seems less hurried and unmetered parking is usually plentiful. Activities vary somewhat at each beach and so does the overall atmosphere. All three beaches, however, are easily accessed from sunrise to sunset from S.R. AlA/Ocean Drive in Jupiter Beach.

Dubois Park is located at 19075 Dubois Road on the south shore of the Jupiter Inlet. The small "pocket beach" has fine scenic views of the 105-foot **Jupiter Lighthouse**, northwest across the inlet. The lighthouse was constructed in 1855 and is still employed by the U.S. Coast Guard. One of the main attractions of the park is the **Harry Dubois home** and museum which was built on an Indian shell mound in 1898. The home has been restored with original "Gay 90's" furnishings. The Jeaga or Jobe Indian mound layers have revealed artifacts of times long before Spanish exploration. Activities at Dubois Park include swimming, snorkeling, scuba, surfing, picnicking, fishing. There are shelters, lifeguards, dock slips, a boat launch ramp, and restrooms.

From Dubois Park it is an easy bridge crossing over a tidal lagoon creek to Jupiter Beach. From the jetty it is a short stroll through an Australian pine grove to the Jupiter Beach parking area and dune crossover. The beach is sloping and narrow along the frontal dunes but widens out farther south enroute to Carlin Park. This was the route the "Barefoot Mailman" took on his southward sandy trek to Miami during the 1870's, before the days of post offices. Beach fare includes swimming with lifeguards, snorkeling, scuba, surfing near the jetty, picnicking with shelters, playground, concessions, showers, and restrooms.

From Jupiter Beach Inlet to Carlin Park the nearly one-mile walk is neither remote nor overbuilt. Carlin Park at 400 AlA is the active recreational "showcase" county park of the three beaches, This popular developed beach park is well used year round by locals and visitors alike. About half of the acreage is found across the AlA highway from the beach. After resting or having some fun here, retrace your sandy steps back north to Jupiter Beach and Dubois Beach. Recreational fare includes swimming (lifeguards), snorkeling, scuba, pier fishing, a playground, and picnicking. There are shelters, a "heart exercise trial," tennis, baseball fields, volleyball, concessions, showers, and restrooms.

Juno Beach Ocean Park/
Loggerhead Park/Juno Beach
Juno Beach/Palm Beach County
Beach Frontage: 3,800 ft. total
Highlights: nature study, swimming, fishing, picnicking shelters, pier, bicycling, tennis, playgrounds pavilion, nature trail, nature study area, observation deck, childrens museum, exercise trail, showers, restrooms

The city of Juno Beach, like Jupiter Beach, has its own "three-in-a-row" set of beach parks. Located north of Donald Ross Road on AlA/Ocean Drive, Juno Beach Ocean Park, Loggerhead Park, and Juno Beach are less than two miles walking distance apart by beach sand, yet they are "miles" apart in regard to available facilities and activities.

Juno Beach Ocean Park is the smallest of the three. Located at 14775 AlA, it is more passive and certainly less developed than Loggerhead, but more built up than Juno Beach. Swimming, lifeguards, fishing, picnicking, shelters, bicycling, showers, a pier, restrooms, and parking are available. It is an easy walk to Loggerhead Park either along the coastline or the oceanfront bike-hike path.

Loggerhead Park, formerly known locally as Pegasus Park before it opened in 1985 as a Palm Beach County Park, has a world of its own to offer to the ocean-going day user. The park is divided by Ocean Drive/AlA. Of special interest to nature walkers, the west landward side features a brief nature trail through sand pine scrub to an observation deck overlook atop a frontal dune. A children's museum dedicated to the study of marine science is situated nearby. The museum hours are Tuesday through Saturday 10 a.m. to 3 p.m. and Sunday 1 p.m. to 3 p.m. A foot tunnel underneath Ocean Boulevard leads to a dune crossover, the beach, and a myriad of beach-related activities: swimming, with life guards, fishing, picnicking. There are shelters, a playground and a "heart exercise trail." Tennis courts are also available. Loggerhead Park is at 111 Ocean Drive/AlA in north Juno Beach.

The third beach, Juno Beach, is one mile south by foot from Loggerhead and is easier to find walking along the seashore than by driving. If you do walk south to Juno Beach, a county park, the pier is the "landmark" to look for. The shore is half a mile long and semi-natural. Juno Beach is partially developed with dune crossovers, restrooms, concessions, and parking west of AIA.

All three beaches are accessible from one hour before sunrise to one hour after sunset. The undeveloped beaches located between Juno and MacArthur are popular with surfers.

John D. MacArthur Beach State Park
North Palm Beach/Palm Beach County
Beach Frontage: 8,000 ft.
Area: 225 acres
Trail Distance: 1.8 mile one-way, 1,600-ft. boardwalk
Highlights: nature study, nature walks swimming, fishing, nature interpretive center

Formerly called Air Force Beach by the locals, John D. MacArthur State Park is one of the outstanding natural east coast beach experiences in southern Florida. The new state park lies in sharp contrast to the developed "mini-Miami" beaches of Singer Island to the immediate south. Easily accessed, the state beach is a prime example of mostly undisturbed subtropical coastal barrier island habitat where exotics (non-native species) are few. Rare and endangered native plants include sea lavender, bay cedar, beach star, and hand fern. May through August, loggerhead, green, and leatherback sea turtles come ashore to lay their eggs in the sloping beach sands. Don't expect to be alone here, especially on weekends when the parking becomes limited and the beach goers are plentiful.

In addition to the pristine beaches there is a popular well-worn walking path that begins before the frontal dunes along the main beach entrance trail. The trail heads north, between the mangrove-edged Lake Worth Cove, a shore and wading bird area, and the 20-foot-high frontal dunes, well covered with native beach plants. The 1.8-mile trail (one way) extends the length of the park where it Ts at a chain link fence. Going east you will cross over the frontal dune to the beach and could walk back along the strand. Going left the trail becomes a service road to A1A. Retrace your steps. Use only the few designated dune crossovers and stay on the path.

At the parking area and main entrance along A1A on the west side of the highway, there is a service road that serves rather nicely as a linear trail. It leads out to a mangrove-covered peninsula that extends into Lake Worth Intracoastal Waterway. Formerly the land point connected to Munyon Island, the site of Dr. Munyon's famous resort and home of "Paw-Paw" elixer at the turn-of-the-century. Retrace your steps.

To reach John D. MacArthur Beach State Park from I-95 in West Palm Beach, exit east on PGA Boulevard/S.R. 786, proceed east across U.S. 1 and continue 2.8 miles to the main parking area at the south tip of Lake Worth Cove. The beach hours are from 8 a.m. to sunset daily. Final development plans are well underway to develop the park with basic amenities such as restrooms, drinking fountains, and developed trails, but the park will remain a part of natural Florida.

Atlantic Dunes Park

Delray/Palm Beach County
Beach Frontage: 650 ft.
Area: 7 acres
Trail Distance: 1/8 mile loop
Highlights: nature study, nature trail,
swimming (lifeguards), picnicking,
shelters, showers, restrooms
Fee(s): metered parking

Atlantic Dunes Park is one of the
few developed beach parks in
Palm Beach County which has a
designated nature trail. Railroad
ties outline and give direction to
the sand and shell pathway that
self-guides as it loops through the
frontal dunes. Labelled plants include sea oats, beach sunflower,

Dune Trail, Atlantic Dunes Park

and sea grape along the dunes, while further back are coastal
hammock gumbo limbo, poisonwood, tamarind, saw palmetto,
spider lily, greenbriar, and wild grape vines. Beach flora encloses
the trail in places, creating an insulated private natural area. The
trail is one loop, interspersed with spurs.

Atlantic Dunes Park is located along AlA/Ocean Boulevard in
Delray Beach. From I-95 exit at Atlantic Avenue and drive east to
AlA, then turn south. Proceed about a mile to the metered parking
lot on the west side of the highway. The residential "cozy" beach
park is owned and managed by the city of Delray Beach and Palm
Beach County.

The beaches north of Atlantic Dunes Park to Lake Worth
Road/S.R.802 are more or less urbanized sandy stretches. In southcentral Palm Beach County, at the ocean end of Lake Worth
Road/S.R. 802, is **R. G. Kreusler County Beach Park** and the city
of **Lake Worth Beach** or **Barton Beach**. Both of these beaches
combine into one, separated only by the impressive pier. The
general atmosphere is a popular "scene" type beach for young and
elderly alike. Surfing is fairly good thanks to the pier. There are
plenty of shops, even a swimming pool and an old "casino" ball-
room. You will find showers, restrooms, swimming, lifeguards,

picnicking, and other beach fare. Parking can be tight. There is metered parking at R. G. Kreusler County beach.

Driving southward on A1A/Ocean Boulevard, just north of the intersection with Ocean Avenue is the developed Lantana Beach Park. It has all the amenities that Lake Worth Park has and fee parking. Continuing south on A1A, at the north jetty of the Boynton Inlet is **Manalapan Beach** and at the south jetty on the other side of the inlet is **Boynton Inlet Park**. Both of these are semi-natural in surroundings and have little in the way of facilities. They are favorite places with surfers, fishermen and those who enjoy unimproved beaches. Further south on A1A at the town of Ocean Ridge is the county-owned **Ocean Ridge Hammock Park**. A fairly undisturbed coastal hammock is found here, bordering the park directly to the south. No trails exist in the hammock presently. It has been preserved by Palm Beach County Parks and Recreation Department and the Florida Department of Natural Resources.

The **Boynton Beach** public beach is at the immediate south boundary of the preserved hammock. All facilities are modern and well designed. The park is especially popular with senior citizens. A $10 winter permit (November to April) is required unless you are a resident of Boynton Beach. Or you can pay a fairly high daily fee for vehicle entry. Further south at Briny Breezes is the developed **Gulfstream County Park**. The usual beach fare of swimming, lifeguards, fishing, picnicking, shelters, showers, restrooms, and fee parking can be expected. The park is popular with scuba divers and a relaxed atmosphere on this bustling east coast is worth a lot.

The last beach before Atlantic Dunes Park is the large **Delray Beach** public beach. It is one of the few beach parks to have a boat ramp but also one of the few without picnicking facilities. There is a fitness trail, boardwalk, lifeguarded swimming, fishing, boat rentals, concessions, and restrooms. Limited parking is found along the city side streets and metered parking on A1A. Many people enjoy walking along the wide sidewalk in the early mornings between the beach and the highway.

All of the aforementioned beaches are located along A1A/Ocean Boulevard from Lake Worth to Delray Beach.

Spanish River Park
Boca Raton/Palm Beach County
Beach Frontage: 1 mile
Area: 79 acres
Highlights: nature study, nature trail, swimming, lifeguards, picnicking, shelters, fishing, docking facilities, observation tower, playground, showers, restrooms, organized group camping
Fee(s): entrance, shelter reservations

Spanish River Park is a day-use facility owned and managed by the city of Boca Raton. The park includes beach frontage as well as forested land areas that are divided by A1A/North Ocean Boulevard. Access to the park is at two entry points: north and south entrances with gatehouses along the west side of A1A/N. Ocean Boulevard. Over 600 parking spaces are available in the circular lots, footsteps away from the picnic facilities. Additional amenities were added in the summer of 1987. A marked short nature trail begins west of the south entrance. The first section of the forested path leads to an observation tower overlooking the Intracoastal Waterway and a lagoon area for boaters. The trail continues northward between the mangrove-lined Intracoastal shore and a hammock. A dry streambed, the former Spanish River before re-channelization, is still obvious in this area. The woodland path makes a 90-degree turn right/east and continues to the north entrance picnic/parking area. You may either retrace your steps or follow the park road south to south gate parking area.

Two tunnels to the beach are on the east side of the park. A healthy stand of sea grape lines the frontal dunes and helps screen out A1A. The beach is sloping, narrow and fairly natural but the beach was renourished during the summer of 1987. The combination of beach and forest makes an ideal oceanside experience. Camping is limited to organized youth groups.

To reach Spanish River Park from I-95 in Boca Raton, exit onto N.W. 51st Street/S.R.794, turn south to N.W. Spanish River Boulevard, then turn east. Proceed to A1A/Ocean Boulevard. Turn south on A1A/North Ocean Boulevard and continue south to the Park entrance. The hours are 8 a.m. to sunset daily.

Gumbo Limbo Nature Center/Red Reef/ South Beach

Boca Raton/Palm Beach County
Beach Frontage: 2 miles
Area: 92 acres total
Highlights:
Gumbo Limbo – nature trails, nature study, nature center, library, auditorium, amphitheatre, programs
Red Reef -- swimming, lifeguards, showers, fishing, picnicking, shelters, turtle sanctuary, golf course
South Beach -- swimming, lifeguards, showers, fishing, pavilion
Fee(s): entrance fee to Red Reef & South Beach.

The best of both coastal worlds, the sandy beach and tropical hammock are preserved at these Boca Raton recreational sites and all three facilities are less than a mile apart. The **Gumbo Limbo Nature Center** at Red Reef Park is a non-profit organization dedicated to providing environmental education for the citizens and visitors of south Palm Beach County. Interpretive displays, aquariums, indoor and outdoor classrooms, a library and auditorium are located in and about the modern rustic nature center. Two short trails, one south and one north of the center are informative and inviting.

The 1/3-mile self-guiding **Coastal Hammock boardwalk trail** begins at the side door of the nature center. A black and white illustrated photo guide booklet to the numbered flora of the hammock is available at a nominal fee. Twenty-eight plants of the tropical coastal hammock and mangrove forest are identified. Protected from the ocean by high frontal dunes plus the modifying effects of the Gulfstream, a warm micro-climate is produced that allows tropical plants to flourish. Rarely seen elsewhere on southern Florida nature trails are Bahama nightshade, black bead, blolly, coin vine, ironwood, snowberry, and white indigo berry. Mature specimens of mastic, pond apple, wild lime, paradise tree, poisonwood, pigeon plum, red, black and white mangroves, and a Tekesta Indian shell mound are also pointed out. An observation tower at midpoint enables visitors to survey the surrounding canopy of the hammock and outreaching landscape.

The quarter-mile labelled **North Trail** heads up on the north side of the nature center. The mulched path leads past an outdoor classroom amphitheatre of excellent design. The trail loops near the Intracoastal Waterway past an old farm, grassflats, mangrove forest and ballast rocks believed to have been used aboard a Spanish galleon to stabilize the ship. The trail returns along the same route. The Gumbo Limbo Nature Center at 1801 North Ocean Boulevard is open 9 a.m. to 4 p.m. Monday through Saturday.

The developed beach area of **Red Reef Park** is accessible 1/4 mile south of the Gumbo Limbo Nature Center. The frontal dunes are well covered with sea grape, sea oats and other native plants. A unique feature of the park is the fenced-off sea turtle sanctuary.

It is a short water-side walk from Red Reef to **South Beach**. South Beach has few facilities other than the pavilion and basically it is a passive, semi-natural undeveloped residential beach. Both day-use beaches are accessible from 8 a.m. to 10 p.m. daily.

To reach Gumbo Limbo Nature Center, Red Reef beach park and South Beach from I-95 in Boca Raton, exit Palmetto Park Road/S.R. 798 and drive east across U.S. 1 to A1A/Ocean Boulevard. The entrance to South Beach is on the east side of the highway at N.E. 4th Street. Red Reef beach parking entrance is approximately 1/4 mile north of South Beach. Fee parking is also available across from the Red Reef park entrance on the west side of the highway. Gumbo Limbo Nature Center is 1/4 mile north and entrance is on the west side of the highway. Limited parking is available.

Hugh Taylor Birch State Recreation Area
Ft. Lauderdale/Broward County
Beach Frontage: 400 ft.
Area: 180 acres
Trail Distance: 1/4 mile self-guiding loop
Highlights: nature study, nature trail, swimming, lifeguards, exercise course, picnicking, shelters, fishing, primitive & youth camping, showers, restrooms, concessions, canoeing, boat launch
Fee(s): entrance, canoe rental, camping, pavilion rental

Hugh Taylor Birch, a Chicago attorney, decided in 1893 to buy land in the formerly rural area northeast of Ft. Lauderdale to escape the windy city winters. For the next half-century Mr. Birch, family and friends enjoyed the quiet remoteness of the land's location next to the Atlantic Ocean. In 1942 at the age of 92 he decided to will the entire acreage to the state of Florida, with the stipulation that it become a public park. Today this green space of beach, hammock, freshwater lagoon, and mangrove forest stands in sharp contrast to the surrounding urbanization and provides a welcome respite from the city's intensity.

The **Beach Hammock Trail**, the only designated nature walk in the park, is a self-guiding loop path with 15 labeled interpretive stations that mainly describe the flora of the endangered coastal tropical hammock. There is a fine vista point overlooking Lake Helen, a dredged pond created from Bonnet Slough by Mr. Birch and named in honor of his daughter. The leisurely walk requires about 20 minutes over a wide high and dry forest path. Guided walks are given during the winter season from November to April. Ask at the park gate for scheduled times and place. The Beach Hammock Trail begins just east of the entrance station between the Garden Center Building and concession area. Consider walking the wide shoulder of the main park road loop where you may find Surinam cherry bushes bearing fruit during mid-winter. An underpass to the beach is near the concession building.

The 'famed' beaches stretching north from the state recreation area to the Hillsboro Inlet are bordered by highly urbanized development and consists of coarse refurbished sandy strips dotted with an occasional coconut palm. The nearly four miles of North Broward County are excellent boy-girl watching and meeting beaches and are mostly public-accessible. Pompano Beach's 875-foot fishing pier is one of the longest in southern Florida.

Hugh Taylor Birch State Recreation Area entrance is at 3109 East Sunrise Boulevard. From I-95 in Ft. Lauderdale exit east on East Sunrise Boulevard and proceed to the park entrance. The park is open daily 8 a.m. to sunset.

Port Everglades Ocean Life Viewing Area
Ft. Lauderdale/Broward County
Area: 1 acre
Highlights: manatee and aquatic life observation site, nature study, picnicking, shelters

Amidst the bustling of this international ocean port, manatees find refuge in the warm outflow waters of the Florida Power and Electric Port Everglades plant. The water, which is 15 degrees warmer, also stimulates aquatic plant life to thrive, thus providing a necessary food source for the vegetarian marine mammals. Manatees are not the only aquatic life to be observed at the viewing area. One hundred and twenty species of sub-tropical and tropical fish, such as angelfish, parrot fish, sergeant majors, sting rays, and barracudas, also frequent this man-made microcosm sanctuary. Colorful interpretive display signs posted along the observation deck identify many of the species.

Aside from the screened observation platform overlook, picnicking facilities are provided in the adjacent landscaped grounds. The Port Authority is currently in the process of establishing an educational center and boardwalk overlook on a refuge channel at nearby John U. Lloyd State Recreation Area. If you want to see aquatic life in a theme park setting, visit the nearby **Ocean World** at S.E. 17th Street Causeway in Ft. Lauderdale.

To reach Port Everglades Ocean Life Viewing Area from I-95 in Ft. Lauderdale, exit eastbound on S.R. 84/S.W. 24th Street. Follow S.R. 84/S.W. 24th Street east into the Port, bear right at the water and proceed to the parking area on the right side of the road just beyond the screened observation platform.

John U. Lloyd Beach State Recreation Area
Dania/Broward County
Beach Frontage: 11,500 ft
Area: 249 acres
Trail Distance: 2.5 miles total
Highlights: nature study, nature trail, swimming, lifeguards, fishing, marina, boat launch, canoeing, scuba, picnicking, shelters, jetty, interpretive programs, showers, bathhouse, restrooms, concessions
Fee(s): entrance, canoe rental

The John U. Lloyd beach experience ranges from watching ships with foreign flags come and go at the busy Port Everglades to quiet remoteness along a coastal hammock trail, from canoeing the mangrove-lined waters of the Intracoastal Waterway to just plain dallying on the warm beach sands. The seemingly isolated narrow barrier island is an ideal setting for a variety of outdoor recreational activities.

The **Barrier Island Nature Trail** is a self-guiding loop trail that begins at the northeast corner of the first parking area past the entrance station on the right/east side of the main park road.

Interpretive markers along the path describe the ecology of the barrier island and the invasion of non-native plants within the coastal sub-tropical hammock. Australian pines are dominant here as they are throughout the park. If you decide not to complete the entire loop, a trail spur shortens the walk.

If you prefer walking near the ocean, cross over the New River Sound on either of the two footbridges located just off the Barrier Island Trail to the service road on the other side. Follow the tree-shaded, firm sandy road in either direction. North will take you to the main beach area and jetty; south leads to the fenced park boundary. This undesignated "trail" makes ideal walking even on a warm summer day.

In the not-to-distant future the Port Everglades Authority in cooperation with the state of Florida will establish an educational complex here for manatee study. The center will feature a refuge water channel for the "mermaids" who frequent the Port and Intracoastal Waterway and will include a boardwalk overlook.

Beaches south of John U. Lloyd State Recreation Area along AlA to the Dade County line include **Dania Beach** (1,000 feet), **Hollywood or South Broward County Beach** (five miles of semi-natural strand) and **Hallandale Beach** (half a mile). All three beaches are developed to some extent and have beach-related activities.

To reach John U. Lloyd State Recreation Area from I-95 in Dania exit onto Stirling Road and proceed east to U.S. 1. Turn north on U.S. 1 and go right/east on East Dania Beach Boulevard and continue to Ocean Drive/AIA. Turn north on Ocean Drive/AlA and drive to the park entrance. The hours are from 8 a.m. to sunset daily. The park is named in honor of a former Broward County lawyer who was a key figure in acquiring the first parcel of land for the park.

Hollywood North Beach
Beach Frontage: 1 mile
Area: 56 acres
Highlights: boardwalk, swimming, lifeguards, biking, jogging, fishing, sea turtle hatchery, 60-ft. observation tower, playgrounds, volleyball, concessions
Fee(s): parking, shelter reservations, sports equipment rentals

This urban regional beach park protects one mile of natural strand along the 23-mile Broward County shoreline. The dune crossovers provide access to over five miles of developed, lifeguarded beach to the south of the park as well as Dania Beach and John U. Lloyd beach to the north.

A walking, biking and jogging path follows the length of the park. Over 500 species of dune plant life occupy the strand at Hollywood North Beach and the park is involved with an Endangered Sea Turtle Protection and Relocation Program, maintaining a sea turtle hatchery. On the backside of the beach, a 1,600-foot boardwalk has been established along the Intracoastal Waterway north of the main park entrance, providing a pleasant place to walk or fish.

Across the Intracoastal Waterway is **West Lake Park**, also a Broward County Park. Over 1,400 acres of coastal mangrove wetlands are preserved, along with numerous threatened and endangered species. Currently under development, the park will feature the 20-acre **Anne Kolb Nature Center** and will include an exhibit and assembly building, nature, canoe, and bicycle trails, a boardwalk and other nature-related facilities and activities. Eighty-eight acres of the park has already been developed for outdoor recreational activities from picnicking to tennis.

To reach Hollywood North Beach County Park from I-95 in Hollywood exit east onto Sheridan Street/C.R. 822 and drive towards the ocean and Ocean Drive. The entrance is at 3501 North Ocean Drive. The telephone number is (305) 926-2444. You will also pass the entrance for West Lake Park, located at 1200 Sheridan Drive. The telephone number is (305) 926-2410.

Bill Baggs Cape Florida State Recreation Area/Crandon Park/Virginia Key Beach

Key Biscayne/Dade County
Beach Frontage: 4.5 miles total
Area: 1,250 acres total
Trail Distance: .5 mile beach trail (Bill Baggs CFSRA)
Highlights:
Bill Baggs – nature study, nature trail, lighthouse tour, bicycling, picnicking, fishing, boat harbor, swimming, lifeguards, primitive youth camp, concessions

Crandon – swimming (lifeguards), fishing, boat ramp, marina, exercise course, picnicking, shelters, bicycling, playground, playfields, golf course, concessions

Virginia Key – swimming, lifeguards, fishing, picnicking, shelters, softball field, future facilities planned

Fee(s): entrance fee to all three parks, lighthouse tours, rentals, golf

The beaches of Key Biscayne are some of the finest, semi-natural strands in Dade County. Although Dade County has miles of ocean-facing shoreline, most of the southern half is inaccessible mangrove forest and the northern half is artificially refurbished urban beach, most notably Miami

Lighthouse, Bill Baggs SRA

Beach. It is not too surprising that for most Miamians, Key Biscayne remains their favorite ocean playground. Three levels of government are actively involved in preserving beachfront parklands on the key.

The south tip of Key Biscayne is known as Cape Florida and the Florida Department of Natural Resources has established Bill Baggs State Recreation Area at this special site. The late Bill Baggs, a Miami newspaper journalist and editor, did a good deal of writing about the natural and social-historical value of Cape Florida, urging its acquisition as a state park. In 1966, the State of Florida purchased the area.The focal point of the park is the 1825 **Cape Florida lighthouse**, the oldest building in southern Florida and sturdy enough to have withstood the power of Hurricane Andrew. The lighthouse and keeper's residence is open to guided and non-guided tours at 10:30 a.m., 1 p.m., 2:30 p.m., and 3:30 p.m. daily except Tuesday. The mile-long sandy beach ends at the sea wall and historical lighthouse. A self-guiding linear nature trail is situated between the beach and the Australian pine forest on the Atlantic Ocean side. Fifteen interpretive stations describe the role of the barrier islands and the exotic and native plant life. Bill Baggs Cape Florida State Recreation Area is open from 8 a.m. to sunset daily.

In the northern half of Key Biscayne is Crandon Park, owned and operated by the Metro Dade County Parks and Recreation Department. The site was a former coconut plantation for copra during the early years of the 20th century. When Crandon Park opened in 1947, the landscaping was nearly complete, with over 10,000 coconut palms gracing the grounds. A wealth of recreational activities are available at this popular beach. The beach park is open from 8 a.m. to sunset daily.

To the immediate north of Key Biscayne is Virginia Key: home of the **Miami Seaquarium, Planet Ocean** and **Virginia Key Beach**. The city of Miami owns and maintains Virginia Key Beach park, the first beachfront park in the city's system. The developed park is planning to include watersports and windsurfer rentals, concessions, horse stables, bridle and nature trails. Currently the Metro Dade County Parks and Recreation Department has scheduled nature walks at Virginia Key. The summer hours of Virginia Key Beach are 7 a.m. to 8 p.m. and winter hours are 8 a.m. to 6 p.m.

To reach the state, county, and city parks from I-95 and U.S 1 ,exit east onto the Rickenbacker Causeway (toll) and proceed to Virginia Key and Virginia Key Beach Road on the east side of the causeway across from the Miami Seaquarium. To reach Crandon Park, continue south to Key Biscayne and Crandon Park Boulevard. Follow the directional signs to the beach area. To reach Bill Baggs Cape Florida State Recreation Area continue south on Crandon Boulevard through the community of Key Biscayne to the park entrance.

Biscayne National Park
Homestead/Dade County
Area: 181,500 acres
Trail Distance: 2.25 miles total
Highlights: nature study, nature walks, historic site, swimming, snorkeling, scuba, saltwater fishing, boating, water skiing, boat tours, backcountry camping, campgrounds
Fee(s): boat tours,snorkeling & scuba trips, island excursions

Biscayne National Park is one of the newest additions to the National Park System. Designated a national park in 1980 after 12 years as a national monument, the vast acreage is 96% offshore in the waters of Biscayne Bay, extending out to a depth of 60 feet in the Atlantic Ocean. Aside from Elliott Key, most of the 44 keys are very small.

Biscayne National Park harbors the northern section of the only living coral reef in the United States and is teeming with marine life and water birds: 200 species of subtropical and tropical fish inhabit the salty waters. Understandably, nature trails and facilities are limited. Aside from the boardwalk and jetty at Convoy Point, hiking is confined to offshore Elliott and Adams Keys, accessible only by boat. The best time to hike is during the cooler winter weather (from January to April) when the insect population, especially mosquitoes which can be fierce on the keys during summer, is lowest.

Convoy Point Information Station and Park Headquarters, located on the mangrove-lined mainland, is the first stop of your visit to Biscayne National Park. The small visitors center features marine exhibits, provides literature, and boat schedules. A half-mile walk out and back along a boardwalk and jetty starts east of the visitors center. Picnicking and saltwater fishing are popular during the park hours from 8 a.m. to sunset daily. Although the park service does not currently provide boat service to the outlying keys, the concessionaire, Biscayne Aqua Center, located next to the visitors center, offers glass boat tours, scuba and snorkeling reef trips and island excursions for picnicking, hiking and camping. A minimum number of passengers are required before the boat departs, so it is best to make reservations by telephone at (305) 247-2400 during park hours. Boat rentals are offered nearby at **Homestead Bayfront Park**, a Metro Dade County facility where fishing, swimming, picnicking, boating facilities and a marina are available.

Offshore, **Elliott Key** is the largest of the park's islands. Black Caesar, a trusted pirate lieutenant of Blackbeard's crew, is believed to have had his hideout on the key. Early settlers cleared most of the hardwood hammock forest, which was composed of a diverse West Indian flora. There are rare isolated stands of Sargent's Palm still remaining. The farmers planted pineapple and key limes in the rich thin soil that overlaid the fossil coral rock, but the fields have long since been abandoned and are revegetating.

The landing dock is at Elliott Key Harbor at bayside, just north of the island's midpoint. A visitor center is open weekends and occasionally during weekdays. Facilities include restrooms, drinking water, picnicking, and a non-fee campground with showers. Backcountry camping is allowed on Elliott and Sands Keys by permit, available from the park headquarters at Convoy Point.

A 1.5-mile round-trip, **self-guiding nature trail** begins at the visitors center and heads east 1/4 mile to the ocean side of the island. The trail then continues along a boardwalk, paralleling the ocean's shoreline. At the end of the boardwalk, it turns west and goes through a lush, subtropical hardwood forest or hammock. The trail ends back at Elliott Key harbor. There are interpretive signs along the way.

Another trail on Elliott Key, is the old **"Spite Highway" trail**, which was blazed in the mid-1960s for developmental purposes. The trail runs down the interior of the island for its entire length of seven miles. Spite Highway can be reached from the nature trail, but is unmarked and unmaintained. Many smaller, unmarked and unmaintained trails can be found by walking the Spite Highway trail, but hikers should use caution when venturing onto these trail spurs. Be advised that mosquitoes can be a problem in the hammock even in winter. Hikers should carry insect repellent and consult with a park ranger before beginning their hike.

Tiny **Adams Key**, just offshore at the southwest tip of Elliott Key, was the former site of the Cocolobo Club built by Carl Fisher of Miami Beach fame in 1920. Presidents Harding and Hoover visited the Cocolobo Club during their administrations. In more recent years the club was owned by Bebe Rebozzo and others. Presidents Nixon and Johnson were occasional guests. A ranger station is located at the old gambling casino, but the main guest house was destroyed by fire in 1968. Picnicking and a nature trail are provided. The trail is a self-guiding quarter-mile loop on the southwest portion of the island.

To reach Biscayne National Headquarters at Convoy Point, 8.5 miles east of Homestead and U.S. 1, drive east on S.W. 328th Street/North Canal Drive to the entrance of the park. The hours are 8 a.m. to sunset daily.

The Gulf Coast

Fred Howard Park/Sunset Beach
Tarpon Springs/Pinellas County
Beach Frontage: 1,000 feet/300 feet
Area: 155 acres/2 acres
Highlights: nature study, picnicking, shelters, windsurfing, swimming (lifeguards), bathhouse, restrooms, fishing, boating, launch ramp, bicycling, horseshoes, soccer, softball, playground

These two beach parks, connected to the mainland by causeways, are within view and close proximity of each other along the Gulf shoreline at Tarpon Springs. Fred Howard is a 155-acre Pinellas County facility developed from property donated by the city of Tarpon Springs. The mainland section of the park features a picnic and active recreation area situated in a shaded grove. A palm-studded, man-made barrier island is connected to the shore by a mile-long causeway. Plenty of parking is available alongside the wide, white sandy beach, which is great for strolling. It is an excellent windsurfing location.

Sunset Beach, a half-mile south, is a Fred Howard park "in miniature." This pocket beach is owned and maintained by the city of Tarpon Springs. For its size, this compact island park offers a fine beach.

Consider visiting the **Tarpon Springs Sponge Docks** while in the vicinity. The Gulf waters in this area are one of the few places in the world where commercial quality natural sponges are found, although the effects of overhunting and pollution have taken their toll. Tours and numerous tourist shops and restaurants are located along Dodecanese Boulevard and the Anclote River juts off by Alternate U.S. 19 in north Tarpon Springs.

To reach these urban beach parks from the Sunshine Skyway Bridge 19, drive north to Tarpon Springs and turn west on Klosterman Road. Before reaching the Gulf, turn north on C.R. 78 and then west on C.R. 80 and proceed a short distance to C.R. 87 or Florida Avenue. Continue north on Florida Avenue to Gulf Drive and turn west to Sunset Beach where the road dead ends at the beach. To reach Fred Howard Park continue north on Florida Avenue to

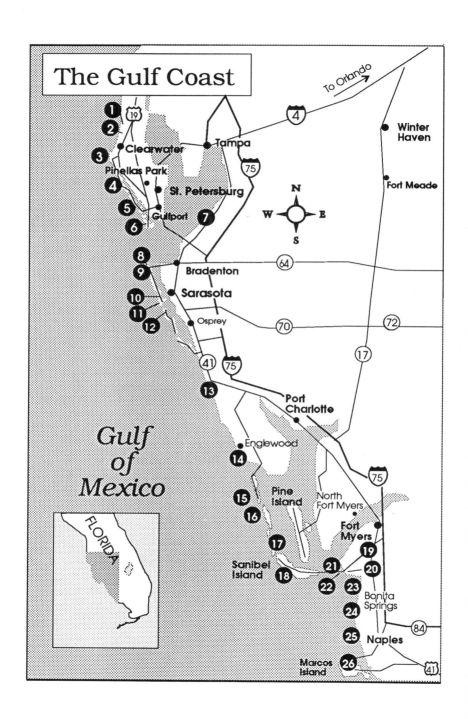

The Gulf Coast

Sunset Drive and then west to the park entrance. Park hours are from 7 a.m. to dark.

Honeymoon Island State Recreation Area/ Caladesi Island State Park

Dunedin/Pinellas County
Beach Frontage: 4 miles
Area: 800 acres total
Trail Distance: 6 miles total
Highlights: hiking, nature study, historical interpretation, windsurfing swimming, lifeguards, fishing, boating, bathhouses, picnicking, shelters, ferry service, restrooms
Fee(s): entrance, ferry service

These barrier islands, created by outwash from the Appalachian Mountains, are more than 5,000 years old. Caladesi and Honeymoon Islands were one island until a hurricane carved a broad channel, appropriately named Hurricane Pass, through the narrow center in 1921. The northern island got its name during the late 1930s when a developer offered contest-winning newlyweds prizes of a free place to spend their wedding trips. After some

1. Fred Howard Park/Sunset Beach
2. Honeymoon Island SRA/Caladesi Island State Park
3. Pinellas County suncoast beaches
4. Clearwater Marine Science Center and Sea Aquarium
5. Suncoast Seabird Sanctuary
6. Fort De Soto Park
7. E.G. Simmons Regional Park
8. Manatee County Beach/Holmes Beach/Anna Maria Bayfront & Beach
9. Coquina/Cortez/Longboat Key Beaches
10. Mote Marine Science Center/City Island Park/Bird Sanctuary
11. North Lido/Lido/South Lido Beaches
12. Siesta Beach & Turtle Beach
13. Palmer Point/Blackburn Point/Nokomis Beach/North Jetty Beach/ South Jetty/Venice Beach/Broward Park/Caspersen Beach
14. Manasota/Blind Pass/Englewood/Port Charlotte Beaches
15. Boca Grande Beaches/Hike & Bike Trail
16. Cayo Costa State Park
17. Lighthouse/Bowmans/Turners/Captiva Beaches
18. Louise Perry Tract/Gulfside Beach
19. San Carlos Bay/Bunche Beach
20. Matanzas Pass Preserve
21. Lovers Key SRA
22. Carl E. Johnson County Park
23. Bonita Beach/Lely Barefoot Beach/Barefoot Beach State Preserve
24. Delnor-Wiggins Pass SRA/Vanderbilt Beach
25. Naples Area Beaches
26. Tigertail Beach/Point Marco Beach/Caxambas Park·

Black skimmers

years of this kind of exploitation, the state acquired the island and opened it as a state recreation area in 1984. Honeymoon Island has the distinction of being Florida's most heavily attended state park. Ther are 400 acres of beach, with sand dunes, marsh, and mangrove swamps for exploration stretching over three miles.

Three miles of footpaths and trail wind through the island's secluded northern tip, which still looks much as it did when the Tocobago Indians, inheritors of the Safety Island culture, made it their home – before European diseases wiped them out. Along these trails, there are still stands of virgin slash pine, where ospreys nest, and huge virgin black mangrove trees in the swamps along the northern beach. Beach activities center along the southwest shore where a nearby picnic ground offers 100 tables and grills.

Undisturbed **Caladesi Island** is accessible only by boat. Every hour between 10 a.m. and 4 p.m. a privately-owned ferry service whisks day visitors in a matter of minutes between Honeymoon Island docks near Hurricane Pass and a quiet, mangrove-lined marina which also houses the park office and concession store. The marina offers private boaters docking for a fee. From there dune-protecting boardwalks lead to the swimming beach, bathhouses, and picnic grounds.

The three-mile **Hammock Loop nature trail,** never out of reach of the sea, takes you from the picnic grounds through the island's interior of live oak, sabal palm, and virgin slash pine flatwoods, then back to the beach strand. The easy to moderate trail takes you past the high stick nests of several osprey.

Shelling is superb on the strand, especially in April and May when the prized common baby's ear, tiger eye and netted olive are likely to be found in quantity. During the summer, sea turtles, including endangered leatherbacks, loggerhead, and hawksbill nest there. Shore, wading, and migratory birds abound but the islands harbor few mammals, reptiles, or amphibians. A list of shells and vertebrates found on the island is available on request at the park office. The park opens at 8 a.m. and closes at sunset year around.

A third island, **Anclote Key State Preserve** is six miles north of Honeymoon Island. This island has been left in its natural state with only a small 1/10-acre compound showing any man-made structure. A 100-year-old lighthouse (still operational) is located on the southern end of the island. The island has four miles of sandy beach with a pine flatwood interior and mangrove-lined eastern shore. This island is also reached only by boat and there are no facilities. The island, long and narrow, totals about 160 acres of upland.

To reach these fine islands from Sunshine Skyway Bridge, drive north on U.S. 19 to Dunedin and turn west on Curlew Road or S.R. 586 to Alternate U.S. 19 and the Dunedin Causeway to the park entrance.

Pinellas County Suncoast Beaches
Beach Frontage: 30 miles
Highlights: beach walks, nature study, swimming, bathhouses, windsurfing, piers, beach-related rentals, scuba, surfing, shelling, fishing, boat ramps, volleyball, concessions, restrooms
Fee(s): metered parking, pier access, beach rentals, toll bridges

Nowhere on the Gulfside west coast has the buildup of highrises, condominiums, commercial businesses and other development reached the limits that Pinellas County Suncoast beaches have experienced. These 30 or so miles of barrier islands have been redesigned to accommodate the tourist and vacation crowds and for those just seeking "the action." Amidst the encroachment, access to the beaches is limited in many sections. With the toll bridges and metered parking, the beaches end up costing more here than further south. Even some of the piers require an admittance fee. Despite the commercialization, these urban sand stretches are still beautiful in their own way and worth a visit, especially if you are looking for company.

Between Clearwater Harbor and the Gulf of Mexico, **Clearwater Beach** lies between Papaya Street at the north and 5th Street at the south end. A municipal beach, these 25 acres of wide white sandy shore have a pier (fee), showers, restrooms, and metered parking. A second municipal beach is between Bay Esplanade and Rockaway Street. This facility has metered parking, a concession stand, showers, and restrooms.There is a small pier here, north of Pier 60, that is free and fine for sunsets. There are also several public access locations at street ends north of the above facilities. Some have parking available on nearby streets. Cabanas, beach pedal "tractors" and other beach paraphernalia may be rented. Skimboarding and kite flying are popular beach activities.

If you feel like setting out on foot three to four miles round-trip to a more remote area of beach, head north towards Dunedin or Big Pass. The people thin out and so does the commercial development. At Dunedin Pass you are only a couple of hundred water yards south from wild and natural **Caladesi Island State Park**.

Driving south on Gulf Boulevard across Clearwater or Little Pass (toll bridge), at the north tip of the island, you will find **Sand Key County Park**. Recently developed, the 95-acre county beach has a minimum of development but includes bathhouses, restrooms and parking. This 2,400-foot high-energy Pinellas County beach has since 1982 acquired 25 additional acres of sand through the natural forces of accretion.

South of Sand Key County Park and past the high rises is the community of **Belleair Beach** and **Belleair Shores**. The beach parking here is restricted to residents, their guests and those who rent property in these communities.

Continuing south on Gulf Boulevard is the community of **Indian Rocks Beach**. Unlike the restrictive parking of the nearby north neighbors, Indian Rocks Beach extends three miles, with public access points at nearly every street end. Read the posted signs closely. Parking is restricted from the late evening to early morning hours, so no overnight parking is permitted. The following streets include limited parking and beach access: 28th Avenue south through 19th Avenue, limited parking at 18th, 17th, 16th, 15th, 12th, 10th, 9th, 8th, 6th Avenues and public access and limited parking at 5th, 4th, 3rd, 2nd, 1st, and Central Avenues. No parking is provided at 28th, 10th, and 5th Avenues. Up until a devastating storm a few years ago, the Big Indian Rocks Fishing Pier was located at 1208 North Gulf Boulevard. The surfing continues to be good here during high waves.

Following Gulf Boulevard south of Indian Rocks Beach you will reach the **Indian Shores** community. Little parking has been provided, but there are pedestrian beach access points at the following Avenues: 201st, 200th, 199th, 198th, 197th, 196th, 195th, 193rd, 190th, and Stella Avenues. Beach and bay access points are provided from 198th Avenue to 190th Avenue. The **Suncoast Seabird Sanctuary** is located at the city limits separating Indian Shores and Redington Shores. The sanctuary is dedicated to saving impaired birds and is open to the public daily. Limited parking is available at the sanctuary.

Redington Shores has eight beach walkway access points to the Gulf but parking is available only on the street: 183rd, Coral, Beach, Atoll, 178th Avenues, 176th Trail, 177th Terrace West, and 176th Avenue. In addition Pinellas County Park Department has established a 3.5-acre beach park at 182nd Avenue that includes benches, showers, restrooms, and free parking. The Long Pier (fee) is at the Gulf end of 175th Avenue.

North Redington Beach has six beach access walkways which are located and marked between 173rd Avenue and Bath Club Circle Drive. Parking may be difficult to find, especially on weekends.

Redington Beach has limited beach access, with walkways to the beach at 157th, 158th, 163rd, and 162nd Avenues and no nearby parking is available. Parking is limited to Redington Beach residents at 160th Avenue.

Madeira Beach has several beach parks, parking, and pedestrian access from the city limits north to John's Pass (2.5 miles). Located between 153rd Avenue and the Tom Stuart Causeway is the five-acre **Archibald Memorial Beach**. Parking is metered. **Madeira Beach Access Park**, a Pinellas County facility that is operated and maintained by the city of Madeira Beach, is a 1.5-acre beach park with 450 feet of frontage, The facilities include parking for 104 vehicles, restroom, and showers. The Madiera Beach Access Park is between Tom Stuart Causeway south and 143rd Avenue. **John's Pass Beach**, at the extreme tip of the island, has three acres of shore and parking for several vehicles. Fishermen will find access to the John's Pass Bridge catwalk where fishing is reported to be some of the best along the Pinellas Suncoast. Beach access, but no parking, is available at the following avenues: 154th, 149th, 148th, 147th, 142nd, 146th, 137th, 136th, 135th, 134th, 133rd, 132nd, 131st, and 130th Avenues.

Crossing south over John's Pass Bridge, **Treasure Island** has some of the best urban beaches along its wide 3.8 miles of strand. St. Petersburg and Treasure Island municipal beach has 75 acres of public beach and is located just south of the Treasure Island Causeway near 112th Avenue. A Pinellas County park is under development at 104th Avenue.

Beach access points are at the end of 127th, 126th, 125th, 124th, 123rd, 122nd, 121st, 120th, 119th Avenues – all north of the Treasure Island Causeway – and 103rd, 102nd, 101st, 100th, 99th, and 97th Avenues, all south of the Treasure Island Causeway. There are several pedestrian access points between 119th Avenue and 103rd Avenue. Bay access is provided at many of the dead ends and picnic facilities, boat ramps, and parking are found at the bayside of 125th and 123rd Avenues. Sunset Beach at the south tip of the island has beach parking at Wacker Park, 88th, 82nd, 77th, 78th, and 79th Avenues.

South of Treasure Island is the 7.5-mile island of **St. Petersburg Beach**, the southernmost developed beach community on the Pinellas County Suncoast. **Upham Beach** and **Pass-a-Grille Beach** are the major public beaches. Nine-acre Upham Beach is adjacent to Blind Pass along Beach Plaza Drive south of St. Petersburg Causeway and includes a playground, concessions, restroom, and parking. At the extreme south end of the island is 27-acre Pass-a-

Grille Beach with restrooms, plenty of metered parking, concessions, and lifeguards. The seawall and jetty are popular spots for fishing along with the bayside walkway. There are numerous rentals for windsurfing, jetskiing, boating, or para-sailing here as elsewhere along the Pinellas Coast. Beach access has been provided at the following points: 55th, 52nd, 51st, 37th and 36th Avenues, south of the St. Petersburg Beach Causeway and north of the Bayway A-19A toll bridge. Beach access points: 35th, 32nd, 30th, 29th, and 28th Avenues are restricted to area residents. Further public beach access points are located at the street end of 27th, 26th, and 23rd Avenues south of the Bayway A-19A toll bridge.

All of the aforementioned Pinellas County beaches are accessible via Gulf Boulevard/S.R. 699 from Clearwater to Pass-a-Grille.

Clearwater Marine Science Center and Sea Aquarium

Clearwater/Pinellas County
Highlights: nature study, exhibits, aquariums, environmental education laboratory, library, research, membership, gift shop
Fee(s): entrance, parking

The **Clearwater Marine Science Center and Sea Aquarium** is making history, both local and international, in its huge building on Clearwater Bay. Visiting it is a vital experience. Its many exhibits include a fascinating variety of aquariums teeming with native and tropical fish, sea horses, stone crabs, lobsters, and other forms of sea life. There's even a "touch tank" and a 500-pound loggerhead turtle named Big Mo, who has a 65,000-gallon tank to call home. Hundreds of turtles have hatched from their eggs at the Center and been released into the sea by the devoted staff. Under construction now is a Sea Aquarium to provide an even more exciting look at local sea life. On the drawing board are plans for converting some of the large holding tanks into communities for other marine organisms of the mangrove swamps, grass flats, and coral reefs. Windows in these additions will let scientists study and visitors view marine life under conditions very close to natural.

The Center is the only facility on the Florida west coast for rescue and rehabilitation of endangered species. Other aquariums in this country and abroad are watching their techniques with a view to setting up similar rescue operations of their own. The Center bought its facility from the city of Clearwater in 1979 for one dollar. Formerly a wastewater treatment plant, the building's enormous holding tanks were its main attraction. The Center is a non-profit institution open to the public. It depends on donations from visitors, gifts, and grants from public and private agencies and foundations.

To reach the Center from Sunshine Skyway Bridge U.S. 19, drive north to Clearwater. Turn west on Gulf-to-Bay Boulevard or S.R.60 to Cleveland Street and onto Memorial Causeway. Turn north at midpoint of Memorial Causeway onto Island Drive and then proceed west on Windward Passage. Metered and limited parking is available at the Center at 249 Windward Passage. The hours are from 9 a.m. to 5 p.m. Monday through Friday, 9 a.m. to 4 p.m. on Saturday, and 11 a.m. to 4 p.m. on Sunday.

Suncoast Seabird Sanctuary
Indian Shores/Pinellas County
Area: 1 acre
Highlights: nature study, tours, wild bird hospital & aviary
Fee(s): donation requested

Walled in between two highrises along the sandy south beach of Indian Shores is what appears to be from a distance a busy avian menagerie or bird rookery. Walking closer one discovers that it is a one-acre beach home that has been turned into a sanctuary for injured birds.

Established in 1972, the Suncoast Seabird Sanctuary was founded by zoologist Ralph T. Heath as a non-profit organization. It all began with an injured cormorant and Ralph's desire to help. Before long everybody who had discovered an injured bird was bringing it to be cared for at the Heath residence. Today as a result of this sensitive effort to aid the helpless birds, the sanctuary is one of the largest in the world. Nearly 90% of the birds brought to the sanctuary have been accidentally or maliciously injured by people. Over 500 species of birds have at one time or another recuperated in the sanctuary's fenced compound. At least 150 to 200 of these unfortunate creatures have been the endangered brown pelican. A qualified small professioal staff is on duty to provide proper health care and to carry on research. An average of 15 to 20 birds are brought in daily. Over 100,000 birds have been restored to health and released back into the wild. Birth of healthy chicks has been achieved by crippled parents who will spend the rest of their days at the sanctuary. The open roof of the wire cages allows rehabilitated birds to fly free as they choose when they feel and hear the call of the wild.

Visitors are welcome to stop by. The sanctuary is open for visitors from 9 a.m. to dark daily. To reach Suncoast Seabird Sanctuary from Sunshine Skyway Bridge U.S. 19, drive north to Alternate U.S. 19, S.R. 595 or 5th Avenue and turn west. Continue on Alternate 19 across Seminole Bridge and bear left onto the Tom Stuart Causeway over Boca Ciega Bay to Gulf Boulevard or S.R. 699 and turn north. Follow Gulf Boulevard to the sanctuary entrance and small parking lot at 18328 Gulf Boulevard in Indian Shores.

Fort De Soto Park
Mullet Key/Pinellas County
Beach Frontage: 5 miles
Area: 900 acres
Highlights: nature study, historical site, picnicking, shelters, swimming (lifeguards), pier, fishing, boat ramp, bicycling, playground, restrooms, concessions, camping
Fee(s): camping and toll bridges

Situated at the mouth of Tampa Bay, scenic and historic Ft. DeSoto County Park is composed of five islands or keys joined together by causeways: **Madelaine Key** (picnic area and boat ramp), **St. Christopher Key** (camping), **St. Jean** (camping), **Bonne Fortune** (service area) and the main **Mullet Key** (picnicking, fishing, pier, swimming beaches, Ft. DeSoto itself, restaurant, gift shop and administrative center). The five miles of natural sandy white beach along the Gulf of Mexico and Tampa Bay are inviting to explore. There are two designated swimming beaches on Mullet Key and the nearby picnic areas are pleasantly designed. If you fish or enjoy the pier atmosphere there is a 500-foot fishing pier on Tampa Bay that has a food and bait concession building. Camping is very popular and the campgrounds are usually filled, but reservations are accepted 30 days in advance in person (not by telephone or mail).

Besides the abundant natural history, the park is rich in human history. Mounds constructed by prehistoric Indians were once evident. Ponce de Leon landed here and engaged hostile tribesmen in armed combat in 1513 and 1521. Confederate Civil War hero

Robert E. Lee once visited and recommended that the keys be built up for defense of the Tampa Bay harbor and coastline. During the Civil War it was a Union stronghold and headquarters for blocking the bay. The fort was begun during the Spanish American War of 1898 and was completed by 1900. But it never fired a shot from its still intact 12-inch mortars. The fort now has public walkways around and on top of the ramparts. Flags from all of the 50 states are displayed daily. It is a fine spot to watch unobstructed sunsets. Most Pinellas County residents agree, as you probably will too, that Ft. DeSoto is their favorite park. To reach Ft. DeSoto County Park from Sunshine Skyway Bridge U.S. 19 (there are good views of the bridge from the park), drive north to Alternate 19A and turn west. Continue west on Alternate 19A to Bayway Road and turn south, then go directly to the park entrance. You will cross two toll bridges enroute. The park is open daily from 7 a.m. until dark.

E. G. Simmons Regional Park

Ruskin/Hillsborough County
Area: 469 acres
Highlights: nature study, manatee sanctuary, picnicking, shelters, swimming, fishing, boat ramp, canoeing, bicycling, playground, restrooms, camping
Fee(s): camping

Formerly a mangrove swamp, the upland portion of this Hillsborough County beach park is entirely composed of reclaimed dredged fill from adjacent Tampa Bay. The man-made islands are surrounded by 200 acres of channels, coves, passes, inlets, and mangrove forest sanctuary, providing a harmonious environment for birds and other wildlife.

Walking areas are limited in the park and are probably best along the beach, with its remaining mangroves and open sweeping vistas of Tampa Bay and the skylines of Tampa and St. Petersburg. Manatees are usually sighted at least once a month, mainly in summer. Additional endangered species sometimes seen include the roseate spoonbill and our national bird, the bald eagle. Bird watching is a popular pastime beside the shallow waters of the outlying mangrove swamp forest. Entirely devoid of vegetation at first, the park was landscaped with over 7,500 native and exotic species. It is one of the few sizeable parks open to the public that borders Tampa Bay.

To reach E. G. Simmons Regional Park from I-75 take S.R. 674 or the Ruskin-Wimauma Road in south Hillsborough County and head west to the city of Ruskin. Turn north on the Tamiami Trail or U.S. 41 and proceed through Ruskin about 1.5 miles to 19th Avenue NW and turn west. The road dead ends at the park entrance after two miles. The park hours are from sunrise to dark April 1st through October 15th, and 6 a.m. to dark October 15th to March 31st.

Manatee County Beach/Holmes Beach/ Anna Maria Bayfront & Beach
Anna Maria Key/Manatee County
Beach Frontage: 16,000 feet
Highlights: nature study, picnicking, shelters, pier, fishing, boat ramp, swimming, surfing, showers, playground, pavilion, restrooms, concessions

Day users will enjoy the small beach town's atmosphere and lapping surf of Anna Maria Key. The sparkling sand is easily accessible by car and then on foot. In the not-so-distant past, authors and other celebrities have found this barrier island an ideal place to live and enjoy the calm quiet. Today's visitor can expect more congestion but may also find the beach has special attractions.

Manatee County Public Beach comprises 10 acres and 900 feet of family fun beach. There is a children's playground, a pavilion with plaza, concessions, showers, and restrooms. Assigned lifeguards watch for swimmers' safety. A terraced picnic spot under Australian pines makes for fine shade and whispers as the breezes blow through the needles. Manatee County Beach is located at the junction of Gulf Boulevard and Manatee Avenue or S.R. 64 west, just after the crossing of Anna Maria Bridge at the community of Holmes Beach.

North along the narrow island's tree-named streets leading to the Gulf of Mexico and the bayside of Sarasota Pass are numerous well marked beach footpaths leading to **Holmes Beach** sands. Parking may be difficult to find on the nearly three miles of strand along S.R. 789 or Gulf Drive. The further northwest one drives on S.R. 789 towards Bean Point, the greater the feeling of being alone with the sea and sand. The most "faraway" portion of the island is the extreme tip north of the village of Anna Maria. Two fishing piers face out to the northeast side and Tampa Bay. Good vistas of Outer Passage Key and the Sunshine Skyway Bridge that spans the bay appear on a clear day. Things seem less hurried out here.

The **Anna Maria Bayfront park** just north of the south pier has swimming, surfing, shelling, fishing, sheltered picnicking with barbecue grills, playground equipment, the bayside beach, historical markers, and restrooms. The sandy beach areas and access points are plentiful on foot due to the limited car parking along Bay Boulevard and North Shore Drive at the extreme north tip of Bean Point. The Bayfront Park is owned by the city of Anna Maria and maintained by the Manatee County Park Department.

To reach Anna Maria Island or Key and beaches from I-75 take the S.R.64 exit 42 west through Bradenton directly to Gulf Boulevard and Anna Maria Island.

Coquina/Cortez/Longboat Beaches
Anna Maria Key & Long Boat Key/Manatee County
Beach Frontage: 5,100 ft. (Coquina & Cortez); 4,000 ft. (Longboat)
Highlights: nature study, fitness trail, swimming (lifeguards), nature walks, limited surfing, fishing, boat ramp & dock, picnicking, shelters, playground, restrooms, showers, concessions

These three Manatee County beach parks offer a full day's outing which includes a fine mix of active and passive urban beach fare. Once connected by land, Anna Maria Key and Longboat Key are now severed by Longboat Pass, but have been reconnected by the Longboat Bridge.

Coquina and Cortez public beaches are located on Gulf Boulevard in the city of Bradenton Beach at Anna Maria Key's south tip and actually are one big beach. The white sandy shore is a mile long on the Gulf side and there is a mile of waterfront on the Sarasota Bay side. There is swimming, shelling, sunning, fishing, a large boat ramp and dock on bayside, a playground, picnicking with shelters, charcoal grills, volleyball, showers, restrooms, and a refreshment pavilion. Locally known as "South End Beach," this 96-acre park was always a favorite summer retreat, even before bridges made it easy to reach. There is plenty of free parking.

The backside or bayside of Coquina Beach has recently added a nature walk on **Leffis Key**. The combination of boardwalk and shell trail weaves along the edge of the mangroves and onto the man-made elevated island, with great views of Sarasota Pass and surroundings. Park in the spacious Coquina Beach area and walk across Gulf Drive to the **Key trail** which is about 3/4 mile long.

Directly south across Longboat Pass is **Longboat Public Beach**, the north end of Longboat Key which is better known locally as Greer Island or "Beer Can Island". Normally quiet and uncrowded, Longboat Public Beach is undeveloped and plans are to keep it that way. The north portion is actually an island that has disappeared and reappeared a few times in this century. Supposedly this is where most of the beer cans are, but it is also the most natural section of the beach. Saltwater shore fishing is reported to be good, with catches of tarpon, grouper, speckled trout, snook, and redfish. Occasionally larger marine creatures such as pilot whales become beached. Current condo growth threatens to reduce the quality of this beach, as has happened along the entire length of 12-mile Longboat Key. Longboat Public Beach is one of the very limited public beach access points on Longboat Key. Parking is limited at North Shore Road and Broadway Avenue on the Gulf side. Wooden dune crossovers direct visitors to the wide sandy beach.

To reach Coquina, Cortez and Longboat Public beaches from I-75 take exit 42 west on S.R. 64 to Bradenton and on through to Anna Maria Key. At Anna Maria Key turn south on Gulf Drive to the south tip of the island and Coquina and Cortez beaches. To reach Longboat Beach proceed south across Longboat Pass to the first road west called North Shore Road. The hours of these three Manatee County beaches are from sunrise to midnight.

Mote Marine Science Center/ City Island Park/Bird Sanctuary

City Island/Sarasota County
Highlights: nature study, bird sanctuary, marine exhibits, tours, lectures, publications, membership, gift shop, nature walk, picnicking, boat launch ramp, boat rentals, boat storage, fishing piers, restrooms
Fee(s): museum entrance, boat rentals & storage at City Island Park

The **Mote Marine Science Center and Laboratory** have made City Island their home since 1978. The Science Center is largely devoted to exhibiting and providing information about sea and plant life indigenous to Sarasota Bay and the Gulf of Mexico. Thirty-five tanks are filled with sharks, clams, fish, lobsters, turtles, shrimp, and other forms of sea life. Displays such as the outstanding shell collection are changed seasonally and give the visitor a good picture of the invisible underwater world that surrounds us.

The Science Center has two important and unique marine habitats: a marine grassflats community and a functioning mangrove swamp. Sea water flowing across the grassflats becomes the source of water for the mangrove swamp which is pumped in from the nearby New Pass. The unfiltered water carries with it seasonal larvae including oysters, mussels, tree crabs and spiders. Other plants and animals found in the exhibits include sponges, scallops, starfish, sand dollars, turtle grass, coral pieces, sea cucumbers, and horse conchs. Even red, white, and black mangroves thrive.

The Mote Marine Laboratory has earned a world-wide reputation for marine science and for its staff of internationally recognized scientists. A day visit to the Center will give you a better under-standing and appreciation of the regional aquatic life. After the Science Center tour you may want to enjoy the picnicking facilities at **City Island Park**. Turn right or east as you leave the Science Center parking lot entrance and drive to the east end of the island. The 83 acres include fishing piers, boat rentals, a boat launching ramp, and fine views of Sarasota Bay and skyline. A **Bay Area Nature Walk** begins behind the aquarium.

To reach Mote Marine Science Center and City Island Park from I-75, take the Fruitville Road/S.R. 780 exit 39 west to Main Street in downtown Sarasota. Follow Main Street to the John Ringling Boulevard and Causeway and cross over the Bay to St. Armands Circle. Continue north on John Ringling Parkway from St. Armands Circle and just before the New Pass Bridge to Longboat Key take a right onto City Island Road and follow the signs. The Science Center will be on your right. The Mote Marine Science Center is open to visitors from 10 a.m. to 4 p.m. Tuesday through Saturday. Sunday hours are from 12 to 4 p.m. The Science Center is closed Mondays. City Island Park is open from sunrise to dark.

Just east of the Mote Marine Aquarium is the **Pelican Man's Bird Sanctuary** which is an educational experience for all. Dale Shields, "The Pelican Man," and numerous volunteers operate the sanctuary for injured native and migratory birds. The sanctuary is open daily and admission is free.

North Lido/Lido/South Lido Beaches
Lido Key/Sarasota County
Beach Frontage: 6,800 ft. total
Area: 200 acres total
Highlights: nature study, nature trail, swimming, lifeguards, fishing, picnicking, playground, horseshoes, volleyball, showers, restrooms, concessions
Fee(s): beach rentals, swimming pool fee

Lido Key is highly condo-ized and developed, as are the rest of the offshore barrier islands near Sarasota. These three popular Lido Key beaches are "in" spots and the limited parking lots fill up quickly on nice days the year around. The nearby St. Armands Circle with its European atmosphere provides the beaches with a cosmopolitan air. The three stretches of strand vary from developed to primitive. **North Lido Beach**, as the name suggests, lies just north of Lido Beach. The undeveloped shore has long been popular for swimming, fishing, shelling, and sunning. This 76-acre section includes a large Australian Pine woodland with several unmarked old road trails ideal for walking. Joggers are commonly spotted along the flat shore. There are no facilities. Park your car in the Lido Beach parking lot and walk north towards New Pass.

Lido Municipal beach is Sarasota's public bathing beach. The wide open strand and the swank "mini" Miami Beach setting offers 23 acres of fine quartz sand plus a swimming pool, lifeguards, bath house, cabanas, casino with concessions, picnicking, playground, showers and restrooms, The sands of Lido are highly sensitive and subject to erosion. Stabilizing plants and artificial offshore reefs help to protect its ever-changing shores.

At the extreme south tip of the once-mangrove island lies **South Lido Beach**. Benjamin Franklin Drive will take you to this pleasantly shaded semi-natural 100-acre Sarasota County Beach. The beach offerings include swimming (lifeguards), shelling, fishing, picnicking, a playground, horseshoe and volleyball courts, restrooms, showers,shelters, and beach trails. An interpretive nature trail has been recently constructed with a boardwalk that leads through a coastal mangrove forest and coastal hammock. Ah observation tower and platform deck with raised boardwalk are in the planning stage. There are good views of the Sarasota skyline across Sarasota Bay and Siesta Key across Big Pass.

To reach Lido Key and its beaches from I-75 take the Fruitville Road/S.R. 780 exit 39 west to Main Street in Sarasota. Follow Main Street west through Sarasota to the John Ringling Boulevard and Causeway over Sarasota Bay. Continue west and go around St. Armands Circle to Benjamin Franklin Drive. The Lido Municipal Beach will be around the first open bend and view of the Gulf of Mexico.

Siesta Beach & Turtle Beach
Siesta Key/Sarasota County
Beach Frontage: 2,400 ft. (Siesta); 2,500 ft. (Turtle)
Highlights: nature study, swimming (lifeguards), windsurfing, surfing, fishing, boat ramps, picnicking, shelters, fitness nature trail, tennis, volleyball, basketball, softball, football, soccer, playground, recreation building, casino, showers, restrooms
Fee(s): recreation building rental, beach rentals

According to a 1950 *National Geographic* magazine article, Siesta Key was considered to be one of the 10 most beautiful beaches in the world. Forty years later the beauty and tranquility are still present amidst the phenomenal development and encroachment that has taken place. It remains one of the best active beaches on the west Gulf coast. Sarasota County Park Department maintains and owns the two distinctively different beaches: Siesta and Turtle. They are connected to the mainland by two bridges at the north tip and center of the island. The white crystal sands of both beaches are 99% quartz that may have drifted from the upper Gulf or possibly from the Appalachian Mountains thousands of years ago.

Mid-key and north of Turtle Beach on Beach Road is **Siesta Key Park and Beach**. No other Gulf coast beach offers more active recreation facilities. The 40 acres of strand is wide and the space accommodates a large number of visitors and their cars. The center of things is the park pavilion or casino which offers concessions, showers, restrooms, and a place to socialize. The nature fitness trail is an exercise course with 20 stations spread out over a mile and leading along shady Australian pine-lined pathways. Picnicking areas, swimming, volleyball, basketball courts, soccer, tennis, play-fields, playground, football, and softball fields are among the offerings here. Surfers are occasionaly seen at the north end of the point near Big Pass. There are numerous access pathways with limited parking at the following points:

- Shell Road, fair surfing, access point near Big Pass.
- Avenida Messinao, fair surfing, access point near Big Pass.
- Columbus Blvd.
- Avenida Navarre.
- Ocean Blvd.
- Calle de Siesta.
- Plaza de la Palmas #1.
- Plaza de la Palmas #2.
- Calle del Invierno.
- Stickney Point Road.
- Point O'Rocks 20, ideal for diving and shelling.

Turtle Beach, located near the southern tip of Siesta Key is the smaller (14 acres), and more private, but offers nearly everything the beach to the immediate north does. The shelling, swimming, and fishing are good and there are sheltered picnicking facilities beneath the Australian pines. Other facilities include playground equipment, a volleyball court, horseshoes, two bayside boat ramps, showers, and restrooms. The parking lot and shell road separates the park from the beach area. A recreational building with indoor rental space is also available along with concessions.

To reach Siesta Key and beaches from I-75 take the S.R. 72/Clark Road exit 37 west. As you near Tamiami Trail/U.S. 41, Clark Road becomes Stickney Point Road and curves southwest. Follow Stickney Point Road west across Tamiami Trail/U.S. 41 and the causeway bridge to Midnight Pass Road, the central throughfare of Siesta Key. Head north to Siesta Key Beach or south to Turtle Beach. Follow the well posted signs. Siesta Drive at the north tip of the island crosses over to Sarasota Florida.

Palmer Point/Blackburn Point/
Nokomis Beach/North Jetty Beach
Casey Key/Sarasota County
Beach Frontage: 5,000 ft.
Highlights: nature study, swimming, surfing, lifeguards, fishing, boat ramps, picnicking, shelters, playground, horseshoes, volleyball, showers, restrooms, concessions

Casey Key is a low-lying, long and narrow barrier island that stretches from Midnight Pass south to Casey Pass/Venice Inlet, a distance of over nine miles. The key was named in honor of Captain John Charles Casey who had surveyed a trusty coastal map of the region south of Tampa Bay. The south tip of Casey Key is where accessibility and the beach is best. Nokomis Beach greets you as you cross over the Back Bay Bridge on Albee Road from the village of Nokomis and the Tamiami Trail/U.S. 41 north of Venice. This wide, active 10-acre beach has a concession stand, sheltered picnic sites, two boat ramps, lifeguards, swimming, fishing, volleyball, and a playground. The parking lot fills quickly during beautiful sunny days year round. The beach walk from Nokomis to North Jetty is recommended since it is under a mile round trip and the two points are in clear view of each other. The name Nokomis is derived from homesteaders who were inspired by Longfellow's poem, *Hiawatha*. Nokomis is an Objibway Indian word meaning "grandmother."

To reach North Jetty Beach by car continue south on North Jetty Road. The projecting seaward north and south jettys have been erected to prevent further erosion and to build up the beaches by directing sand flow. The jettys also provide boats an easier passage to the sea through the inlet. It so happens that the jettys have also created the best surfing on the west coast of Florida. Casey Pass was established when men with shovels and other hand equipment dug out the connecting land bridge early in the 20th century.

The North Jetty Beach has a fishing camp with concessions and fishing bait. Friendly pelicans mix with visitors. Manatees have been seen in the back bays. The wooded Australian pine area of the park offers picnicking under rustic shelters, playground equipment, horseshoe pits, and restrooms. The sandy white beach is walkable to Nokomis Beach at the north. In between is South Nokomis Beach, with one acre and 300 feet of beach frontage.

To complete your visit of Casey Key drive north on Casey Key Road past beach homes and a very narrow ribbon of strand to the extreme north tip of the island. **Palmer Point Conservation District** is a 24-acre sanctuary with native vegetation and wildlife, fishing, picnicking, and swimming. Palmer Point lies at the end of a private residential road where Casey Key Road bears east on Blackburn Point Road/S.R. 789. Before you reach the bridge over

Little Sarasota Bay, you will see Blackburn Point Park on the north side of the road. The pocket park offers five acres of fishing, picnicking and fine vistas of Midnight Pass along its mangrove-lined shore.

To reach Casey Key from I-75, take the Venice exits 34 and/or 35 to Venice Avenue and drive west to the Tamiami Trail/U.S. 41 By-pass. Go north across Curry Creek and Dona Bay and turn west on Albee Road. Drive directly to Nokomis Beach. Turn south on Casey Key Road and proceed to North Jetty Beach. In addition, southbound traffic only may exit from I-75 at S.R. 681 exit 36 to Laurel via Tamiami Trail/U.S. 41. Continue south on Tamiami Trail/U.S. 41 to Albee Road and turn west.

South Jetty/Venice Municipal Beach/ Broward Park/Caspersen Beach

Venice/Sarasota County
Beach Frontage: 5.5 miles South Jetty to Caspersen Beach
Highlights: nature study, nature trail, fitness trail, swimming, surfing, diving, fossil collecting, fishing, boating, boat ramps, lifeguards, picnicking, shelters, pier, volleyball, showers, restrooms, concessions

Venice beaches range from highly developed to pleasantly semi-wild and have a "scene" for nearly every beachgoer. The City of Venice and Sarasota County Parks and Recreation Department maintain these high quality beaches. A unique feature of the Venice littoral is the deposits of shark teeth and fossils. From Venice south to Sanibel Island, along with beaches in California and Maryland, are the best areas to find fossilized shark teeth in the United States. The usually dark-shaded teeth are 1.5 million years old and originate from mako, tiger, lemon, sand, bull, dusky, and hemipristis sharks. Recent shark teeth are white. The average shark produces and loses thousands of teeth in a lifetime. Also washing ashore from the long sloping continental shelf are such Pleistocene fossils as mammoth, cave bear, and saber-toothed tiger fragments. Shell collectors will find good yields as well. The best finds follow a storm.

South Jetty is a two-acre municipal beach park where such activities as fishing, surfing and boatwatching are popular. Built in the 1930's, the boulder-lined jetty projects into the Gulf waters to temper the highly erosive waves and to protect the boats that come and go from Lyons, Dona, and Roberts Bays. South Jetty is at the end of Tarpon Center Drive from The Esplanade and West Venice Avenue about a mile north of the Venice City Beach. Enroute to South Jetty Park on the east side of Tarpon Center Drive is the 1.2-acre **Higel Park**. This marine-oriented city park provides access for boats to Roberts Bay, along with picnicking and restrooms.

The five-acre **Venice Municipal Beach**, operated by the Sarasota County Parks and Recreation Department, has the usual beach fare and atmosphere: swimming, sunbathing, lifeguards, playground, picnic tables and shelters, grills, fishing, volleyball, a fitness trail, showers, and restrooms, plus plenty of boy and girl watching. Concessions may be purchased at the hyperbolic-shaped beach casino, which is designed to reflect the sun's searing rays and to deflect the wind and rain. If you feel like strolling a few city blocks, try the landscaped walk up and down adjacent West Venice Avenue median.

South of the Venice Municipal Beach about two miles, and south of West Venice Avenue on Harbor Drive, is the 65-acre **Brohard Park** and **Venice Pier**. Brohard Park originated from airport property donated to the city of Venice by the Federal Government. The Venice Pier has recently undergone repairs and a fee is charged for day use. Due to the erection of sea walls to control the heavy erosion, the walk to Venice Pier from Venice Municipal Beach is not recommended. South of the city of Venice the vistas are more open, unmarred by highrise buildings and the vegetation is more natural. Swimming, shelling, fossil collecting, sunning, fishing, picnicking, restrooms, concessions, and exploring are offered. Parking is available at the pier and other access points. The beach frontage is over a mile and merges with Caspersen Beach, the next strand park to the south.

If you continue your drive south on Harbor Drive, you will enter the 327-acre **Caspersen Beach Park**, administered by Sarasota County Parks and Recreation Department. One of the most natural stretches of shore along the Gulf coast, the park's 740-foot boardwalk and dune crossovers give access from the spacious parking areas to the sandy beach. For the adventuresome, you could make a day hike from Caspersen's Beach south to Manasota Public Beach and return. Picnic tables with grills have been provided in a sabal palm hammock near the parking area, along with showers and restrooms.

A 1/3-mile interpretive trail winds through a salt marsh and coastal beach hammock. Sea oats and other native beach vegetation have been planted to prevent erosion and restore the natural character. You can enjoy the widely used bluff walk along an old paved roadbed where the entrance road ends. The old road bed follows the shoreline south through revegetating dune hammock. This is a good alternative to the beach on windy days. Activities at Caspersen's Beach include

The Old Road, Caspersen's Beach

swimming, shelling, wildlife observation, and fossil collecting. Reportedly this is the best beach for locating large ancient shark teeth. Caspersen's is a first-class park thanks to the help of several govermental agencies. Definitely a model for other beach parks.

To reach the Venice beaches from I-75 take the Jacaranda Avenue exit 34 or Everglades Boulevard exit 35 west to Venice Avenue. Follow Venice Avenue to Harbor Drive; turn south on Harbor Drive for Venice Pier, Brohard Park and/or Caspersen's Beach, or continue westward along West Venice Avenue towards Venice Beach (which is also enroute to Higel Park and South Jetty Park).

Manasota/Blind Pass/Englewood & Port Charlotte Beaches
Manasota Key/Sarasota and Charlotte Counties
Beach Frontage: 10,000 ft. total
Highlights: nature study, nature trails, swimming, lifeguards, limited surfing, fishing, boating, boat ramps, picnicking, shelters, showers, restrooms, concessions, beach rentals
Fee(s): beach rentals

Numerous beach homes but few highrises line the Gulf shore and back bay of Manasota Key – a barrier island that has managed to retain an uncrowded beach atmosphere. The wide strand enables the day tripper to walk or jog the entire length from Caspersen's Beach to the south tip of Manasota Key at Stump Pass, Port Charlotte Beach State Recreation Area, barring the few places where heavy erosion has created sea walls and makes passage difficult.

Near the north end of the key is **Manasota Public Beach,** a 14-acre, 1,300-foot sand and surf beach administered by Sarasota County Parks and Recreation Department. Picnicking, with sheltered tables and grills, is popular, along with swimming, fishing, shelling and sunning. A lifeguard is normally on duty year round. A bathhouse, restroom facilities, and dune walkovers have been provided. A boat ramp and scenic boardwalk has been recently constructed on Lemon Bay near Manasota Bridge. This is at the east side of the road across from the parking area. Unmarked paths weave through the sabal palm hammock north of the parking and picnic areas. This is a fine beach for walking either north to Caspersen's Beach or south to Stump Pass. Be advised: parking fills up quickly on nice sunny days.

Driving southward on Manasota Key Road past well landscaped and unobtrusive beach homes for nearly four miles, you will arrive at **Blind Pass Beach.** This Sarasota County beach is highly susceptible to erosion and sands come and go with the storms. Plenty of parking is found on the east side of the road. Sunning, swimming, and shelling are the main beach things to do on this 1/4-mile-long beach The county hopes to make improvements in the near future, which would include picnic facilities, restrooms and a nature trail.

Further south across the line into Charlotte County is **Englewood Beach.** It is a county-administered beach with a city beach feeling. Charlotte County's only beach is 11 acres of white sands, sea oats, picnic tables and shelters, boardwalks, paved parking lots, concessions with beach rentals, and plenty of space to socialize.

Locally known as "Stump Pass Beach," **Port Charlotte Beach State Recreation Area** lies directly south of Englewood Beach about one mile. This 25-acre finger-like projection of sand at the extreme southern tip of Manasota Key has over one mile of beach frontage. Two associated islands, Petersen and Whidden, located on the Lemon Bay side of the key, are also part of the holdings. The two plant communities of coastal strand and mangrove swamps are well developed but the exotic Australian pines and Brazilian pepper have made a strong invasion. There is a complete list of the plants at this natural undeveloped beach available from the district office at Oscar Scherer State Park. As with all Manasota Key beaches, prehistoric black shark teeth are commonly found along the beach. Due to the limited parking at the closed entrance gate to Port Charlotte Beach at the end of Gulf Boulevard, it is best to park at Englewood Beach and walk down via the boulevard (seawalls prevent beach entry).

Shark's teeth, Port Charlotte

Just south across Stump Pass is Knight Island, Don Pedro Island and Little Gasparilla Island, accessible only by boat or ferry at Panama Boulevard on Placida Road/Charlotte County 775. The Department of Natural Resources is considering buying 130 acres of prime beachfront land on Don Pedro Island. Currently, residents of the islands have the best access and use of the beaches.

Another park to enjoy while in the Englewood area is Indian Mound Park along Lemon Bay. Once the site of a prehistoric Calusa Indian village dating to 400 B.C., the point is now a Sarasota County Park with swimming, picnicking with shelters, fishing, boat ramp, restrooms and mound exploration along the short trails through sabal palms and live oaks. There are good views of Lemon Bay and the back sides of Manasota Key from the remaining burial mound and shoreline. Indian Mound Park is at the end of Winton Avenue on Lemon Bay, accessible from West Dearborn and County Road 775 or Indiana Avenue in Englewood. Just follow the brown and white lettered signs.

To reach Manasota Key from I-75, take the Venice exit to Tamiami Trail/U.S. 41 south to C.R. 775 at South Venice. Turn west on the Manasota Beach Road from Tamiami Trail/U.S. 41. The beaches are located along the Manasota Key Road and North Beach Road.

Boca Grande Beaches/Hike & Bike Trail

Boca Grande/Gasparilla Island, Charlotte & Lee Counties
Beach Frontage: 1,000 ft.
Trail Distance: 6.5-mile hike & bike trail
Highlights: nature study, hiking, bicycling, swimming, fishing, picnicking, shelters, historical sites, restrooms, concessions
Fee(s): toll bridge crossing, bicycle rentals

A day visit to out-of-the-way Gasparilla Island at the mouth of Charlotte Harbor is a slow-paced experience of white sugar sand beaches, historic lighthouses and the small village atmoshere of Boca Grande, one of the world's outstanding tarpon fishing centers. The quiet atmosphere is a far cry from the days when it was inhabited by the infamous pirates Jose and Leon Gaspar in the late 18th century.

South of the Boca Grande Causeway and toll bridge, at the Lee and Charlotte County line, and on the east side of Gasparilla Road is the north terminus of the 6.5-mile Boca Grande bicycle and walking path, established in 1985 by Lee County and the people of Boca Grande. Continue south on Gasparilla Road to the town center of

Boca Grande Lighthouse, 1891

Boca Grande. Bicycle rentals are available at East Third Street one block south of the bike/hike path. The paved trail continues south to First Street then heads west two blocks to Gulf Boulevard. It follows the east side of the boulevard south to the southern terminus at Port Circle Drive, entrance to the SDB Railroad property. Along the west side of Gulf Boulevard from First Street south are the public beaches maintained by the Florida Department of Natural Resources.

Boca Grande Beach, now called **Gasparilla Island State Recreation Area**, offers sheltered picnicking, grills, swimming, shelling, fishing, and restrooms. Dolphin observation is very good here as well as along the entire length of the island. The friendly marine mammals frolic in and out of the surf pursuing fish or other dolphins. A 1927 lighthouse is a major feature.

From Boca Grande Beach you can walk north along the sea wall to the undeveloped city beaches of Boca Grande. Foot access streets include West First, West 5th, West 7th, West 10th, West 11th, West 12th, West 13th, West 17th, and West 19th Streets. South of the lighthouse, you can walk around the sea wall to the other beach access points, then up along the road edge of Gulf Boulevard a brief way, past the old pilings of the former fishing pier, to the south tip of Gasparilla Island State Recreation Area and Boca Grande Pass. Bicyclists can continue on Gulf Boulevard from the trail's south terminus to Boca Grande Pass. An abandoned 1927 church, an 1891 Coast Guard lighthouse and two cottages (the whole scene reminiscent of Sanibel Island's Point Ybel) are the main historical attractions at Boca Grande Pass. Sheltered picnicking, fishing, swimming, and shelling are the main recreational activities. The park service is considering ferry service across Boca Grande Pass to Cayo Costa State Park. Incidentally Boca Grande, "Big Mouth" in Spanish, refers to Charlotte Harbor, the deepest natural channel in Florida.

To reach Gasparilla Island beaches, historical sites and the bike-hike trail from I-75, exit south and west from the exchanges at south Venice, exit 35 North Everglades Road; or exit 34 River Road; or the two exchanges at North Port, exit 33 Sumter Boulevard or exit 32 Toledo Blade Road. On reaching U.S. 41/Tamiami Trail, go south from south Venice on S.R. 775 and proceed to Englewood Island. From North Port continue south on U.S. 41 to S.R. 776 just

Sand dollars, Cayo Costa

north of Murdock and go west and south to S.R. 771 near Gulf Cove. S.R. 771 will continue to Placida and the toll bridge to Gasparilla Island.

Cayo Costa State Park
LaCosta Island/Lee County
Beach Frontage: 6 miles
Trail Distance: 5.5 miles
Area: 2,000 acres
Highlights: nature study, hiking, swimming, shelling, boat docks, fishing, picnicking, primitive tent camping, cabins
Fee(s): boat charter service, tent camping, cabin rental

Accessible only by boat, Cayo Costa ("Coast Key") State Park is without doubt the best primitive beach experience on the Gulf coast of Florida. Other than a few private homes, the seemingly remote barrier island is 90% undeveloped and future plans are to keep it in a pristine state. The wild beaches stretch about six miles from Boca Grande Pass south to Captiva Pass. Shell "shunters" will discover an abundance of treasures along the sandy shores, including cockles, whelks, olives, conch, and sea dollars to name a few. Osprey or "fish eagles" nest high in Australian pines along the dunes and southern bald eagles and frigate birds are often seen. Crescent-shaped sand spits or bars, attached to the north gulfside of the barrier island, have created quiet lagoons. High tides and beached uprooted Australian pines may force you to leave the beach temporarily and walk along the unmarked dune paths.

The established and maintained nature trails follow old roads at the north end of the island. The 5.5 miles of trails are mainly north of the tram road between the bayside landing dock and park office (on the one side) and the cabin and campground area on the gulf side of the island's north portion. Setting out on foot from the park office in the direction of the campground (about one mile), you will see trail signs that direct you north past the old water tower and small pioneer graveyard to a "T" junction. Right is the **Pineland Scrub Trail** which leads to the bayside picnic area of **Quarantine Docks** and eventually to **Gulfside Trail** and Boca Grande Pass. Quarantine Docks was where ships and crew suspected of carrying contagious disease were held in isolation from the shore port. Left or west at the "T" leads to Gulfside Trail, Boca Grande Pass, and the campground and cabin area. All trails interconnect in a loop pattern. The north interior of the barrier island is covered with sabal palm hammocks, slash pine forest, and sparsely vegetated dune or former beach ridges. Gumbo limbo trees are outstanding enroute on the .3-mile spur to the picnic area at the Quarantine Docks. Hikers be advised that there are sandspurs, poison ivy, chiggers, mosquitoes, and biting sand flies, but little evidence of fire ants. Wild hogs and snakes are occasionally spotted on the beach or in the forest but are normally afraid of humans.

The 12 cabins, tent campground, and picnic area are located one mile west of the park office along the north Gulf shore. A free tram service is available. The small cabins are furnished with six bunks and a table and can be reserved by calling the park. Cold showers, flush toilets and water are also furnished. The tent campground lies just south of the cabins beneath a shady Australian pine grove. Boat dockage for overnight park campers is located on the gulf side near the cabins. No saltwater fishing license is required. All camping supplies must be provided by campers.

To reach Pineland Marina, or the *Tropic Star* charter ship and other charters to Cayo Costa State Park from I-75, exit 26 west at Bayshore Road in North Fort Myers. Continue west on Pine Island Road/S.R. 78 to Pine Island. On Pine Island, at Pine Island Center, Pine Island Road/S.R. 78 will come to a "T" with S.R. 767. Proceed north on S.R. 767 and drive about three miles, then turn west/left at the Pineland Marina sign. Follow the curving road about two miles to the Pineland Marina. Plenty of free overnight parking is available. For day visitors the park opens at 8 a.m. and closes at sunset year round.

The Florida Department of Natural Resources is planning a ferry Service from Gasparilla Island State Recreation Area at the south tip of Gasparilla Island across Boca Grande Pass to the park office at Cayo Costa State Park.

Lighthouse/Bowmans/Turners/ Captiva Beaches
Sanibel & Captiva Islands/Lee County
Beach Frontage: 7 miles
Highlights: nature study, swimming, shelling, fishing, pier, historic site, restrooms
Fee(s): bridge toll, parking fee at Bowman's Beach

The broad white sandy beaches of Sanibel and Captiva Islands are among the most beautiful and enchanting along the Gulf coast of southern Florida. **Sanibel Island** is named for Santa Isabella, the Queen of Spain and Castile (1474-1504) and wife of Ferdinand II, who aided Columbus. These barrier islands are famous worldwide for their yield of a vast variety of colorful seashells – the third best place in the world after the Philippines and southern Africa. Four hundred different types of shells can be found on these Florida islands. Be aware that the shells are well sought after. Local restrictions limit you to two live shells per species per person. The best shelling times are 15 minutes before sunrise, after a northern storm, preceding the full moon, and at a new moon.

Five-acre **Lighthouse Beach Park** at Point Ybel is the first beach available from the causeway. Two public parking areas are located at the extreme south tip of Sanibel. The picturesque 1884 lighthouse and sun-bleached cottages add charm to this historic beach by San Carlos Bay. This site is listed in the National Register of Historic Places. A 168-foot fishing pier has been constructed on the back bayside and restrooms can be found by the nearby lighthouse. An interpretive display near the west parking lot describes the beach flora and fauna, from molluscs to sea turtles, and the dynamics of the ever-changing beaches. Unmarked walks wind through the interior woodlands of mangrove, Australian pine, Brazilian pepper, seagrape, and cacti. The Gulf-facing beach is wide open for walking from Point Ybel to Bowman's Beach and Blind Pass. Administered by the city of Sanibel and the United States Coast Guard, Lighthouse Beach Park may be reached by driving southeast on Periwinkle Way/Lighthouse Road to the island's end from the first four-way stop after crossing the causeway.

Bowman's Beach, on the north end of Sanibel Island, is named in honor of pioneer Robert Bowman. This Lee County beach park has 2.25 miles of natural beach and sandbar. Swimming, picnicking, shelling, sunbathing, and fishing are popular on this undeveloped beach. There is a most enjoyable walk along the curving strand towards Blind Pass to the north. Few intrepid souls venture here. Old roadpaths through the Australian pines are an alternative to hiking the beach. **Turner's Beach** is situated at Blind Pass. Retrace your steps.

To reach Bowman's Beach turn west on Periwinkle Drive at the first four-way stop after crossing the causeway from the mainland. Continue on Periwinkle Drive until you reach the three-way stop at Tarpon Bay Road. Turn north/right and proceed a short way to the junction with Sanibel-Captiva Road/S.R.867, where you turn west. Continue on Sanibel-Captiva Road/S.R. 867 for about six miles to Bowman's Beach Road and turn left/south. The public fee parking area is located at the end of the road to the right. It is a short walk to the beach across the wooden bridges over the bayou. There are restrooms but no drinking water.

Turner's Beach is located at the extreme north end of Sanibel Island and the extreme south end of Captiva at Blind Pass that separates the islands. Lee County Parks and Recreation purchases the 2.5 miles of Gulf front beach in 1962. Erosion from pounding waves and high winds have been serious in recent years at this "high energy" beach. Blind Pass has been opened and closed at various times by the southward moving "river of sand." Picnicking, swimming (be careful of the powerful undertow), fishing, and shelling are the activities here. Restrooms have been provided. Parking is limited and the lot is often full.

Captiva Island beaches lie just to the north of Turner's Beach. The once wide beaches have been subject to heavy erosion in recent years and groins have been built to prevent further depletion. Nonetheless shelling and sunsets, swimming and fishing remain ideal along the northwest shore. The Gulfside beaches of Captiva are accessible from the Sanibel-Captiva Road/S.R. 867. Pedestrian foot access points are located on street ends at Post Office Corner, Cemetery, Andy Rosse Lane, Wightman Lane, South Seas, and Laika Lane. The furthermost point reachable by motor vehicle has a small parking area. Take Sanibel-Captiva Road to the jog of Coconut Road, then continue north on South Seas Plantation Road to "land's end" parking area. Formerly Captiva Island was connected by a land bridge to North Captiva Island by a spit of land called the "narrows," until a 1921 hurricane created Redfish Pass. Captiva is named for a band of women held hostage in the early days by pirates.

To reach Sanibel and Captiva Islands from I-75 at Fort Myers, exit Palm Beach Boulevard/S.R. 80 west to First Street downtown. Continue west on First Street to McGregor Boulevard/S.R. 867 to the Sanibel Causeway toll bridge.

Louise Perry Tract/Gulfside Beach
Sanibel Island/Lee County
Beach Frontage: 1,000 ft
Area: 34 acres
Highlights: nature study, swimming, lifeguards, picnicking, fishing, restrooms

The **Louise Perry Bird Sanctuary Tract** is a 3.31-acre parcel of undeveloped gulf frontage beach with a small pond that was donated to the U.S. Fish and Wildlife Service in 1963 by Louise Perry. A medical doctor by profession, Mrs. Perry enjoyed shelling and the study of molluscs as a hobby since 1924, when she first arrived as a winter resident on Sanibel Island. In 1940 she published *Marine Shells of the Southwest Coast of Florida*. The preserve boundaries are marked by U.S.F.W.S. flying blue geese signs.

Just west of the Louise Perry Tract is the city of Sanibel's **Gulfside Beach** park of 30 acres. The property was also owned by Louise Perry prior to selling it to friends who "beached" a converted New Orleans ferryboat into a home here. Gulfside Beach is sometimes called by the locals "Algiers Beach" after the ferryboat that is now long gone. General public parking is permitted. Picnic tables have been provided in the shade of Australian pines and restrooms are nearby.

To reach Louise Perry Tract and Gulfside Beach from I-75 at Fort Myers take the Daniels Road exit west, which becomes Six Mile Cypress Road, and cross U.S. 41. Go left on Summerlin Road which takes you to Sanibel Causeway and toll bridge. After crossing the causeway turn right/west on Periwinkle Way at the first four-way stop. From Periwinkle Way turn south onto Casa Ybel Road, drive 1.5 miles and turn left on Algiers Road, a shell road that leads directly to a parking area adjacent to Gulfside Beach. Although spacious, the parking area will at times be filled, especially during winter and summer weekends.

If you continue on Casa Ybel Road to Gulf Drive to Tarpon Bay Road at the four-way stop, you will arrive at Tarpon Bay Beach. Tarpon Bay Beach is at the gulf side end of Tarpon Bay Road. Public parking is available at beachside and at a nearby overflow lot on Tarpon Bay Road. The beach is undeveloped. You may also reach the nearby Bailey Tract of the "Ding" Darling National Wildlife Area by driving immediately north on Tarpon Bay Road, turning left at the entrance parking area.

San Carlos Bay/Bunche Beach
Ft. Myers/Lee County
Beach Frontage: 3,600 ft.
Highlights: nature study, swimming, fishing, windsurfing

Quiet and secluded overlooking San Carlos Bay, **Bunche Beach** is situated between the hustle and bustle of Estero Island and Sanibel Island. Windsurfers find the quiet and shallow San Carlos Bay water ideal for their sport. The beach is bounded on the north and south by watery canal inlets.

Mangroves were once common along the shoreline but have been removed to create more beach frontage. There is little shade, since there has been an effort to remove the Australian pines and other exotics, which will allow for native sabal palms and sea grapes to regain a foothold. The shallow offshore waters and mudflats provide an excellent habitat for shore birds. Plovers, sandpipers, terns, gulls, herons, egrets, willet, ruddy turnstone, marbled godwit, whimbrel and short-billed dowitcher can be observed here. It is a fine beach to relax and watch the shrimp and other boats come and go from Matanzas Pass. There are no restrooms or drinking water available.

To reach Bunche Beach from I-75 take Daniels Road exit west to U.S. 41 south, then to Gladiolus Drive and then west to Summerlin Road. Turn south on John Morris Road enroute to Sanibel Island. Drive approximately two miles on the shell road that will dead end at the beach. Plenty of parking is available. The hours are from sunrise to sunset.

Matanzas Pass Preserve
Ft. Myers Beach/Lee County
Area: 42 acres
Trail Distance: 3/4 mile
Highlights: nature study, nature walk

This secluded "wilderness" is at the "back door" of the commercial Ft. Myers Beach frontage on the Gulf of Mexico. Dedicated January, 1979, the 42 acres of barrier island, with mature oak hammock, coastal marsh and undisturbed mangrove forest, can be explored by boardwalks and bridges built by the local high school students. Wooden rustic benches have been provided at key rest points. A pavilion classroom and observation pier deck gives day visitors an overlooking watery vista of Matanzas Pass and the mangrove-dotted bay. The Matanzas Pass Preserve is held in trust by The Nature Conservancy.

To reach the nature sanctuary from I-75 at Ft. Myers take Daniels Road exit 20. Drive west and cross the Tamiami Trail/U.S. 41/Cleveland Avenue to Summerlin Road. Take Summerlin south or left to Highway 865 at San Carlos Boulevard. Drive south on San Carlos Boulevard across Matanzas Pass bridge onto Estero Boulevard, the main street of Ft. Myers Beach. Approximately one mile from the stop light at Matanzas Pass bridge, turn left at Bay Street. The preserve is directly behind the Ft. Myers Beach Elementary School, where parking for 15 cars is available. The property is open to the public.

Lovers Key State Recreation Area

Ft. Myers Beach/Lee County
Beach Frontage: 4 miles
Area: 469 acres
Highlights: nature walk, nature study, fishing, shelling, picnicking, canoeing
Fee(s): entrance, canoe, kayak rentals

Lovers Key SRA adjoins Carl Johnson County Park, which is to the immediate south. Portions of Black Island and Lovers Key, as well as all of Inner Key, comprise the state recreation area. Although the islands are sandwiched between Bonita Beach to the south and Ft. Myers Beach to the north, the distance is far enough to give the feeling of remoteness amidst natural surroundings. Future plans call for limited development.

From the parking area, two boardwalks lead over the tidal lagoons to the beach. The boardwalks provide an ideal place to fish and birdwatch. If you are seeking a long walk along the Gulf of Mexico, this beach is recommended. Try walking south from Big Carlos Pass to Hickey Pass and Carl Johnson Park. Efforts are being made to return the strand to its natural state. Australian pines and other exotics are being removed. Areas are roped off along the foredunes to encourage shorebirds to nest and dune vegetation to re-establish itself. The beach is seldom crowded.

Lovers Key SRA entrance is about one mile north of Carl Johnson County Park across the highway from the boat launch ramp (see Carl Johnson directions from I-75). Park hours are from 9 a.m. to 5 p.m. daily.

Carl E. Johnson County Park

Ft. Myers Beach/Lee County
Beach Frontage: 2 miles
Area: 278 acres
Highlights: nature study, nature trail, swimming, picnicking, shelters, fishing, canoeing, boat ramp & dock, pier, playground equipment, tram, showers, restrooms, concessions
Fee(s): entrance, rentals

Pinched between Ft. Myers Beach and Bonita Beach, Carl E. Johnson County Park occupies Black Island, Inner Key, and Lovers Key: an enchanting and pristine landscape along Florida's south-

Shrimp boat, Carl E. Johnson Park

west Gulf coast. Dedicated as parkland in 1967, the Lee County Park is named in honor of Carl E. Johnson, a surveyor who was later responsible for the public bridge accesses to the barrier islands.

The beaches, bays, and estuaries provide a setting for diverse recreational activities. Past the entrance gate is a half-mile nature walk to the beach. Several interpretive markers identify and describe the common and conspicuous plants of the mangrove swamp and their role in island building: saltworts, red, white, and black mangroves. A pier connects Long Key to Lovers Key and makes a fine place to fish, photograph, and observe feeding birdlife at low tide. A tram service is available for those who prefer to ride rather than walk to the beach.

The beach is the hub of most activities. Canoes can be rented, the shelling is excellent, concession stores are available, shelters for picnicking are provided, along with grills. The swimming is fine, and there is a playground, plus showers and restrooms. The two-mile, pure white level beach is great for walking or jogging, but you swim at your own risk since there are no lifeguards. You can walk north along the strand to Lovers Key and Big Carlos Pass. The narrow coastal strand vegetation is indigenous, with the exception of the Australian pines, which provide welcome shade. A boat ramp and wayside picnic shelters are scattered along the four-mile causeway of S.R. 865 outside the main entrance, between Big Carlos Pass and Big Hickory Pass.

For those who seek the more active commercial beach scene, Estero Island or Ft. Myers Beach lies directly north of San Carlos Pass. Fort Myers Beach Park and Lynn Hall Memorial Park are located at the north end of Estero Island near the Matanzas Bridge and Estero Boulevard. Shrimp boats are often seen since shrimping is the islands' largest source of income besides tourism. A nice, less congested walk may be taken by walking north from Ft. Myers Beach Park to the island's north tip near Estero Pass.

To reach Carl E. Johnson Park from I-75, take exit 18 west on Bonita beach Road/S.R. 865. Head directly west towards the beach on Bonita Beach Road/S.R. 865, turning north at Hickory Boulevard/S.R. 865. Proceed north through Bonita Beach. The park entrance is about one mile north of Big Hickory Pass on the left/west side of the road. Plenty of parking spaces are available. The park hours are from sunrise to sunset.

Bonita Beach/Lely Barefoot Beach/ Barefoot Beach State Preserve

Bonita Beach/Lee and Collier Counties
Beach Frontage: 4 miles total access
Highlights: nature study, swimming, volleyball, picnicking, fishing, concessions, restrooms
Fee(s): fee parking at Lely Barefoot Beach

To the beachgoer, **Bonita Beach** and **Lely Barefoot Beach** are one beach although administered by two separate County Parks and Recreation Departments: Lee and Collier. To the north, coastal homes and apartments jam the two-mile beach frontage to Big Hickory Pass, but the wide beach allows for plenty of body room. Walking southward about two miles along the undeveloped shore, you come to **Barefoot Beach State Preserve** and Wiggins Pass. Recently, an access road has been built to the State Preserve via Bonita Bay condominiums. Unfortunately, this has brought crowds. This four-mile section of strand ranges from over-developed to natural. Crowds dwindle and only a few intrepid souls will be encountered in the direction of Barefoot Beach State Preserve. Most of the activity is found at Bonita Beach and adjacent Lely Barefoot Beach.

The walk to Barefoot Preserve passes along a coarse shell and sand beach ridge studded with sabal palm, sea grape and, of course, the invasive Australian pine. Hints of development appear, as "No Trespassing" signs and red boundary markers block off parts of this once remote strand. Although development degrades the natural beach experience, the developer cannot revoke the right of passage along the shoreline. Here coastal plantlife is largely intact, birdlife is plentiful and shelling is fine. It is a perfect walk for the adventuresome, lovers, naturalists and those who have all the time in the world.

Barefoot Beach State Preserve is separated from Delnor-Wiggins State Recreation Area by 100 yards of the Cocohatchee Little Hickory Bay tidal passage to the gulf, known as Wiggins Pass. The nearly one-mile beach, comprising 156 acres, contains an excellent representation of native Florida plants. A vehicle-wide road cuts through the back dunes, providing an up-close look at the vegetation. Exotic control has eliminated many of the Australian pines and Brazilian peppers, allowing the natives to grow. Be advised that chiggers inhabit the dune vegetation year round. Barefoot Beach activities include nature study, fishing, picnicking, canoeing in Little Hickory Bay, swimming, and beachcombing. Retrace your steps north to Lely Barefoot and Bonita Beaches. Low tide exposes the level and firm sands that make walking or jogging ideal here.

From I-75 take the Bonita Springs exit 18 west towards the Gulf of Mexico. Follow Bonita Beach Road/S.R. 865 directly to Bonita Beach and Lely Barefoot Beach parking areas. Limited parking is free at the 600-foot Lee County Bonita Beach, while fee parking is available at the neighboring 600-foot Collier County Lely Barefoot Beach. Parking may be limited during the peak winter tourist season and during the hot weekends of summer.

Delnor-Wiggins Pass
State Recreation Area/Vanderbilt Beach
Vanderbilt Beach/Collier County
Beach Frontage: 5 miles total
Area: 167 acres total

Highlights: nature study, swimming (lifeguards), fishing, observation tower, picnicking, shelters, boat launch, canoeing, bathhouses, naturalist programs, restrooms
Fee(s): entrance at Delnor-Wiggins SRA, parking at Vanderbilt Beach

In the shadow of recently constructed condominiums is the quiet peninsular strand of **Delnor-Wiggins Pass State Recreation Area**. This "sand spit" of a barrier island is divided into coastal strand, hammock and 80% mangrove forest swamp. The tidal pass is the natural outlet for the Cocohatchee River and Little Hickory Bay. The recreation area

Vanderbilt Beach

is named for Delora Norris, the wife of Mr. Norris, who donated the land for the park, and Joe Wiggins, the first settler, who ran a trading post in 1882.

The gulfside is composed of clean calcareous shell-rich natural beach. Stands of sabal palms and Australian "beefwood" pines create an ideal picnic setting for a day's outing. The plant life is well diversified and largely intact, but efforts are being made to re-establish the beach vegetation where it has been disturbed. Boardwalks help to reduce the human impact and connect the beach to the parking lots, making the shore accessible for handicapped persons. Birdlife observation is excellent and you may see frigate birds and cormorants along with herons and other shore and wading birds.

A boat ramp is provided on the back bayside for access to Little Hickory Bay and the Gulf of Mexico via Wiggins Pass. Cast-netting for mullet and surf fishing for trout, redfish, snook, and tarpon are popular activities. Summer is reported to be the best time for fishing and the park is open all night to fishermen. The one-mile shore of **Barefoot Beach State Preserve** consists of 156 acres of natural Florida and lies directly across Wiggins Pass to the immediate north. Access to the preserve was possible only by boat or long-distance walking (about two miles) south along the shore from Bonita Beach or Lely Barefoot Beach at Bonita Springs. But now there is a road to the preserve from Bonita Beach.

The beaches of Wiggins Pass are popular nesting sites for sea turtles that come ashore during warm summer nights to lay their eggs. The ornate diamondback terrapin, gopher tortoise, and the Atlantic loggerhead are three types of turtles identified at the park. A turtle watch walk program is conducted by park rangers. A vertebrate identification list is available on request from the park entrance station. The parking area fills up quickly during the tourist season from December to April. Once filled, the main gate will close to other prospective beachgoers who arrive by car. The park opens at 8 a.m. and closes at sunset year round.

To reach Delnor-Wiggins Pass State Recreation Area from I-75, take the Naples-Immokolee Road/S.R.846 exit west. The road changes names three times (David C. Brown Highway, 11th Avenue, and Bluebill Avenue) enroute to the park but it remains the same road. Continue westward across the Tamiami Trail/U.S. 41 to where the road dead ends at the park entrance.

Vanderbilt Beach is about 1.5 miles south of Delnor-Wiggins Pass State Recreation Area at the intersection of North Gulf Shore Drive and Vanderbilt Beach Road/S.R. 862. Plenty of fee parking is available on the south side of Vanderbilt Road by the Collier County Parks and Recreation Department. No other amenities exist at the.present time.

If you feel like walking from Wiggins Pass south to Clam Pass it is nearly four miles one-way. You can avoid the condominium and hotel expanse by beginning at Vanderbilt Beach instead of Wiggins Pass. Although Collier County owns only one acre of beachfront, it provides access to several miles of natural strand. Vanderbilt Beach is rated as one of the best wild beaches along the Gulf coast. However additional high-rise development appears imminent on the backside of the beach ridge.

A common sight along the shore are gulls, terns, sandpipers, pelicans, and occasional vultures in search of fish carrion left along the high tide line. Coral, cat's paw, turkey wing, calico scallop, olive shell, and tellins are but a few of the shells found. Sargassum seaweed, finger sponges, beached jellyfish and coconuts accumulate along the drift line. Excellent narrow stands of sabal palm line the dunes and coastal hammock, intermingled with exotic Australian pines. Sea grape, yucca, agave, beach bean, railroad vine, sea oats, and crowfoot grass are some of the more common beach flora. If barefoot, do watch for sandspurs and prickly pear cactus spines.

Naples Area Beaches
Naples/Collier County
Beach Frontage: 8 miles
Highlights: nature study, swimming, showers, picnicking, shelters, fishing,restrooms, concessions, rentals at Naples pier

Naples beaches are urbanized stretches of quartz sand, shells, surf, parks, elegant homes and condos and, with the exception of undeveloped Clam Pass beach, hotels hovering on the horizon. From Gordon Pass in south Naples to Clam Pass in the Pelican Bay area, the beach is uninterrupted for the walker except by Doctors Pass. Aside from the seemingly endless buildings, the silver strand is clean and unhurried. No "Coney Island" atmosphere exists in this refined community. The city of Naples and the county of Collier recognizes their valuable natural resource. The area's economic well-being is dependent on beach preservation.

The focal point and community landmark of Naples Municipal Beach is the **Naples Pier**, located downtown at 12th Avenue south and Gulf Shore Boulevard. The pier makes a fine starting place to stroll or fish. Fishing rods are rented on the pier and bait is available. Unobstructed sunsets are special here. The pier is open 24 hours. The pier was first built in 1888 as a freight and passenger dock and even the post office provided service on the wooden structure. Fire and hurricanes have destroyed the pier four times but it was rebuilt every time.

Heading south from the pier to Gordon Pass, about 2.5 miles, you will pass a well-preserved beach with healthy stands of sea oats and other strand vegetation. Beautiful homes face the Gulf waters and add architectural interest to the walk. Shelling is good along this section of:quiet beach where few people will be seen. Beach access is from 13 Avenue south to 18 Avenue south, 21st Avenue south walkway, 32nd Avenue south and 33 Avenue south.

North of the pier is the most active section of the beach extending about two miles up to **Lowdermilk Park**. Lowdermilk is a developed beach park with easy access and ample parking from Gulf Shore Boulevard at Banyan Boulevard west. Picnicking in the pavilion or on the grass, lazing in the sun and people-watching are some of the activities. Swimming, fishing, showers, restrooms, and concessions are also available. Occasional artists with easel and canvas are seen here painting the seascape. Lowdermilk City Park is open from 8 a.m. to sunset.

The beach walk to Doctors Pass continues for nearly a mile from Lowdermilk Park but is obstructed by encroaching condominiums built without proper setbacks before the erosive loss of beach occurred. You will have to walk the concrete seawalls unless you don't mind wet feet. Coquina rock boulders serve as erosion-preventive groins and jetties. Doctors Pass is a popular spot for fishermen. Beach access is at all avenues, North Lake Drive, and South Gulf Drive.

Northward of Doctors Pass is **Park Shore coastal barrier island**, stretching nearly two miles to Clam Pass. From Doctors Pass north to Seagate Beach Club and Drive, condominiums rule. If you enjoy beach recreation in the shade of the highrises, this may be your section of sandy paradise. Access points are limited but can be found along Gulf Shore Boulevard at Via Miramar, Vedado Way, Horizon Way, and Park Shore Beach. Gulf Shore Boulevard is reached from the Tamiami Trail/U.S. 41 in North Naples at Harbour Drive and Park Shore Drive.

North of Seagate Beach Club and Drive is **Clam Pass Beach**. Except for trash barrels, Clam Pass Beach is undeveloped at the moment and is owned and maintained by Collier County Parks and Recreation Department. The Australian pines, sabal palms, and sea grapes provide some screening and welcome shade from the highrise encroachment that seems inevitable. Red, black, and white mangroves line the back bay shoreline of Outer Clam Bay. Wading birds find the rich estuarine waters filled with fish. Fishermen in motor boats zip in and out of Clam Pass. North across the pass lies Vanderbilt Beach. Shelling is best at low tide or after a storm and may lead to such finds as angel wings, left-handed welks, sand dollars, starfish, and possibly the rare junonia.

To reach Clam Pass Beach from North Tamiami Trail/U.S. 41 in North Naples, go west on Seagate Drive to the dead end parking areas or from Park Shore Drive to Gulf Shore Boulevard, then north to the dead end parking area. To reach Naples from I-75, take exit 16 west onto Pine Ridge Road/S.R. 896 and proceed to Tamiami Trail/U.S. 41 or exit 15 south on Isle off Capri Road/S.R.951, the last exit before or the first exit after the toll booth at Alligator Alley. Turn west on S.R. 84 or Davis Boulevard and proceed to Tamiami Trail/U.S. 41 and then on into downtown Naples.

Tigertail Beach/Point Marco Beach/ Caxambas Park

Marco Island/Collier County
Beach Frontage: .5 mile
Area: 36 acres
Highlights: nature study, swimming, volleyball, playground, picnicking, shelters, boat launch, boat rentals, concessions
Fee(s): parking fee at Tigertail, boat launch fee at Caxambas

Largest of the Ten Thousand Islands, **Marco Island** is the least accessible beach along the southern Gulf coast. The greater portion of the island's 3.5-mile beach frontage, like so much of the south Florida coastline, is filled with hotels, condos, and other private beach facilities, but fortunately sections have been set aside for public use.

Tigertail Beach, the largest beach park on Marco Island, is well managed by Collier County Parks and Recreation Department. The wooden entrance sign, pavilion, picnic shelters, playground, the natural landscaping, all complement and blend harmoniously with the beachscape. Handicapped parking is available. A bicycle rack is provided for those who peddle to the beach. Outdoor showers and restrooms are provided. Sailboats, windsurfers, and Hobie Cats can be rented at the shore. No lifeguard is on duty. The south beach section of Tigertail is closer to the highrises, while the north section towards Big Marco Pass is more natural, private, and fun to explore. A thought to muse over while walking the strand is the possibility that there is an offshore submerged Calusa Indian village, since the water line has risen 30 to 40 feet since the first white settlers came here.

Tigertail Beach

Shelling is regarded as "unexcelled" along the sandbars at low tide. Some of the shells that can be collected are sun rays, olives, tulips, jingles, cones, cockles, lions paws, sand dollars, murex, whelks, and conch. You may see a southern bald eagle or an osprey, along with herons, spoonbills, ibis, and other avian seashore life.

To reach Tigertail Beach from Collier Boulevard at the northwest section of the island, turn northwest onto Kendall Drive, then southwest on Hernando Drive and continue to Tigertail Beach at the end of the road.

At the near southwest tip of Marco Island near Caxambas Pass is the undeveloped one-acre **Point Marco Beach**. This small strand is pinched between the highrises of Sea Winds and Sand Piper and is popular with tourists and locals alike.

More remote is **Caxambas Park**. This water-oriented Collier County facility harbors a boat ramp, picnic area, concessions, and restrooms. It is a fine spot just to relax and watch the boats come and go. There is a 51-foot Calusa shell mound reported in this area. The beach hours for Caxambas and Tigertail parks are from dawn to dusk.

To reach Caxambas Park, take Collier Boulevard to the extreme southeast end of the island where it turns into Collier Court and dead ends at the water's edge. Caxambas Park will be on your right, on Collier Court past the Water Edge condominiums.

Marco Island is 16 miles southwest of Naples. From I-75, take exit 15 south on Isle of Capri Road/S.R. 951, the last exit before or the first exit after the Alligator Alley toll gate. Continue southwest on Isle of Capri Road/S.R. 951 to Marco Island, crossing the Tamiami Trail/U.S. 41. After crossing the Marco River Bridge, the highway becomes Collier Boulevard.

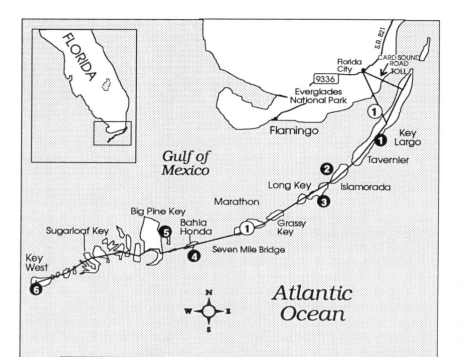

The Keys

1. John Pennekamp Coral Reef State Park
2. Lignumvitae Key State Botanical Site/ Indian Key State Historic Site.
3. Long Key State Recreation Area
4. Bahia Honda State Recreation Area
5. Key Deer National Wildlife Refuge
6. Key West Nature Places

The Keys

From Soldiers Key in the northern waters of Key Biscayne National Park to Key West, the Florida Keys are about 150 miles in length. This archipelago forms a curving arc from the Atlantic Ocean southwestward into the warmer waters of the Gulf of Mexico. Over 800 keys or islands of vegetated coral and limestone are scattered along this near-tropical chain reef, but only 30 or so are inhabited. The Keys vary in size from less than one acre to 28-mile-long Key Largo. Most Keys are one to two miles wide. The highest elevation point is 18 feet at Windley Key but the average is five feet above sea level.

Formerly attached to the mainland, the Keys were isolated by the rising ice age waters 12,000 years ago They are about one degree north of the Tropic of Cancer, and the subtropical climate favored an ecosystem similar to the not-so-distant Bahama Islands. The flora is a mixture of plants from the Caribbean, mainland Florida, and those that are endemic to the Keys. The fauna originated primarily from the mainland, but several local subspecies have developed such as the Key deer, Key Vaca raccoon, Key Largo woodrat, reptiles, and mollusks. Urbanization is undoubtedly the greatest threat to the natural areas and wildlife of the fragile Keys.

The overseas Highway U.S. 1 leads down through what many consider the "American Caribbean." From one mile past Florida City at MM 126, the road leads south to the corner of Whitehead and Fleming Streets in Key West (MM 0). Green and white numbered mile markers are posted along the roadside and are very helpful in locating beaches, parks, or attractions. Forty-two bridges span the islands and the Seven Mile Bridge that connects Knight Key to Little Duck Key is the world's longest segmented bridge. At numerous points both the Atlantic Ocean and Florida Bay are seen at the same time.

It should not be surprising that the limited land mass of the Keys has few public-accessible natural areas to explore, but the Keys do have their share. State parklands provide the best walking. The virgin tropical hammock of Lignumvitae Key is the best wilder-

Beached

ness experience. Bahia Honda State Recreation Area is generally regarded as the best natural beach, and beaches are few in the Keys. Key West has several nature-related attractions, parks and garden tours among them. Recently the north tip of Key Largo was purchased by the state of Florida for development as a state park.

As throughout southern Florida, winter remains the choice time to explore, when temperatures are cooler, little rain falls (only about half of the mainland total), little threat from hurricanes exists and the insect populations are at their lowest. The only poisonous snake found in the Keys is the Eastern Diamondback Rattlesnake. The Keys are a popular destination for visitors and residents during the winter season, so expect to put up with a certain amount of congestion, especially in the campgrounds. Take the time to stray off the main road, U.S. 1, and explore the "back roads," particularly in the Lower Keys such as Torch, Sugarloaf, and Boca Chica. Old state highways and county roads here can be used as trails.

John Pennekamp Coral Reef State Park
Key Largo/Monroe County
Area: 56,320 acres
Trail Distance: .5 mile total
Highlights: nature study, nature trails, swimming, snorkeling, scuba, windsurfing, sailing, canoeing, boat launch, picnicking, shelters, bicycling, pavilion, nature center, glass bottom boat trips, dive shop, marina, fishing, showers, restrooms, campgrounds, bathhouse, gift shop, concessions, ranger programs
Fees: entrance, camping, glass bottom boat tours, sailboat rental, windsurfing rental, canoe rental, snorkeling and scuba tours, certified scuba instruction, dive shop rentals, motorboat rental

John Pennekamp Coral Reef State Park is the first and to date only underwater state park in the continental United States. The park is

Keys sunset

named in honor of "Mr. Conservation," as John Pennekamp, a Miami newspaper editor, was known. It was he who worked for the establishment of the state park in 1957, as he did for the Everglades National Park. The aquatic park is a favorite of boaters, snorkelers, and scuba divers, who explore the offshore coral reef where 40 varieties of coral thrive along with 300-650 varieties of fish. An underwater sea garden features a nine-foot bronze statue of "Christ of the Deep." Adjoining east of the state park waters is **Key Largo Coral Reef National Marine Sanctuary**. The marine sanctuary measures 21 by 8.5 nautical miles wide and preserves 100 nautical square miles from Molasses Reef to Turtle Reef.

Even though the park is almost entirely underwater, land lubbers will enjoy the visitor center's natural history exhibits, displays, slide show, touch tank, and the **Patch Reef Tank**: a large aquarium simulating a coral reef filled with a variety of colorful fish. The visitor center is open from 8 a.m. to 5 p.m.

The two brief nature trails explore two separate habitats: a mangrove forest and tropical hardwood hammock. The 1/4-mile **Mangrove Boardwalk** loop trail is a 15-minute leisurely walk winding through mangroves and across a tidal creek. The seven-station labeled trail interprets the ecology of the mangrove forest. An observation overlook provides tree top-views of the salt water surroundings. The marked boardwalk begins just south of the swimming beach parking area. The sandy beach is very limited along the mangrove-lined shore.

West of the visitor center is the **Wild Tamarind Trail**. This 20-minute self-guiding loop trail explores the upland limestone area of a tropical hardwood hammock. Tamarind, as well as gumbo limbo, mahogany, and poisonwood are the dominant trees.

John Pennekamp Coral Reef State Park entrance is located at MM 102.5, U.S. 1 northbound, in Key Largo. This is the northernmost and largest of the Keys, one hour south of Miami. The park is open daily 8 a.m. to sunset.

Lignumvitae Key State Botanical Site/ Indian Key State Historic Site
Islamorada/Monroe County
Area: 280 acres (Lignumvitae Key); 10 acres (Indian Key)
Trail Distance: 2 miles each key
Highlights: guided nature and historic walks
Fee(s): tour fee

Lying offshore between Upper and Lower Matecumbe Keys are three state parks that comprise Lignumvitae Aquatic Preserve. **Shell Key State Preserve**, the most northeasterly of the Keys, is currently closed to the public, but Lignumvitae and Indian Keys are open. For current tour information and reservations contact the park office at Long Key State Recreation Area, (305) 664-4815. Be advised mosquitoes are especially abundant on Lignumvitae Key year round.

A short boat ride one mile west of Indian Key Fill, MM 78.5, is **Lignumvitae Key State Botanical Site**. The undisturbed key was acquired through The Nature Conservancy, who in turn deeded the land to the state of Florida in 1971. The visitor center is located west of the docking area in the former Matheson House. The self-sufficient wind-powered, wooden home was built in 1919 of imported Dade County slash pine by Mr. Matheson, a wealthy chemist. The focal point of the island is the two-mile guided tour of the virgin tropical hammock forest of West Indian trees. Diversity is a mark of the hammock where 44 tree species are found, several rare and endangered. The mid-canopy lignumvitae or "wood of life" (referring to the mythical medicinal value of the wood), are quite old. Stunted by the inhospitable conditions, this member of the Caltrop family (Zygophyllaceae) is especially significant to the people of Jamaica and the Bahamas, where it is the official national tree.

Three-quarters of a mile southeast of Indian Key Fill lies **Indian Key**. Although Indian Key is small in acreage, it is rich in colorful history. Precolumbian Indians, Spanish explorers, British colonists, Bahamian fishermen and foresters, and dreaded pirates preceded American occupation and settlement. Starting with the days of cargo-laden Spanish galleons, salvaging reef-wrecked ships was the major reason for the development of Indian Key. Under the direction of Jacob Housman, a ship salvaging business developed on Indian Key in 1831 that soon rivalled that of Key West. Three wharves, warehouses, a carpenter's shop, general store, private homes, and the Tropical Hotel (where James Audubon stayed during his 1832 visit) were constructed. Tons of topsoil was imported for gardens in 1838. So powerful was Housman's influence, he had the State Legislative Council establish Dade County in 1836 and proclaim Indian Key the county seat. Dr. H. Perrine, physician and pioneer agriculturist, moved to Indian Key and established an experimental nursery on nearby Lower Matecumbe Key.

Decline set in for Housman's salvage business at the outset of the Second Seminole War in 1835 and his island became endangered. News that Housman petitioned the state government to buy Seminole Indian scalps angered the already hostile Indians. Seeking powder and much needed supplies, 100 warriors attacked Indian Key, killing several inhabitants, including Dr. Perrine. All buildings but the post office were burned. Jacob Housman left the island in 1840 and returned to Key West. After his death by accident in 1841, he was later buried here near his home site. Indian Key has only been used sporadically since the town's destruction in 1840.

Today visitors walk the former busy streets where ruins are still visible. Dr. Perrine's early experiments in tropical agriculture are still evident, particularly the sisal hemp plant. An observation tower overlooks the island and surrounding seascape. Indian Key is open to the public from 8 a.m. to sunset daily.

Golden orb spider

Long Key State Recreation Area

Layton/Monroe County
Beach Frontage:1.5 mile
Area: 1,015 acres
Trail Distances: 2 miles total
Highlights: nature study, nature trails, swimming, fishing, canoe trail, snorkeling, scuba, picnicking, shelters, ranger programs, campground, restrooms
Fee(s): entrance, camping

Long Key State Recreation Area is situated south of Layton in the Middle Keys between Lower Matecumbe Key and Conch Key. Historically, diverse groups such as the Calusa Indians, Spanish explorers, Bahamian fishermen, and American settlers have occupied the area. Henry Flager's 128-mile-long Florida East Coast Railroad to Key West regularly stopped near here for about three decades before its destruction by the 1935 hurricane. Mr. Flagler was the founder of the Long Key Fishing Club, an elite social organization for saltwater fishermen of leisure. Not exactly fitting the social mode, Zane Grey, ardent conservationist and novelist, was elected the first president of the prestigious fishing organization. Zane Grey Creek, named in his honor, begins in the state recreation area at Long Key Lake.

Two nature trails allow access to some of the best hiking in the Keys and in particular the Golden Orb Trail. The **Layton Nature Trail** begins north of the park entrance at MM 68.5 on U.S. 1, just south of the city limits of Layton and next to the Long Key Fishing Club Historical Marker. The 1/4-mile, 20-minute loop walk will provide a view of Long Key's rocky bayside shoreline and Florida Bay. Some tropical plants are labeled. A linear spur trail bisects the main loop down the middle to make two shorter loops.

Access to the **Golden Orb Trail** begins on the boardwalk adjacent to the restrooms in the northeast picnic parking area. Take a left at the "T" road past the entrance station to get there. Interpretive labeled stations describe such topics as mangrove forests, tidal lagoons, food chains, nursery grounds, wildlife, Calusa Indians, birdlife, occupation by early settlers, charcoal from buttonwood, dunes, and general ecology. An observation overlook allows vistas of the tidal lagoon and seascape. The boardwalk crosses the tidal lagoon to the trailhead of the Golden Orb Trail where the boardwalk "T's": right is the beach and left is the trail.

The Golden Orb Trail is the longest and the best self-guiding hike in the Keys. The one-hour labeled loop walk leads through five mature plant communities. The trail follows the shoreline dunes be-

Silver Palm Trail

tween the ocean and lagoon and loops back through a tropical hardwood hammock of West Indian plants. Torchwood, crabwood, Jamaican dogwood, stopper, pigeon plum, gumbo limbo, and poisonwood are found in the higher ground. Poisonwood, a close relative of poison ivy, produces the same itchy red rash but grows as a tree whose splotchy bark resembles sea grape or pigeon plum, with leaves similar to gumbo limbo. Golden orb spiders may or may not be seen along the path and the large, nonpoisonous weaver spider is also a resident of the hammock. The 1.5-mile trail ends at the parking area. The entrance to Long Key State Recreation Area is at MM 67.5 on the south side of the highway. The recreation area is open daily from 8 a.m. to sunset.

Bahia Honda State Recreation Area
Bahia Honda/Monroe County
Beach Frontage: 1,548 ft.
Area: 300 acres
Trail Distance: .5 mile
Highlights: nature study, nature trail, swimming, snorkeling, scuba, windsurfing, fishing, boating, boat launch, picnicking, shelters, ranger programs, dive shop, concessions, bayside cabin rental, campground, showers, restrooms
Fee(s): entrance, cabin rental, camping, windsurfing & diving equipment rental

Bahia Honda or "deep bay" provided one of the few safe harbors in the Keys for ships of the Spanish explorers. Today Bahia Honda State Recreation Area is the most natural such preserve in the Keys, if not of all south Florida. The combination of sky, sea, vegetation and soils with the ever-changing sunlight makes this a beautiful place to visit. The Atlantic-facing strand is the largest and touted as the best beach in the Keys, closely resembling the Bahamas. The park preserves rare West Indian plant species and has been since 1870, an area for botanical studies. Jamaica morning glory, West Indian yellowwood, spiny catesbaea, and wild dily are not found elsewhere in the continental United States. Hurricanes, ocean waves, birds, and man act as agents of seed dispersal. Geologically, Bahia Honda marks the transition from Key Largo limestone of the Upper Keys to the Miami oolitic of the Lower Keys.

The Silver Palm Trail provides an excellent opportunity to view the largest collection of silver palms in the state of Florida. The 20-minute leisurely subtropical walk alongside a tidal lagoon, through a coastal hammock and along the beach begins at the northeast end of the parking area and Sandspur Beach. An undesignated trail segment of about half a mile one-way continues northwest from the main trail along the inner dunes to connect with a service road. Eleven interpretive stations correspond with a trail guide available from the entrance station. A birdlist is also available.

The entrance to Bahia Honda State Recreation Area is at MM 37 along U.S. 1 on the south side of the road, 12 miles south of Marathon. The park hours are from 8 a.m. to sunset daily.

Key Deer National Wildlife Refuge
Big Pine Key/Monroe County
Area: 4,383 acres
Trail Distance: .66 mile
Highlights: nature study, nature trail, fishing

Established in 1954, this day-use national wildlife refuge's main mission is to protect the remaining endangered Florida Key Deer, a subspecies of the white-tail deer and the smallest race of North American deer. Substantial numbers once ranged from Key West to Duck Key, but by 1947 only 50 deer remained. The current population is placed between 250 and 300, now restricted mainly to Big Pine Key and 16 surrounding islands. Authorities believe the mainland white-tail deer migrated thousands of years ago across a land bridge. As ice age waters melted, the ocean rose, isolating the deer, which then evolved into a distinct subspecies. The "Bambi-like" deer are just over three feet in length, and 24" to 28" inches tall at shoulder height. The females weigh 45-65 pounds and the males 55-75 pounds. Key Deer prefer the well-vegetated pine and hardwood habitat with a year-round freshwater supply, but will seasonally migrate to outlying adjacent islands. Rutting occurs primarily in September, peaks in October, and then decreases gradually during November and December. Fawns are usually born from April through June. Their diet is composed of a variety of vegetation including silver and thatch palm berries and red mangrove leaves. Early morning, late afternoon, and early evening are the best times to view the deer on Big Pine and No Name Keys, where 60% to 70% of the population resides. Be advised it is against the law to feed the Key Deer. Humans are now their only predator, with several killed by cars each year.

The only designated trail in National Key Deer Refuge is the **Pine Wood** or **Jack C. Watson Nature Trail** located 3.3 miles north of the intersection of Key Deer Boulevard/S.R. 940 and U.S. 1, MM 30.5, or 1.5 miles north of the intersection of Key Deer and Watson Boulevards. A well-illustrated and informative trail guide is available at the trailhead box or from the refuge headquarters located about one mile west of the intersection of Key Deer and Watson Boulevards. Compiled listings of birds, mammals, reptiles, and amphibians are also available from the refuge office.

Eighteen numbered stations are posted along the slash pine and palm woodland loop trail. Visitors will become familiar with the plant life, soils, geology, and the ecology of the unique forest. The numerous sinkholes provide reservoirs of drinking water for the Key Deer. Jack C. Watson became the first conservation officer to protect the Key Deer in the early 1950's and was officially honored by the National Wildlife Federation for his dedicated service. Another point of interest is **Blue Hole**, an old limestone rock quarry located 1.3 miles north of the intersection of Key Deer and Watson Boulevards, due south of the Jack C. Watson Nature Trail. There is an undesignated but conspicuous footpath encircling the margin of the pond.

Key West Nature Places
Key West/Monroe County
Highlights: beaches, historic sites, aquarium, botanic gardens, museums, sunset pier
Fees: entrance

The Spanish explorers referred to the island that lay 90 miles north of Cuba as "Cayo Hueso" or the "island of bones." The former resident-writer Ernest Hemingway once called the southernmost United States city the "island in the sun." Today, natives affectionately call their four-by-two-mile island of Key West the "rock." Key West is a unique aberration: part of the "American Caribbean" with a cosmopolitan flavor. The people who live in this tiny speck of the U.S.A. are as diverse as the island's past history. The county seat of Monroe County, Key West is also considered the capitol of the so-called "Conch Republic" (Conch is what the natives call themselves). Although independent in spirit, the "last resort" remains dependent on tourism, the main source of revenue.

There is a natural side to Key West, but no real wilderness and if you are prone to claustrophobia the congestion may lead to "island fever" – not quite as bad as cabin fever. It would be a more pleasant place if cars were banned and everyone rode bicycles or scooters. The island's size and climate would be conducive to that.

Most of the Atlantic-facing side of the island is publicly accessible sandy strand. The 3/4-mile city-owned **George Smathers Beach** or **Rest Beach** is most especially popular with tourists. From 8 a.m. to sundown, swimming, fishing, boating and picnicking take place along South Roosevelt Boulevard. North across the boulevard, half a mile west of East Martello Tower (a fine art museum) is the entrance to the **Thomas Higgs Wildlife Refuge**. Behind the usually locked green gate are the Old Salt Ponds where migratory birds may be viewed along a wooden pier overlook. If the gate is locked, call 294-2116 for access. Further west between White and Reynolds Streets along Atlantic Boulevard is the **Monroe County Higgs Memorial Beach and Astro Park**. The beach park is developed on both sides of Atlantic Boulevard and includes swimming, fishing, pier, picnicking, shelters, playground and concessions. The hours are from 8 a.m. to 11 p.m. Near the center of the beach is the **West Martello Tower Garden Center**. What was a Civil War fortress a century ago is now a botanic garden maintained by the

Key West Garden Club. The free admission includes a checklist of 92 plants growing in the subtropical garden. The hours are 10 a.m. to 4 p.m. Wednesday to Sunday, closed Monday and Tuesday. The Key West Garden Club also maintains a five-acre hardwood hammock with mowed trails and labeled plants on adjoining **Stock Island** to the immediate north. Warblers, gray kingbirds, white-crowned pigeons and other birds frequent the hammock. From U.S.1, cross over Cow Key Channel to Stock Island and turn north/left onto Junior College Road, then drive approximately half a mile. The unmarked botanical garden hammock is across from the Bayshore Manor Home and between the Monroe County Mosquito Control District Office and the Humane Society on Aquieno Circle. Parking is available along the road.

Continuing west from Clarence Higgs Memorial Beach, you come to the city-owned **South Beach** at the south end of Duval Street. This small undeveloped "pocket beach" is a popular spot with the young local crowd and nearby street parking is difficult to find. The hours are 8 a.m. to 11 p.m. The beach is about a block away from Southernmost Point at the end of Whitehead and the intersection with South Street. Tourists enjoy posing with the red-striped buoy which reads, "90 miles from Cuba."

The last Atlantic-facing public beach is at **Ft. Zachary Taylor State Historic Site** on the west tip of the island. This is by far the most natural beach on Key West. Shaded picnicking and shelters along the bluff top overlook the beach and Atlantic Ocean. Tours are conducted through Ft. Zachary Taylor by a park naturalist from 8 a.m. to 5 p.m. Wednesday to Sunday, closed Monday and Tuesday. The three-story, trapezoid-shaped fortress played a key role in the defeat of the Confederacy. The fort was designated a National Historic Landmark in 1973 and has the largest collection of Civil War cannon in the United States. Access to Ft. Zachary Taylor Historic Site and Recreational Area is via the U.S. Naval Station at the end of Southard Street. Directional signs will guide visitors through the maze to the entrance station. The park is open 8 a.m. to sunset daily.

North of Southernmost Point, two historic homes lie close together on Whitehead Street. **Ernest Hemingway** owned and resided at 907 Whitehead from 1935 to 1961. The Nobel Prize winner planted many of the trees and shrubs around his Spanish Colonial style home. The one-acre house and garden is a registered National Historic Landmark. There is an admission fee and the hours are 9 a.m. to 5 p.m. daily. Walking north seven blocks, you encounter the restored 1830 **Audubon House and Garden** at 205 Whitehead. The house was owned by Captain John Geiger when naturalist-painter Audubon visited Key West in 1832. A self-guiding booklet is available for your tour of the garden, which includes practical as well as ornamental plantings of the period. Audubon painted a white-crowned pigeon perched on a Geiger tree in the garden during his stay. Now owned by the Florida Audubon Society, the daily hours are from 9:30 a.m. to 5 p.m. There is a fee for the house and garden tour.

The **Key West Municipal Aquarium** at 1 Whitehead Street in Mallory Square is two blocks north of the Audubon House and Garden. The numerous aquariums of various sizes display the marine life of the Keys. A special feature is the 50,000-gallon Atlantic Shore exhibit. There are narrated guided tours and feedings at 11 a.m., 1, 3 and 4:30 p.m.

Turtle Kraals at Lands End Village and Waterfront, at the Gulf of Mexico end of Margaret Street, has a free historic museum and exhibit. The open air bar and restaurant is in the original Thompson Green Turtle Soup Cannery. "Kraals," a Dutch South African word for "pens," were used to corral captured green sea turtles until they were slaughtered and canned for commercial use. The adjoining original kraals feature live green sea turtles on display and a boardwalk pier leads to the historic museum with exhibits of the turtle cannery. The kraals and museum and bar restaurant are open 12 p.m. to 12 a.m. year round.

Finally to end your day with a celebration, visit the **Mallory Square Docks** at Front and Duval Street downtown. Artisans of diverse talents perform while the sun is setting; an appropriate finale to one of the greatest daily shows on earth.

Other Nature Sites in the Keys

MM 98.5 **Everglades Ranger Station**. Picnicking available at bayside. Information available about Everglades National Park.

MM 92.5 **Harry Harris County Park.** Harry Harris was a bar owner elected to public service as a Monroe County Commissioner for 25 years. The county park is an Atlantic Ocean beach with swimming, fishing, boating, snorkeling, diving, picnicking, shelters, playground, north of Tavernier.

MM 89 **Florida Keys Native Nursery.** If you are interested in native plants especially those suitable for Florida landscaping, stop here.

MM 84.5 **Theater of the Sea.** World's second oldest marine park, established in 1945. Natural lagoon setting with "hands on" marine life experiences and shows. Windley Key.

MM 81.5 **Islamorada County Park.** Located bayside behind the public library in Islamorada. Picnicking, swimming, playgrounds, boat ramp.

MM 80 **Upper Matecumbe County Park.** 200 feet of shoreline on Atlantic Ocean. Picnicking, swimming, fishing. Just north of Lignumvitae and Indian Keys.

MM 79 **Indian Key Fill Picnic Area.** Picnic tables, boat ramp. Ferry boat dock provides tours to nearby Lignumvitae and Indian Keys.

MM 69 **Sea World Marine Science & Conservation Center.** Staffled tours of marine life.

MM 68.5 **Sea World's Shark Institute.** Bayside Layton at Long Key. Shark exhibits and tours.

MM 59 **Dolphin Research Center.** Grassy Key at Marathon Shores. Formerly Flipper's Sea School. Currently providing tours and dolphin encounters. Non-profit organization.

MM 50 **Stanley & Wanda Switlick County Park.** Also called Sombrero Beach. Popular beach scene at end of Sombrero Road at Marathon Key and Boot Key. 8 a.m. to sunset.

Perky Bat Tower

MM 50 **Crane Point Hammock.** Wilderness sanctuary and natural history museum. Hours 9-5 Monday tbrouqh Saturday; Sunday noon to 5.

MM 49.5 **Marathon Chamber of Commerce Beach.** End of 33rd Street. Small, no facilities.

MM 47 **Old Seven Mile Bridge.** Proclaimed the world's longest fishing, walking, jogging, bicycling pier.

MM 40 **Little Duck Key Veterans County Park.** Developed park just before the Seven Mile Bridge, going north, or at the south end of the bridge on the Atlantic Ocean side.

MM 30 **Big Pine Key County Park.** Undeveloped county park along Pine Channel.

MM 17 **Perky Bat Tower.** Lower Sugarloaf Key. R. C. Perky, real estate developer, built this Dutch-style tower for bats who would, he hoped, rid the area of mosquitoes. It didn't work. Perky dedicated the tower "to good health" in 1929.

Cities & Suburbs

"Woe unto them that join house to house, that lay field to field, till there be no place that they may be placed alone in the midst of the earth."

Isaiah 5:8 Old Testament

Southern Florida offers many opportunities to experience nature even in the midst of the cities and their suburbs, where over 80% of all Floridians live. Before the 20th century, southern Florida was largely a wilderness, nearly untouched by man. But the unprecedented growth in population since that time has forced planners to seek ways of including parklands close to where the people live. A goal of 30 acres of parkland per 1,000 population has been established, but the increase in population outpaces governmental efforts to purchase available sites.

Unlike many of the other parks in this book, with their miles of nature trails, city parks are usually filled with playgrounds, tennis courts, ballfields, and other recreation facilities. Some parks, however, are simply islands of green, where city dwellers can make contact with nature and breathe the open air. It is also in the urban areas where most of the botanical gardens, zoos, and natural history museums are found.

Southeast Florida

Brevard Zoo
West Melbourne/Brevard County
Area: 56 acres
Trail Distance: several miles of paved walking paths
Highlights: zoological/botanical gardens, picnicking, gift shop, membership
Fee(s): entrance, membership

The recently opened Brevard Zoo is a not-for-profit organization providing recreation, entertainment, and education for the residents and visitors of Melbourne and south Brevard County. The 56 West Melbourne acres are home to hundreds of wild species of

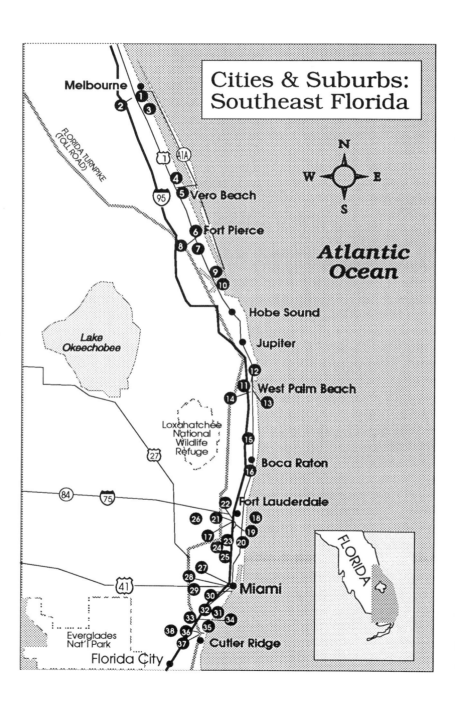

Cities & Suburbs:
Southeast Florida

Melbourne

Florida Turnpike
(Toll Road)

1

Vero Beach

Fort Pierce

Hobe Sound

Jupiter

West Palm Beach

Loxahatchee
National
Wildlife
Refuge

Boca Raton

Fort Lauderdale

Lake
Okeechobee

Atlantic
Ocean

N
W   E
S

Miami

Everglades
Nat'l Park

Cutler Ridge

Florida City

FLORIDA

exotic and native animals from around the world. Florida's indigenous animals as well as other North, Central, and South American, African, Asian, and European animals are represented at the new zoological/botanical park in a natural habitat setting. The zoo is divided into four geo-continental areas. Felines are particularly plentiful and include the North American cougar, African lion, Indian leopard and tiger, South American black jaguar, North and Central American ocelot and the North American bobcat. There are opportunities to become a zoo "parent" with the Adopt-An-Animal Program.

1. Brevard Zoo
2.. Erna Nixon Park
3. Turkey Creek Sanctuary Park
4. Environmental Learning Center
5. Coastal Hammock Nature Trail
6. Heathcote Botanical Gardens
7. The Savannas Recreational Area
8. Fort Pierce City Parks
9. Martin County Environmental Studies Center
10. Possum Long Nature Center
11. Society of the Four Arts Botanical & Sculpture Gardens
12. Mounts Botanical Garden
13. Drehr Park Zoo & Nature Area/S. Florida Science Museum & Planetarium
14. John Prince Park
15. Morikami Park, Museum & Gardens
16. Deerfield Island Park
17. Tradewinds Park
18. Fern Forest Nature Center
19. John D. Easterlin Park
20. Colohatchee Natural Park
21. Discovery Center/Museum of Archaeology
22. Secret Woods Nature Center
23. Buehler Planetarium & Observatory
24. Tree Tops Park
25. Flamingo Gardens
26. Markham Park
27. Oleta River SRA
28. Greynolds Park
29. Arch Creek Park
30. Simpson Park & Alice Wainwright Park
31. Vizcaya Museum & Gardens/Museum of Science & Space Planetarium
32. Planet Ocean
33. Fairchild Tropical Garden
34. US Subtropical Horticulture Research Station
35. Old Cutler Hammock Nature Center
36. Miami Metrozoo
37. Castellow Hammock Nature Center
38. Preston B. Bird & Mary Heinlein Fruit & Spice Park

The Brevard Zoo is located one mile east of I-95 on U.S. 192/West New Haven Avenue near Suntree in West Melbourne or Rockledge, Florida. From I-95 take exit 73 east onto Wickham Road and drive a short distance to Murrell Road and the entry area. The telephone number is (407) 254-3002.

Erna Nixon Park

West Melbourne/Brevard County
Area: 52 acres
Trail Distance: 2,700 ft.
Highlights: nature study, nature walk, natural history room, picnicking, special programs

The late preservationist Erna Nixon once described the hammock she loved and saved from commercial development as "an island of hardwoods in a sea of pines." Thanks to her foresight and dedicated efforts, today's visitor can enjoy the green environs of this exceptional nature-oriented Brevard County Park.

The loop boardwalk trail begins and ends at the open-air pavilion adjacent to the parking lot. Several picnic tables are situated near the natural history room, which features park-related information and restrooms. The park ranger naturalist, whose office is next door to the natural history room, is available to answer your questions regarding the natural life of the park. Sixty-eight posted stations are identified with a corresponding trail guide which may be obtained on loan from the ranger. The sanctuary has three distinct ecological communities: pine flatwoods, wet transitional zone, and a low-lying oak-palm hammock. The trail heads to the right through the longleaf and slash pine flatwoods which feature pennyroyal, saw palmetto, prickly pear, bracken fern, tarflower, wire grass, and Spanish moss. After 12 stations, the wooden pathway enters the wetland plant community of red maple, dahoon holly, American elm, coastal plain willow, black tupelo, buttonbush and other aquatic plants such as arrowhead, pickerel weed, and saw grass. The impressive oak-evergreen hammock begins at station #27. Cabbage palm and live oak dominate the canopy while nakedwood, French and red mulberry, red bay, marlberry, guava, dogwood, and persimmon occupy the understory. Various ferns, vines, and wildflowers abound on the hammock floor. Winding on, the trail re-enters the pine flatwoods at station #59. Identification of wild grape, shiny and white lyonia, reindeer and British soldier mosses, shiny blueberry, greenbrier, cinnamon fern, and the wildflower "innocence," rounds out the walk. There are four vista points with rest benches to enable the visitor to observe at leisure. The boardwalk is closed during times of rain due to the build-up of blue-green algae that makes the wooden surface slippery. Tours of the park are available by appointment. The trail is designed for handicapped accessibility.

To reach Erna Nixon Park from I-95, exit east onto U.S. 192/New Haven Avenue to Evans Road. Turn north on Evans Road and drive approximately two miles to the park entrance on the west/left side of the road. From U.S. 1 proceed west on New Haven Avenue to Evans Road and turn north. Parking is available for 40 or 50 vehicles. The park is open for visitation from 9 a.m. to 5 p.m. daily. The telephone number is (407) 952-4525.

Other Sites in the Melbourne Area

Botanical Gardens at Florida Institue of Technology. The botanical gardens are actually an old growth native sabal palm hammock. Over a mile of nature trails wind througb the preserve where benches and picnic shelters have been provided. Students are often seen studying between classes in the green oasis, so the best time to visit may be on weekends when parking is also more available along the Babcock Street-Southgate Avenue campus parking lot next to the gardens. The gardens are open from 6 a.m. to 6 p.m. For additional information call (407) 768-8000, ext. 6123.

Crane Creek Promenade. This streamside pocket park is reputed to be a good spot for observing manatees. There are plenty of benches along the 100 yards of landscaped boardwalk and street parking is available. Another pocket park that is landside and east of the promenade is **Bean Park**, suitable for picnicking. West of the promenade is the developed **Holmes Park** which features manatee sculpture. These city parks are located along Melbourne Avenue near the U.S. Highway 1 bridge over Crane Creek and the railroad bridge in historic downtown Melbourne.

Wickham Park. This large 490-acre county park offers plenty of activities, but little in the way of hiking paths (only 2,000 feet). Located in north Melbourne at 2500 Parkway Drive. Daily hours are 7 a.m. to dark. Telephone (407) 255-4307 for further information.

Turkey Creek Sanctuary Park
Palm Bay/Brevard County
Area: 60 acres
Trail Distance: 1 mile boardwalk
Highlights: boardwalk, nature study, photography, manatee sanctuary, fitness trail

Traversing the riparian bluff tops of Turkey Creek, the word scenic aptly describes this nature walk. The Sanctuary is owned by the City of Palm Bay and the Florida Audubon Society. Developed by local public, private, and corporate funds and grants from the State of Florida, this enclosed sanctuary contains, in addition to the boardwalk trail, a separate active exercise course.

From the trailhead you enter a sand pine ridge forest where interpretive signs identify the sandy soil as ancient ocean dune, the animals (gopher tortoise, skunk, squirrel, deer, turkey, rattlesnake, indigo snake), and plants (sand pine, gopher apple, myrtle and live oaks, scrub paw-paw, wire grass, saw palmetto, pignut hickory, French mulberry) that inhabit this southern Florida community. After several hundred feet the wooden trail forks at a handsome shady gazebo. Continuing due east the trail follows alongside the elevated bluffs of the meandering stream. Three vista overlooks have been provided with benches that provide ideal observation points looking down into the valley. Turkey Creek's inhabitants include the alligator, turtles, garfish, otter, bass, mullet, water moccasin, water snakes, and the endangered manatee. In 1983 Turkey Creek was declared a year round sanctuary for the "gentle giants" and in 1985, an Aquatic Reserve. The trail culminates at the "treehouse," where the elevated boardwalk reaches into the branchworks of a high live oak. Retrace your steps back to the trail fork at the gazebo.

Follow the boardwalk fork to the south and the stream bottom's floodplain hammock. A trail sign informs you that the soil of the floodplain is composed of peat, muck and clay, the vegetation is sabal palm; hardwoods (oaks, hackberry, sweet bay), ferns, vines (poison ivy and grape). The animal residents include raccoon, opossum, grey fox, skunk, and banana spider. Benches and vista observation points have also been provided on this segment of trail. A canoe deck has been built that provides access to Turkey Creek and downstream Palm Bay and Indian River lagoon. The trail loops around to the gazebo and the trail entrance. The beauty of the preserve and the opportunity to observe wildlife, especially the rare manatee, makes the walk worthwhile. The hours of the preserve are from 7 a.m. to sunset daily. Group tours can be arranged. Future plans include building a Nature Interpretive Center and Archaeological Museum.

To reach Turkey Creek Sanctuary Park from U.S. 1 in Palm Bay turn west onto Port Malabar Boulevard and drive 1.5 miles to the Palm Bay Community Center and City Library. The trailhead entrance is adjacent to the Palm Bay City Library. Parking is available in adjoining lots. The address is 1520 Port Malabar Boulevard. For more information call (407) 952-3400.

Environmental Learning Center
Wabasso/Indian River County
Area: 51 acres
Trail Distance: 600 ft. boardwalk
Highlights: nature study, nature walk, nature center, picnicking, shelter, guided tours

Everyone is welcome to visit and enjoy the non-profit Environmental Learning Center located on Wabasso Island along the Indian River. If your senses are open to exploring the natural surroundings, the center is bound to fill them with the dynamics of the Indian River lagoon.

You will want to visit the nature center first to view the exhibits and get oriented to the new facility. Outside the door the boardwalk begins near the picnic shelter. The elevated "trail" leads out into the mangrove-fringed shore and to an open vista of the lagoon, where many "wet" lab experiments are conducted. The boardwalk returns to the nature center and parking lot, forming a loop. Canoe excursions and guided tours are also given.

Future plans include the construction of laboratories, an auditorium, headquarters for the Pelican Island Audubon Society, Coast Guard Auxiliary, as well as a gift shop and exhibit area.

To reach the Environmental Learning Center from U.S. 1 in Wabasso, north of Vero Beach, go east on C.R. 710 across the causeway to the base of the arching bridge over Indian River. Go right/south onto Wabasso Island Lane and proceed to the next immediate right/south or Live Oak Drive. Go 0.2 mile to the entrance on the right/west side of the road. The center's hours are Monday through Friday 9 a.m. to 5 p.m. and weekends 1 to 4 p.m.; telephone (407) 589-5050.

Coastal Hammock Nature Trail
Vero Beach/Indian River County
Area: 20 acres
Trail Distance: .25 mile
Highlights: nature study, nature trail

The Pelican Island Audubon Society, with the cooperation of the Indian River County School Board, have established a short nature walk through a coastal hardwood hammock adjacent to the Beach-land Elementary School on Orchid Island, directly east of down-town Vero Beach. Easily accessible, the trail winds and loops about the interior of the shady, mature upland forest and is self-guiding.

The local Audubon Society members have produced an informative and detailed trail pamphlet identifying the abundant flora and fauna at 35 posted stations. Common and scientific names are given, along with a scientific description of the plant life. Common names include French mulberry, wild coffee, golden polypody, myrsine, Spanish moss, wild orchid, indigo berry, and Spanish bayonet. In addition, poisonous, edible, dye, landscaping, and wildlife food plants are pointed out and described. An outdoor "classroom" and council ring accomodates nature classes under the closed canopy of sabal palms and live oaks. The trail guide is available from the Pelican Island Audubon Society or the principal's office at the close-by Beachland Elementary School. The trail is hikeable daily during the daytime hours.

To reach Coastal Hammock Trail from U.S. 1, turn east on 23rd Street and follow Royal Palm Boulevard across Merrill Barber Bridge onto Beachland Boulevard. Turn north at Mockingbird Drive. The school is at the corner of Beachland and Mockingbird. The marked trailhead lies 50 yards north of the school near a fire hydrant. From S.R. A1A, turn west on Beachland Boulevard and drive two blocks to Mockingbird Drive. Parking is available along the quiet residential street.

Other Parks in Vero Beach and South Indian River County

Riverside Park. This large park is just a few blocks west and then east of the **Coastal Hammock Trail** at the east approach of Barber Bridge on S.R. 60. Basically an active park with recreational facilities, it does have a mile-long jogging trail and a picnic area. In addition, a trail leads to Indian River or Memorial Island sanctuary, an eight-acre island in the Indian River, accessible at the cul de sac of Dahlia Lane. Manatees frequent the river area.

The Florida Medical Entomology Lab. The lab's primary mission is the biological control of mosquitoes through research. Walking paths lead through a virgin sabal palm hammock and the **Bill Bidlingmayer Nature Trail** loops through a West Indian hammock, with outstanding stands of stopper or nakedwood. Stop by the office for a guided tour of these "plant islands." The lab is near the small community of Oslo. Turn east on the dead end Oslo Road driving towards Indian River. The facility and entrance are on the left/north side of Oslo Road. Park in the rear of the building and enter the office.

Harbor Branch Oceanographic Institution. This non-profit institution, founded in 1971, is one of the top three marine science research centers in the US (Scripps in LaJolla, CA and Woods Hole in Woods Hole, MA are the other two). Two-hour tours are given daily beginning at the visitors center. A fee is charged. The 480 acres include laboratories, ships, aquarium displays, a sculpture garden, gift shop and more. Harbor Branch is open 10 a.m. to 2 p.m. and is located along the Indian River between Vero Beach and Ft. Pierce, east of U.S. 1/Dixie Highway.

Heathcote Botanical Gardens
Ft. Pierce/St. Lucie County
Area: 3.5 acres
Trail Distance: .5 mile total
Highlights: botanical gardens, horticultural education, workshops, classes, lectures, gift shop, bookstore, membership
Fee(s): entrance

Formerly a commercial nursery, Heathcote Botanical Gardens was recently established as a nonprofit horticultural education center to serve the Ft. Pierce area and southeastern central Florida where public botanic gardens are a rarity. The planting model emulates the Marie Selby Botanical Gardens of Sarasota, Florida.

Trails weave throughout the specialty gardens of roses, hibiscus, cacti, and succulents. A palm forest and a Japanese garden, featuring bonsai tree specimens, adds to the botanical richness. The greenhouse contains orchids, African violets, ferns, bromeliads, and other exotic plants. A demonstration home landscaping design concentrates on native indigenous plants oriented to the southern and central Florida climate. Rest areas and a picnic spot allow further enjoyment of the garden's beauty.

The charming house of the former resident now shelters the administrative office, workshops, class and lecture rooms, gift shop, horticultural book store and a non-circulating reference library for members and interested persons. The Heathcote Botanical Gardens are beautiful year round. There is a blooming flower for every season.

To reach Heathcote Botanical Gardens from U.S. 1 in south Ft. Pierce, turn east on Gardenia Avenue to South Third Street. The parking lot and garden entrance are located on South Third Street. The gardens are open daily from 10 a.m. to 5 p.m. except Mondays. A labeled guided map is available at the entrance booth. Free admission is offered to students with instructor and there are special group rates. The mailing address and telephone number are Heathcote Botanical Gardens, 210 Savannah Road, Ft.Pierce, Florida 34982; (407) 464-4672.

The Savannas Recreation Area
Ft. Pierce/St. Lucie County
Area: 550 acres
Trail Distance: 1.5 miles
Highlights: nature study, nature walks, swimming, fishing, boating, boat launch ramp, boat rental, boat tours, picnicking, shelters, playground, petting farm, botanical garden, camping, group camping, water & dump station, concessions, camping,
Fees: entrance, boat rentals, boat tours

Within the city limits of Ft. Pierce, seven miles south of the central business district, lies a relatively undisturbed freshwater wetland. Once utilized as the city's main drinking water reservoir, this watery plain became a St. Lucie County parkland in 1970.

Sunrise, Savannas

There are three brief nature walks traversing the 100 acres of higher dry land bordering the aquatic shallows. After you obtain a bird checklist from the entrance station, the walk to the bird observation tower is about half a mile one-way. The main park road serves as the trail, passing between the campgrounds, past the petting farm of sheep, pigs, and cows, on through the picnic area and playground to the tower, which is at the extreme northeast corner of the park, literally at "land's end." From the tower, there is a sweeping view as far as the eye can see, to the sabal palms lining the south and east horizons. Early morning, late afternoon and early evening are the best times to witness the numerous avian residents, including the Everglades kite. Natural marshlands and a chain of small lakes stretch southward for nearly 10 miles to Jensen Beach, in Martin County. So unique are these wetlands, the Florida Department of Natural Resources has purchased some of the area south of The Savannas and will purchase more as funds become available. Besides birding, bass fishing is considered excellent.

The second walk also begins near the entrance station. If no groups are camping on **Palm Island**, the area is open to walkers. Follow the park spur road about 100 yards to the island, which has picnic shelters and restrooms. A narrow undesignated trail crosses over the footbridge and follows the spoilbanks south another 100 yards to the botanical garden, but does not cross over the deep channels to access the garden. The weedy path brings you close to the park's birdlife.

The third nature walk leads though the informal botanical garden, situated alongside the entrance road, where parking is allowed.

Enter across the footbridge. None of the native plants are labeled, but the setting is peaceful and pleasant.

The Savannas outdoor recreation area is in south Ft. Pierce at 1400 E. Midway Road, 1.2 miles east of U.S. 1. Unless you are camping, visitor hours are from 8 a.m. to sundown. The best way to experience the watery world of the park is on a boat tour conducted by a local naturalist.

Fort Pierce City Park
Fort Pierce/St. Lucie County
River Frontage: 3,000 ft.
Highlights: manatee observation, cultural facilities, special events

The downtown Indian River Lagoon area of Ft. Pierce is one of the 25 manatee sanctuaries in the State of Florida. The warm discharge waters of the Henry D. King Municipal Power Plant, just north of the central city district along North Indian River Drive, has created one of the several artificial "hot springs" for the heat-seeking aquatic mammals in winter. The busy waterfront has an idle speed limit for motor boats from November 15th through March 31st.

There are several accessible points to observe the manatees. Immediately south of South Bridge or Peter P. Cobb Bridge, S.R. A1A, is City Park, easily reached from South Indian River Drive. Paved walkways and benches can be found along the entire length of the river shore in the park. Additional observation spots are behind the adjacent art gallery and outdoor amphitheatre. Just south of these cultural facilities is the colorful Municipal Yacht Basin and Park, where recreational river- and ocean-bound boats come and go. From here to Orange Avenue behind the library there is more river frontage. Even if you do not spot any manatees, enjoy the city's cultural amenities during your day's outing. The Ft. Pierce City Park and adjoining facilities are two blocks east of U.S. 1 in downtown Ft. Pierce.

Martin County Environmental Studies Center
Jensen Beach/Martin County
Area: 4-5 acres
Trail Distance: 0.5 mile
Highlights: nature study, nature walk. marine museum, hammock botanic garden, Seminole chickee, wet lab, gift shop, special community programs and events

With open vistas of the Indian River Lagoon, the Spanish Colonial style schoolhouse is home to Martin County's renowned alternative outdoor education program, where the environment is explored with a friendly "hands-on" approach. It is administered by the Martin County School Board, and the public is encouraged to visit. The center is open 9 a.m. to 3 p.m. Monday through Friday during the school year months from September to June. There are no summer hours from June through August.

After parking on the circle drive in front of the building, stop by the visitors' office and gift shop, the first door to the right, for a self-tour guide leaflet to the coastal hardwood hammock landscaping example and an orientation on what to see. Former classrooms harbor a small marine museum, a collection that includes the local biology of the adjacent Indian River and nearby Atlantic Ocean. Another classroom or "wet lab" contains 30 saltwater aquariums containing an octopus, shark, starfish, loggerhead and green sea turtles, and other aquatic life collected by the students. An authenic Seminole Indian chickee or thatched shelter is around the corner of the grassy courtyard plaza. The Native Plant Society has a small exhibition slat house of indigenous plants that are sold at school fund-raising events. The model coastal hammock is found beside the south side of the school. Twenty-eight native plants are identified by their common and scientific names, and include the paradise tree, satin leaf, jamacia caper, wild lime, and torchwood. The entire visit may require one hour.

To reach the Martin County Environmental Studies Center at Jensen Beach from U.S. 1, turn east on Jensen Beach Boulevard/S.R. 707A, drive 3.5 miles to Indian River Drive and turn north. The center is on the west side of Indian River Drive, a half-mile north. The address is 2900 N.E. Indian River Drive. The telephone number is (407)334-1262.

Possum Long Nature Center
Stuart/Martin County
Area: 4.5 acres
Trail Distance: .3 mile total
Highlights: nature study, nature walks, botanical garden, horticultural conservatory, exhibition house, special programs, field trips, Audubon Society membership
Fee(s): special programs, field trips

The Possum Long Nature center was established in 1973, by the Martin County Audubon Society, from the one-acre homestead and former plant nursery of Charles W. "Possum" Long. The nature center, located in a residential district near the center of the city of Stuart, maintains in addition to a maze of short nature walks, a botanical garden, horticultural conservatory and environmental education program. School groups visit Possum Long during field trips. Workshops, classes, films, meetings, and guest speakers are sponsored and often held at the nearby Florida Institute of Technology auditorium at Jensen Beach.

An exhibition house contains numerous plants raised by the members that are offered for sale during Possum Long Week in November. An annual Pancake Breakfast and a fruit and foliage fashion show are also held during the event to raise money for maintainence of the nature center.

There are several interconnecting, wood-chipped paths that weave through the densely shaded hammock of 4.5 acres. Plants are labeled to make the walk more informative. Nature walkers can enjoy the trails during daylight hours. Conducted and self-guided walks are held Monday and Thursday mornings at 10:30 or by appointment. The nature center buildings are open at that time.

To reach Possum Long Nature Center in Stuart from U.S. 1, exit north on Palm Beach Road and drive 1.3 miles to 7th Street. Turn east on 7th Street and proceed to Hibiscus Avenue, the first street to the left. The Nature Center will be on the west side of Hibiscus Avenue where conspicuous identification signs are posted. Parking is limited to about 10 cars.

Additional Martin County Audubon facilities include the **Treasure Coast Audubon Wildlife Hospital** at 2800 S.E. Bridge Road, Hobe Sound and the recently acquired 160-acre **Martin County Nature Sanctuary** on Loop Road in Stuart.

The neighboring community of Palm City has the **Gift Gardens Botanical/Fine Art Park** that is also worth a visit. The 24-acre park features an art collection and gallery, outdoor sculptures, a lakeside pathway and a Life Wall with bronze masks of famous individuals. There is an entrance fee. To reach the park from U.S. 1 in Stuart go west on Monterey Road and turn left onto Mapp Road.

Continue on Mapp Road to C.R. 714 and turn right. Continue 0.8 mile on C.R. 714 to Palm City School Road. The park is next to the Palm City elementary school at 3400 S.W. Palm City School Road. The telephone number is (407) 283-2828.

Society Of The Four Arts
Botanical & Sculpture Gardens
Palm Beach/Palm Beach County
Area: 3 acres
Trail Distance: .3 mile
Highlights: botanical garden, sculpture garden, library, seashell display, special events, membership

The Society of the Four Arts is a non-profit organization supported by public membership. It was incorporated in 1936, to promote appreciation of art, music, drama, and literature through presentation of cultural programs. The office, library, botanical, and sculpture gardens are located at the Four Arts Plaza in the City of Palm Beach. The Garden Club of Palm Beach maintains the Four Arts Gardens adjacent to the library and the sculpture garden. The new Sculpture Garden was made possible by membership donations.

The formal plantings of the Four Arts Gardens are comprised of several small demonstration theme gardens, including a Boxwood, Rose, Herb, Moonlight, Chinese, Balm, Jungle, Rock, Tropical, Madonna, and Fountain Garden. Statuary, urns, gateways, brick and stone pathways, and patios further accent the tranquil setting.

Just east of the botanical gardens is the Four Arts Sculpture Garden where significant pieces of sculpture are displayed on the landscaped grounds. Visitors may enter from the botanical gardens or from the street side off Royal Palm Way. House and Garden Day is a special annual tour held the first Sunday in March, followed by the Flower Show in April. Both events are sponsored by the Garden Club of Palm Beach.

The Four Arts Gardens are open to the public from 10 a.m. to 5 p.m. Monday through Saturday from November 1 to May 1 and Sunday 2:30 to 5 p.m., January 1 to April 1. Summer hours are from 10 a.m. to 5 p.m. Monday through Friday, May 1 to April 15.

To reach the Four Arts Gardens and Plaza from I-95, exit Okeechobee Boulevard/S.R. 704 east. Stay on Okeechobee Boulevard all the way across Royal Palm Bridge over Lake Worth intracoastal waterway onto Royal Palm Way. The Four Arts Complex is the first street, Lake Drive, to the left off the bridge.

While you are in Palm Beach, try walking or bicycling the 4.8-mile one-way South Lake Trail. You can begin the hike-bike path south section at the Royal Palm Bridge next to the Society of the Four Arts Plaza and head south past immaculate landscaped homes along Lake Worth to Phipps Beach Ocean Park on South Ocean Boulevard/S.R. A1A. The 1,300-foot beach has high frontal dunes with thatched chickee picnic shelters. The Gulf Stream comes closer to the east Florida shore here than elsewhere. This is the best natural beach along the Palm Beach coast.

The north section of the bike-hike trail begins at Worth Avenue and continues to the Lake Worth Inlet or north end of the island. From the Society of the Four Arts Plaza, the trail runs north, along Lake Worth to the Sailfish Club, then inland east and north to the Port of Palm Beach and the inlet.

Organ pipe cactus, Mounts

Mounts Botanical Garden
West Palm Beach/Palm Beach County
Area: 14 developed acres
Trail Distance: 1,500 ft.
Highlights: nature study, nature walk, picnicking, guided tours, horticultural programs, plant shows, plant & craft sales, reservable pavilion, weddings & receptions, membership, newsletter

Southern Florida home gardeners interested in learning which subtropical and tropical plants they can cultivate should take advantage of Mounts Botanical Garden. The demonstration areas have come a long way since the mid-1950s, when Palm Beach County Agricultural Extension Agent Marvin "Red" Mounts first planted tropical trees in the 'back acres' of the Extension office for public display. Generous assistance from several governmental and educational agencies, plant societies, garden clubs, nurserymen, and individuals alike, has established a botanical garden of thousands of trees and plants. They are arranged in landscaped settings and labeled for easy viewing from the winding, concrete pathways. The labels give both common and scientific.names, family, native country, and fruit or plant description. A pamphlet can be obtained from the Garden office. The pamphlet lists the following areas in the garden:

- Food Crops
- Low Water Area
- Salt Tolerant Area
- Shade and Flowering Trees
- Hibiscus
- Hedges
- Palms
- Herb Garden
- Shrubs

- Rose Garden
- Begonias
- Lake Worth
- Citrus and Tropical Fruit Trees
- Foliage Rain Forest
- Rose Garden
- Lake Worth
- Island

Mounts Botanical Garden can be reached from I-95 in West Palm Beach. If you are coming from the south, exit at Southern Boulevard and go west to Military Trail. Turn right/north on Military Trail. The garden will be on your left, directly behind the Agricultural Building at 531 North Military Trail. If you are driving from the north, exit at Beleveddere Road and go west to Military Trail, then turn left/south. The garden will be on your right. The garden hours are Monday through Saturday, 8:30 to 5 p.m. and Sunday from 1:30 to 5 p.m. with a one-hour tour starting at 2:30. The garden is closed on holidays.

Drehr Park Zoo/South Florida Science Museum & Planetarium/Drehr Park Nature Area

West Palm Beach/Palm Beach County
Area: 99 total acres
Trail Distance: 2 miles total
Highlights:
Zoo - zoological gardens, gift shop, concessions, special events, membership
Museum - science museum, planetarium, observatory, aquarium, programs, tours, gift shop, membership
Nature Area - arboretum, picnicking, shelters, bike trail, fishing, foot trails
Fee(s): entrance to zoo, museum, planetarium

A full days outing is in store for visitors to these West Palm Beach cultural and recreational facilities. Although small, the zoo, museum and nature area are first class. All are located back-to-back in a natural parkland setting. The **Drehr Park Zoo** exhibits over 260 native and exotic subtropical animals, of which 15 are considered rare and endangered. The zoo has achieved recognition as the first in the nation to exhibit Goeldi monkeys outdoors year round. Visitors will see Central American marmosets and Brazilian tapirs, African Diana monkeys, Malaysian sun bears, Florida panthers and an outdoor reptile display. The North American male black bear, Hammer, starred in the "Gentle Ben" television series and is here to be seen. The river otter exhibit has an underwater window for easy viewing. There is a walk-through butterfly exhibit. A petting zoo is a favorite with children. The Betty Cardinal Trail features many plants that Paul Drehr, the original owner who donated his land for the park, collected on his trips around the world. The Drehr Park Zoo hours are 9 a.m. to 5 p.m. daily except Thanksgiving, Christmas and New Year's Day. The address is 1301 Summit Boulevard.

The main mission of the South Florida Science Museum and Aldrin Planetarium is to promote science education in Palm Beach County. The numerous exhibits and diplays cover adaptive anatomy, archaeology, astronomy, biology, chemistry, computers, herpetology, marine sciences, oceanography, paleontology, physics, and space science. A major exhibit is the South Florida Aquarium,with a simulated coral reef from the Atlantic and Pacific Oceans and a Touch Tank. Beyond the back door of the museum is a 300-foot nature walk through six south Florida plant communities. Special events and traveling exhibits occur frequently.

The **Aldrin Planetarium** has a seating capacity for 100 persons during the daily Sky Shows. Multi-media presentations and laser concerts are shown on weekend evenings. Another attraction is the Gibson Observatory, one of the largest in south Florida, with its 16.5 inch Newtonian Reflector Telescope.

The **Science Museum** hours are 10 a.m. to 5 p.m. Tuesday through Saturday, Friday evenings from 6:30 to 10 p.m. and noon to 5 Sunday and Monday. The Planetarium shows are at 3 p.m. daily and Friday evening at 8 p.m. The observatory is also open Friday evenings from 8 to 10, if skies are clear for viewing. The address is 4801 Drehr Trail North.

Drehr Park's wooded and lagoon-studded acres provide sheltered picnicking, lagoon fishing, baseball fields, a model airplane field, a children's play structure, walking and jogging paths, a bike trail, and an arboretum. Dedicated in 1987, the **Nature Area**, at the north end of the park near Southern Boulevard, features a quarter-mile linear trail that passes 10 family groupings of woody and herbaceous plants such as palm, ginseng, bromeliad, arum, lily, and day flower. The plants are identified by a single marker to a plant family. Park hours are from 8 a.m. to sunset daily.

To reach Drehr Park Zoo, South Florida Science Center and Planetarium and Drehr Park Nature Area from I-95 in West Palm Beach, exit onto Southern Boulevard, drive east to Park Avenue and turn south/right. Proceed on Park Avenue to Summit Boulevard and turn west/right. The zoo parking lot will be on the right side of Summit Boulevard before the I-95 overpass. The Museum can be reached by following the park road north past the zoo into Drehr Park. Continue to the end of the park road to reach the Nature Area.

John Prince Park
Lake Worth/Palm Beach County
Area: 1,053 acres
Trail Distance: 1 mile
Highlights: nature study, nature trail, Heart Trail, wheelcourse trail, bike path, picnicking, shelters, playgrounds, playing fields, tennis courts, basketball, golf range, model plane ramp, pier, fishing, boat ramps, boating, waterskiing, water sports, concessions, day camp, camping, Kravis Performing Arts Center, Palm Beach Junior College
Fee(s): boat rentals, reserved group shelters & facilities, camping

Established in 1939, John Prince Park is the second oldest county park in the state of Florida. Located in the city of Lake Worth, this large regional park offers a pot pourri of recreational pursuits in or along Lake Osborne, ranging from rigorous to leisurely and laid back.

The **Custard Apple Nature Trail**, maintained and sponsored by the local Everglades Chapter of the Audubon Society, is situated at the park's south end near the campground. The main trailhead begins across from the campground entrance office. Successful efforts have been made by the Everglades Chapter to landscape some of the open areas with native hardwood hammock plant material, although the unwelcome Australian pine is the predominant tree. Numerous trailside plants are identified by tag labels. Trail spurs connect the main trail from the offroad parking area along the main park road west of the campground. The lower portions of the trail can be wet and muddy, but recent efforts have been made to fill these in with mulch.

The most natural portion of the loop trail is the boardwalk that overlooks a cattail marsh where waterfowl and wildlife are often seen. This wetland area also supports the custard apple tree. Audubon-guided tours are led every Saturday from January through March beginning at 9 a.m. The Everglades Chapter also leads field trips to other surrounding Palm Beach County sites. In the not-so-distant future, Palm Beach County Park Department plans to construct a nature center and develop hiking trails at Lake Worth Nature Park, as well as to upgrade and establish nature trails at the existing county facilities.

To reach John Prince Park at 2700 6th Avenue in Lake Worth from 1-95, exit South 6th Avenue and drive west to Congress Avenue/S.R. 807. Turn north on Congress to Lake Worth Road, turn east and drive to the main park.entrance. The park hours are one hour before dawn to one hour after dusk.

Other Nature Parks in West Palm Beach

Pine Jog Environmental Education Center. Two short nature trails begin and end at the nature center. They pass tbrougb pine flat-woods, sawgrass marsh, live oak-sabal palm hammock, past a freshwater pond and an open meadow. The limited bours are 1 to 4 p.m. on weekends. To reach the center from I-95 go west on Southern Boulevard to Jog Road and turn south/left. Proceed to the junction of Summit Boulevard and Jog Road, where the center is on the northeast corner of the intersection.

Okeeheelee Park. Continue south from Pine Jog Environmental Education Center on Jog Road and turn right/west on Forest Hill Boulevard. Drive a few miles further and you will reach the 900-acre Okeeheelee Park. The Palm Beach County park was created from a reclaimed shell pit and at first appearances the park is little more than an open space of atbletic fields, small lakes, picnic areas, and landscaped grounds. But by following the park roads to the rear of the property you will find the nature center and over five miles of hiking trail leading through 90 acres of pinelands and wetlands. The nature center is open during the afternoons from 1-5 p.m., but scheduled hikes are often conducted. Enter the park from Forest Hill Boulevard just east of the Florida Turnpike.

The Morikami Park, Museum & Gardens
Delray Beach, Palm Beach County
Area: 155 acres
Trail Distance: 1 mile
Highlights: nature study, nature trails Japanese gardens, bonsai exhibit, museum, picnicking, shelters, gift shop, reference library, tours, special events & programs
Fee(s): entrance, reservable picnic shelters, special programs and events

George Sukeji Morikami (1886-1976) donated his land to the county of Palm Beach in 1974 with the request that his former pineapple fields be developed "to enhance Japanese-American cultural understanding." Under the ownership and management of Palm Beach County Parks and Recreation Department, The Morikami Park, Museum, and Gardens were opened to the public in 1977. The park visitor will not only learn about traditional and modern Japanese culture, but will discover a subtle atmosphere of tranquility here. To best appreciate your visit, see the museum first, then the gardens and nature trail. Finally, have a picnic on the grounds if you wish.

The Museum of Japanese Culture has several permanent and traveling folk art exhibits on display. They can be found in separate rooms of the traditional Japanese home, centered around an open courtyard garden. Visitors are greeted by a museum host, who provides paper slippers in exchange for shoes (a Japanese custom), to be used while walking on the tatami mats. The rooms of the museum feature pottery, paper wares, toys, dolls, an authenic tea room, bedroom, furniture, and a history of the local Yamoato Colony and Japanese heritage in Florida. A gift shop stocks Japanese cultural items for sale, including a guide book to the garden.

The two-acre Japanese Garden surrounding the museum is designed with both authenticity and adaptation to the Florida climate in mind. Groupings of carefully placed rocks, trees, plants, sand, mounded hills, and water are arranged in a controlled, though seemingly unplanned natural scheme. The Edward N. Potter Memorial Bonsai exhibit displays Florida native trees in miniature. A 20-foot-high waterfall cascades into a small pond filled with Koi fish (ornamental Japanese carp), and visitors are encouraged to feed them with dispensed food pellets at Moon Bridge. A memorial to the astronauts who perished in the Challenger explosion is near the waterfall. The museum and garden loop goes on to interconnect with the nature trail.

Twenty Interpretive stations have been placed along the self-guiding loop through a slash pine flatwoods grove. The pine trees filter the warm sun in the open understory. The trail follows the border of the property on a wide path and ends at the picnic ahd parking area. To complete your visit, enjoy a leisurely picnic at the sheltered tables. Check at the museum for information about guided tour programs and special events. A tea house is planned for construction in the near future.

The Morikami Park, Museum, and Gardens are three miles west of Delray Beach at 4000 Morikami Park Road. From I-95, exit at Linton Boulevard and drive west to Carter Road, then turn south to Morikami Park Road. From the Florida Turnpike, take exit 32 and go east on Atlantic Avenue/S.R. 806 to Carter Road, then turn south to Morikami Road. Follow the directional signs.

The Morikami Museum is open daily 10 a.m. to 5 p.m. and closed Mondays and major holidays. The grounds are open 8 a.m. to sunset daily.

Deerfield Island Park
Deerfield Beach, FL/Broward County
Area: 55 acres
Trail Distance: 1.4 mile total
Highlights: nature study, nature walks & boat trip tours, picnicking, shelters, boating, ten-slip dockage, playground, volleyball, horseshoes, youth camp, concessions
Fee(s): boat transportation, shelter reservation

Accessible only by boat, Deerfield Island Park is an ideal day-use retreat at the mouth of the Hillsboro Canal, where it flows together with the Royal Palm Waterway and the Intracoastal Waterway at the Broward and Palm Beach County line. If you don't have a boat, reservations for boat transportation to the island, on Wednesday mornings and Saturday afternoons, can be arranged through the Broward County Park and Recreation Division, the island's owner and steward. Normally, the boat leaves at 8:30 a.m. from the dock of the Riverview Restaurant, 1741 Riverview Road, Deerfield Beach, and returns at 12 noon. On Saturday afternoons, the boat leaves from Pioneer Park in nearby northeast Deerfield Beach. If you do have a boat, Pioneer Park has the nearest boat ramp to the island. To make the necessary reservations, telephone (407) 428-5474. Once in the boat, the ride from the Riverview dock is only 10 minutes to Deefield Island, a man-made, triangular island created from dredged spoils. Nature has been quick to cover the limestone spoils with a green mantle. Wildlife has also made the island home, with armadillos, raccoons, grey fox, and various sea birds. The island is also a state refuge for the gopher tortoise.

Naturalist-guided tours are conducted on arrival. Two nature trails traverse the island: **Mangrove Trail** and **Coquina Trail**. The .6-mile Mangrove Trail winds through a red, black and white mangrove swamp forest on the northwest portion of the island. 1,500 feet of the trail is boardwalk. The slightly longer .8-mile Coquina Trail

Double-crested cormorants, Deerfield Island

follows the east edge of the island alongside the Intracoastal Waterway. Coquina limestone is a soft whitish material formed from broken shells and corals and it is readily exposed along the path. The plant life on this side of the island is coastal dune and hammock species.

After your return to the mainland, consider visiting the beach at **Deerfield Beach**. The over half-mile, sandy strand stretches along A1A and offers picnicking, shelters, swimming, fishing, a pier, and concessions. Parking is available from N.E. 7th Street south to S.E. 10th street at the city's boundary with Hillsboro Beach.

To reach Riverview Restaurant, where the boats depart for Deerfield Island, from I-95, exit at Hillsboro Boulevard/S.R. 810 and drive east towards the beach. Riverview Road is just before the Deerfield Chamber of Commerce on the left/north side of Hillsboro Boulevard. Drive to the end of Riverview Road, where parking is available at a public lot next to the restuarant.

Pioneer Park can be reached from Hillsboro Boulevard by driving north on Dixie Highway to the Hillsboro Canal and the Broward/Palm Beach County line. Pioneer Park entrance is on the right/east side of the Dixie Highway.

Tradewinds Park
Coconut Creek/Broward County
Area: 540 acres
Trail Distance: 3,200 ft.
Highlights: nature study, nature walks, museum, butterfly world, landscape garden, jogging trail, petting zoo, pony rides, bicycling, marina, boat launch ramp, fishing, picnicking. shelters, playfields, playgrounds, miniature golf, general store, concessions
Fees: entrance (weekends & holidays only), shelter reservations, boat rental, bicycle rental, guided pony rides, ballfield reservations, miniature golf

Tradewinds Park is a large regional Broward County day-use facility that offers something for everyone. The widespread tract of land is divided into two separate parcels by West Sample Road, fittingly referred to as Tradewinds North and Tradewinds South. Tradewinds North is the smaller half, at 190 acres, but it is by no means short on recreation. This more passive side offers lakeside picnicking, playgrounds, guided pony and horse rides, a scenic

Dutch-style windmill, a barnyard petting zoo, two short cypress forest boardwalks, a museum and landscape gardens. Two raised boardwalks, both 100 yards in length, crisscross and encircle the 1.5-acre bald cypress stands in the north property. The **McLean Ranch** house has been restored to a walk-through-museum that reveals western Broward County farm life in the early days of this century. The small landscaped garden features 200 exotic plant species from various areas of the world. Peacocks wander the garden.

Tradewinds South is the more active park. There are baseball, softball, football, and soccer fields, marina and boat rentals, miniature golf, playgrounds, a jogging trail and bicycling. Of special interest to nature walkers is the 3,000-foot-loop **Cypress Trail** at the extreme south end of the park, where the park road ends and the trail begins. The boardwalk trail winds through 100 acres of the largest tract of cyress and red maple forest remaining in Broward County. Fortunately, it was bypassed by agricultural drainage projects and urban development. The outstanding botanical features of this second-growth forest are the resurrection-fern-covered pond apple trees at the center of the slough. A Cypress Trail guide booklet is available at the park office. The text corresponds with the 16 numbered green pond-apple symbols along the boardwalk. Trees, shrubs, ferns, air plants and animal residents are identified and described.

The first butterfly "farm" in the U.S. is in the southern half of Tradewinds Park. Built by Meta-Science, Inc., the four-acre site features a screened rainforest dome or insectarium which houses thousands of butterflies and where visitors can walk. There is also a breeding laboratory, an international collection of butterflies in the butterfly museum and a botanical garden. **Butterfly World** is open daily 9 a.m. to 5 p.m. and Sunday 1-5 p.m., including the gift shop. Tradewinds Park can be reached from I-95 in northeast Broward County by exiting west on Sample Road and driving directly to the north or south entrance at 3600 West Sample Road. Tradewinds is open daily from 8 a.m. to 6 p.m., November to April.

Nearby **Quiet Waters Park**, another Broward County Park, provides camping facilities. A unique camping feature is the rent-a-tent site that is already set up and waiting for occupancy. Quiet

Waters Park is located at 6601 North Powerline Road in West Deerfield Beach, about three miles northeast of Tradewinds.

Fern Forest Nature Center
Pompano Beach/Broward County
Area: 255 acres
Trail Distance: 1.5 miles total
Highlights: nature study, nature walks, picnicking, nature center, amphitheatre, assembly hall, guided tours
Fee(s): amphitheatre and assembly hall rental

Tucked away in a secluded natural environment, Fern Forest Nature Center is one of Broward County Parks Division's most recent acquisitions. The curving boardwalk approach to the "hidden" nature center accents its seclusion. The modern center provides an overview introduction to Fern Forest with its 10 plant communities and its wildlife residents. The walk-through simulated "oak-palm community" display includes "singing" birds. Aptly named, Fern Forest includes 32 identified species of ferns in the preserve. A trail guide book is available for a small fee at the center. The trails begin at the back door.

Cypress Creek Trail is a .5-mile raised boardwalk that encircles a well-preserved, cypress-maple plant community. Sixteen numbered stops correspond with the trail booklet. Plants, animals, and general forest ecology of Cypress Creek are the main themes. Rest benches and observation overlooks are provided.

The **Prairie Overlook Trail** is a one-mile loop walk through an oak-sabal palm hammock that skirts an open prairie. A boardwalk overlook of the prairie is located at mid-point. American kestrels and red-tailed hawks hover overhead in search of prey and numerous wildflowers grace the treeless opening. West of the observation overlook, the oak-sabal palm hammock has several large tree specimens.

Unfolding ferns

A third trail, the **Maple Walk**, is currently under construction near the beginning of the Prairie Overlook Trail. Pure stands of red maple comprise one of the 10 plant communities at Fern Forest. Some of the other plant communities include cypress-maple, oak-cypress-sabal palm, oak-pine-sabal palm, ficus-tropical hardwood, mixed temperate-tropical hardwood hammock, prairie, and Brazilian pepper-guava-exotic. The lovely natural setting and publicly available modern facilities make the park a popular place for weddings.

To reach Fern Forest Nature Center from I-95 in south Pompano Beach, exit west on Cypress Creek Road/N.W. 62nd Street and drive to N.W. 31st Avenue; turn right/north and proceed 1.8 miles (underneath an overpass of the Florida Turnpike) to the park entrance at 201 Lyons Road South, on the left/west side of the road. Fern Forest is open daily 8:30 a.m. to sunset.

John D. Easterlin Park
Oakland Park/Broward County
Area: 46 acres
Trail Distance: .75 mile
Highlights: nature study, nature walk, fitness course, picnicking, shelters, playground, horseshoes, volleyball, shuffleboard, camping
Fee(s): entrance (weekends and holidays only), picnic, shelter rental, camping

Established in spring of 1965, this is a nature-oriented "picnic and camping" park, owned and managed by Broward County Parks and Recreation Division. The property is the remnant of a bald cypress and mixed cypress woodland that survived development and drainage. Surrounded by streets, a railroad, canal, and apartments, the park's dense vegetation acts as a green buffer, creating a more insulated natural environment for park visitors.

A short wood-chipped nature trail loop begins just west of the park office and parking area. The narrow path follows the property's forested edge underneath a shady canopy of red bay, pond apple, dahoon holly, sabal palm, oak, red maple, strangler fig, and bald cypress. Many of the bald cypress trees, especially in the picnic area at the north end of the park, are nearly 100 feet tall and 300 years old. Exotic trees include Brazilian pepper and guava. Wild coffee is particularly abundant in the understory. A variety of ferns carpet the damp forest floor. Since drainage altered the water pattern, the mixed cypress forest is in a transitional state, evolving to hardwood hammock. The trail may be wet and muddy in low sections near the campground. The nature trail ends at a laurel oak woods on the east shore of Easterlin Pond. Cross the open grassy area to the northwest, where you may see peacocks, and walk back to the parking area,

To reach John D. Easterlin Park, exit I-95 at Oakland Park Boulevard and drive east to Powerline Road. Go north to N.W. 38th Street, then west across the railroad tracks to the park entrance on the south side at 1000 N.W. 38th Street. The park hours are 8 a.m. to sunset daily.

Colohatchee Natural Park
Wilton Manors/Broward County
Area: 6 acres
Trail Distance: 1,800 ft.
Highlights: nature study, nature walk, picnicking, shelters, boating, launch ramp, basketball, horseshoes, volleyball
Fee(s): picnic shelter reservations

Located on the mangrove-lined north shore of the Middle River's South Fork, Colohatchee Natural Park is a day-use facility owned and managed since 1975 by the City Park and Recreation Department of Wilton Manors. Adjacent to the four-acre red and black mangrove forest is the sunny, open, two-acre upland recreational area that features horseshoes, volleyball and basketball courts, a picnic pavilion, playground, and restrooms. Seven additional picnic shelters are provided along the 1,800-foot boardwalk loop. The boat ramp is directly across N.E. 15th Avenue from the main park and parking area.

Dredging, channelization, and canal construction have altered the natural freshwater stream flow patterns and allowed the ocean waters to sweep further inland, creating a brackish water habitat that has destroyed the riparian species that are not salt-tolerant, such as coastal plain willow and bald cypress. Red mangrove now grows close to the river's edge. They display curving, pole-like roots, while the black mangroves are recognizable by their vertical tube-like projections called pneumatophores. The dominating mangroves and the inundation of high water does not allow a plant understory to thrive. This makes for easy observation of the

Mocking bird in red mangrove, Colohatchee Natural Park

wildlife, especially herons that frequent the low tidal mud flat floor.

Interpretive signs displayed near the boardwalk entrance provide the visitor with information about the park's historical past. William C. Collier, early settler and farmer, established a citrus grove in the area during the 1890s. Collier befriended the neighboring Seminole Indian families and they affectionately referred to him as "Colo." Since he resided near the river or "hatchee," Collier and his farm were called "Colohatchee." It is doubtful that mangroves flourished along the river in Collier's time.

To reach Colohatchee Natural Park in Wilton Manors from I-95, exit eastbound onto Sunrise Boulevard and drive to N.E. 15th Avenue, then turn north/left. Continue north on N.E. 15th Avenue to the parking area on the west/left side of the avenue. This is just beyond the city limits bridge over the South Fork of the Middle River. The address is 1975 N.E. 15th Avenue. The hours are 9 a.m. to sunset daily except Tuesdays. A park ranger is on duty during the park hours.

The Discovery Center/Museum of Archaeology
Ft. Lauderdale/Broward County
Highlights: museums, gift shops, special events, workshops, classes, memberships
Fee(s): entrance

These non-profit educational institutions are close to one another in the Himmarsha Village area near the New River in downtown Ft. Lauderdale, and each displays fine exhibits about the natural and social history of southern Florida.

Founded in 1977, the **Discovery Center** is essentially a children's museum that houses displays and exhibits (many "hands-on"), of art, history, and science. The Center is located in the historic New River Inn, Ft. Lauderdale's first hotel. Three stories of 40 rooms and hallways feature unique exhibits waiting to be "discovered," such as the Florida Reef Room, Insect Room, Reptile Hall, a mini-planetarium, Everglades Room, and Backyard Workshop Nature Center. Be prepared to explore with your senses and to find out why and how things work. The Discovery Center is not only for children.

The Discovery Center is open Tuesday to Friday noon to 5 p.m., Saturday 10 a.m. to 5 p.m. and Sunday 12 noon to 5 p.m. The Center is closed Mondays. The address is 231 S.W. 2nd Avenue. Plans are under way to construct a new science center.

The **Museum of Archaeology** is about two blocks north and east of the Discovery Center at 203 S.W. 1st Avenue, where it was re-opened in 1987. "Man, His Culture and Environment" is the main exhibit, with special emphasis on the former inhabitants of the Broward County area: the prehistoric Tequesta Indians. The archaeological and geological exhibits deal with such subjects as the geological formation of south Florida, Pleistocene glaciation, world tribal arts, Pre-Columbian artifacts, osteology (the branch of anatomy dealing with bones), pottery, homonid evolution, a simulated exploratory dig in Broward County, and a great deal of Tequesta Indian information. Members and volunteers engage in actual excavation of prehistoric Indian sites throughout southern Florida.

The Museum of Archaeology's hours are from Tuesday to Saturday 10 a.m. to 4 p.m. The Museum is closed during the summer months of June, July, and August.

If time allows, consider visiting the **Ft. Lauderdale Historical Museum** at 219 S.W. 2nd Avenue and the **King-Cromartie House,** restored pioneer home at 229 S.W. 2nd Avenue. These two non-profit institutions are situated just north of The Discovery Center.

To reach the museum from I-95, exit east on Broward Boulevard and drive to downtown Ft. Lauderdale.

Secret Woods Nature Center
Fort Lauderdale/Broward County
Area: 37 acres
Trail Distance: 4,400 ft. total
Highlights: nature study, nature walks, naturalist service, photo blind, amphitheatre, assembly hall, programs
Fee(s): amphitheatre and assembly hall rental

As its name implies, this is a forested retreat that beckons day visitors to enjoy the splendors of nature. Situated on the South Fork of New River in Ft. Lauderdale, Secret Woods was the first interpretive center established by Broward County Parks Division in 1972. The park remains today a world away from urban noise and bustle.

Beginning directly behind the nature center, the two self-guiding nature trails provide a close-up look at the four plant communities thriving within its 37 green acres: laurel oak hammock, freshwater cypress-maple wetland, pond apple, and mangrove. New River Trail is a 3,200-foot boardwalk loop with 21 stations that are identified by red maple leaf symbols. A finely illustrated trail guide booklet is available for a nominal fee from the office. The shady, wooden pathway follows the north boundary along the mangrove-lined shore of the increasingly saline New River. The hammock in the park's interior is undergoing a successional struggle between the native and exotic plant life. Several of these plant species are identified in the trail booklet.

Slightly higher in elevation, the **Laurel Oak Trail** is a 1,200-foot ground level, wood-chipped walk through semi-pure stands of what are sometimes referred to as "diamond-leaf oak." The tree is widely planted in the southeastern U.S. for the cool shade cast from its dense broad, round crown. Several hundred turkey vultures roost in the trees at night. The labeled interpretive stops focus on sensory awareness. Visitors are invited to touch, smell, and visually examine (no tasting) the identified plants of the hammock. Several rest and observation benches have been provided on both trails.

Secret Woods Nature Center is open Monday through Friday 8:30 a.m. to 5 p.m. weekends and holidays. The Center is half a mile west of I-95 at the S.R. 84/S.W. 23rd Street exit in south Ft. Lauderdale. The address is 2701 West State Road 84.

Other nearby nature-oriented parks with active recreational facilities including short nature trails and boardwalks, are **Snyder Park** and **Topeekeegee Yugnee** or "TY" park. The 92-acre wooded Snyder Park, a Ft. Lauderdale city facility, features a 150-foot boardwalk, picnic pavilions, swimming beach, spring-fed lakes, and various recreational rentals. There are abundant live oaks here. The park is half a mile south of S.R. 84 at 3299 S.W. Avenue, next to the busy Ft.Lauderdale-Hollywood International Airport, "TY" park, a Broward County regional park, is one mile west of I-95 in Hollywood at 3300 North Park Road and Sheridan Street. Nature paths, playfields, picnic pavilions, and a campground surround the 40-acre lake. Both parks charge entrance fees.

Buehler Planetarium & Observatory
Davie/Broward County
Highlights: planetarium shows, observatory viewing

Named for Emil Buehler, pioneer in aeronautics, the Buehler Planetarium is one of the largest in the world and has served the public since 1965. Recent renovations of the planetarium include tiltback seats, a new star dome and a new Zeiss Model 1015 star projector. The public is invited to "see the universe" at the "star theatre" on Thursday evenings at 7:30 and Sundays at 2:30 and 3:30. In addition, 10- and 12-inch telescopes are available for public viewing after the planetarium shows on Thursday evening, weather permitting. Six special "star studded" programs are featured each year.

The Buehler Planetarium is on the Broward Community College Campus at 3501 Southwest Davie Road, Fort Lauderdale, Florida 33314. To reach the Broward Community College campus from I-95, exit westbound on S.R. 84/S.W. 27th Street and drive 3.5 miles to Davie Road, then turn south to the well-marked college entrance. For further information telephone (407) 475-6680.

Tree Tops Park
Davie/Broward County
Area: 257 acres
Trail Distance: 4,843 ft. total
Highlights: nature study, nature trails, Tree Tops tower, picnicking, shelters, bridle paths, playground, marina, boat launch ramp, concessions
Fees: entrance (weekends & holidays), picnic shelter reservations, boat rentals, pavillion building rental

Tree Tops Park conjures up images of the huge, epiphyte-festooned live oaks that thrive along the Pine Island Ridge of western Broward County. The Seminole Indians lived here underneath their sheltering, spreading boughs and futilely fought to keep it that way during one of the battles of the Second Seminole Wars (1835-1842). Two interconnecting, level ridge trails allow visitors to sample the natural and cultural history of this unique oak-hammock forest that is owned and operated by the Broward County Parks Division.

The **Live Oak Trail** is a 2,843-foot loop trail that begins across the main park road from the marina and concessions area, where parking is available. After a short distance, the paved path portion leads to the 30-foot-high Tree Tops Tower. You are welcome to climb to the top, but there are no sweeping vistas of the parkscape. Instead, the top platform gives a gray squirrel's eye view of the miniature world of plants, insects, and birds that live in harmony amidst the oak limbs. Live oaks are called, "live" because they are evergreen, unlike northern species, which shed their leaves in autumn. In late January or February, however, the live oak does drop its old leaves as new leaves mature. In March or April it produces springtime "flowers." The acorn fruits mature annually and are sweet and edible. Painted acorn symbols identify the 12 stations that line the sandy forest trail. A corresponding trail book is available from the marina and park office for a small fee.

At the north point or terminus of the Live Oak Trail is the junction of the **Seminole Trail**. The 2,000-foot forest path continues toward the backside of the park office and exhibit pavilion. It follows the ridge system, historically known as Sam Jones Island, having been named for a Micasukee Indian leader. There are interpretive signs that describe the geological and botanical background, as well as the history of the Seminole Indian occupation of Pine Island Ridge and Sam Jones Island. The trail begins and ends directly behind the park office.

To reach Tree Tops Park from I-95, exit west on S.R. 84 in south Ft. Lauderdale and proceed seven miles to Pine Island Road, then turn south from there onto Orange Drive. Follow Orange Drive west to S.W. 100 Avenue/Golden Shoe Road and turn right/north, continuing to the park entrance at 3900 S.W. 100th Avenue, Davie. The park hours are from 8 a.m. to sunset daily.

Flamingo Gardens
Davie/Broward County
Area: 60
Trail Distance: approximately 1/2 mile botanical/museum walk
Highlights: botanical garden, Everglades Museum, horticultural library, petting zoo, plant nursery, tram ride through citrus groves, Gator World, Transportation Museum, gift shop, special events, education classes, garden membership
Fee(s): Separate entrance fee for botanical gardens and museums. Additional fee for other attractions.

Flamingo Gardens is for nature walkers who want a chance to see massive trees and learn about the Everglades through displays and exhibits. Situated along the Pine Island Ridge in western Broward County, the original Flamingo citrus groves and 12-acre botanical garden were established by Floyd and June Wray in 1927. Today, 60-plus years later, 60-acre Flamingo Gardens has become a tourist attraction with a theme park setting. Of special interest are the botanical gardens and Floyd Wray Everglades Museum. A single ticket purchase will admit the visitor to both facilities, but not to the other attractions.

The main feature of the botanical garden of exotics are the 24 designated official champion trees – the largest in the state of Florida, according to the Florida Division of Forestry. Two trees, a cluster fig (Ficus racemosa) and a dynamite tree (Hura crepltans), are the largest in the continental United States. Nearly all of the plants are labelled and a guide brochure is available with ticket purchase at the garden entrance. Orchids, heliconias, gingers, tree ferns, aroids, cycads, palms, and fruit trees are some ot the plants you will encounter beneath the shady canopy of the giant trees. The introduction of new and rarely planted sub-tropical plant material has become a major goal of Flamingo Gardens.

Banyan, Flamingo Gardens

Adjoining the botanical garden is the **Floyd Wray Everglades Museum**. The old Wray homestead was recently reconverted to shelter a museum dedicated to the natural and social history of the Everglades. Inside there are large photomurals depicting the sawgrass landscape, natural history exhibits of its wildlife inhabitants and prehistoric Indian artifacts, as well as historic Seminole tools, clothing, and a bald cypress canoe. After completing the tour, feel free to sit on the porch swing and gaze out on the lawn with its 200-year-old live oaks. Stop by the Garden Shop, which sells many of the unusual plant species that are found in the gardens.

In addition to the gardens and museum, Flamingo Gardens includes a petting zoo, Gator World, a Transportation Museum with antique cars (next to the Everglades Museum), and a narrative tram ride tour of the citrus groves. Additional facilities near the parking entrance are a gift shop and a fresh fruit patio restaurant.

Flamingo Gardens is open daily 9 a.m. to 5 p.m. To reach the gardens from I-95 in Ft. Lauderdale, exit west on State Road 84, drive approximately 10 miles to Flamingo Road and turn south. The address is 3750 Flamingo Road, Davie, Florida. Phone (305) 473-0010.

Markham Park
Sunrise/Broward County
Area: 665 acres
Trail Distance: 0.8 mile
Highlights: nature study, nature walk, interpretive programs, horse trail, observatory, picnicking, shelters, playground, swimming pool complex, boating, boat launch ramps, clubhouse, basketball, volleyball, tennis, racquetball, fishing, model airplane field, outdoor target range, youth camp, campground, special events, concessions
Fee(s): entrance (weekends & holidays), boat/canoe rentals, shelter reservation rental, bicycle rental, target range fee, swimming pool fee, tennis & racquetball courts, camping

Formerly a cattle farm ranch bordering the Everglades in western Broward County, C. Robert Markham Park, named for the former owner, is now a popular outdoor recreational park in a rapidly developing suburban area. Opened in 1973, this is the second largest park in Broward County. Star gazers will enjoy the Fox Observatory which is free and open to the public on the second and fourth Saturday of each month, if the weather permits. The nature trail begins west of the park entrance, where off-road parking is available. The trail penetrates two dominant plant communities: a young bayhead (a wetland dominated by bay trees) of subtropical broadleaf evergreens such as red bay, dahoon holly and sabal palm along with an exotic Australian pine, melaleuca and Brazilian pepper community. A trail with 21 interpretive stations and a corresponding guidebook has been established. A short trail follows the west perimeter of the man-made lake.

To reach Markham Park from I-95, exit at S.R. 84 and drive west 13 miles to the park entrance located on the north side of the state bighway at 16001 West State Road 84 in Sunrise, Florida. The park bours are from 8 a.m. to sunset daily.

Oleta River State Recreation Area
North Miami Beach/Dade County
Area: 900 acres
Trail Distance: under development
Highlights: nature study, bike trail, picnicking, shelters, canoe launch ramp, swimming, bathhouse, camping, concessions
Fee(s): entrance

Opened in 1986, Oleta River State Recreation Area is currently undergoing trail and primitive youth camping development. Located in the

Florida box turtle, Oleta River

Graves Tract, this segment of the Oleta River remains closest to its natural state. Approximately eight miles long, the river is a coastal stream that has been greatly altered by channelization and riparian plant removal and now suffers salt water intrusion. A public boat ramp is at the Blue Marlin Smoke House, on state property just west of the park entrance. The facility offers pleasant surroundings for day-use recreation in this metropolitan area.

Oleta River State Recreation Area is on North Miami Beach Boulevard/S.R. 826 in North Miami Beach. From I-95, exit onto North Miami Beach Boulevard/S.R. 826 and proceed east across U.S. 1 to the park entrance on the south side of the Sunny Isles Causeway. The park hours are from 8 a.m. to sunset daily. The address is 3400 N.E. 163rd Street.

Greynolds Park
North Miami Beach/Dade County
Area: 232 acres
Trail Distance: 1.5 miles total
Highlights: nature study, nature trails, picnicking, shelters, bird rookery, observation tower, golf course, paddleboat rental
Fee(s): entrance, paddleboat rental

Upstream from Oleta River State Recreation Area, along the west bank of the Oleta River, is Greynolds Park. The Metro Dade County Park facility is divided into two sections (East Greynolds and West Greynolds Parks) by U.S. 1. East Greynolds offers picnicking accommodations along the shores of Oleta River and Maule Lake. The main activities are found at West Greynolds. Sheltered picnicking, paddleboat rentals, a pavilion, a nine-hole golf course, lagoon, lake, bird rookery, observation mound, and nature trails are the main activities and facilities.

The four short nature trails include the **Scrub Oak Trail** (.25 mile), **Squirrel Hollow Trail** (.25), **Oleta River Trail** (.25), and the **West Lake Trail** (.75 mile). The longest trail, West Lake, encircles a former limestone quarry lake that is now home to many wild and domestic birds. The man-made observation mound appears like a fortress tower and is the highest "natural" point in Dade County.

East Greynolds Park is located along U.S. 1, north of North Miami Beach Boulevard and West Greynolds is at 17530 West Dixie Highway/U.S. 1 in North Miami Beach. From I-95, exit onto North Miami Beach Boulevard/S.R. 826 and proceed east to U.S. 1.

Just south of West and East Greynolds Parks is the **Ancient Spanish Monastery and Gardens** – 16711 West Dixie Highway/U.S. 1 at 167th Street. The monastery was actually imported, block by block, from Sacramenia, Spain by William Randolph Hearst in 1925 and, after long storage in a Brooklyn warehouse, was erected here in 1954. The Monastery dates to 1141 A.D. and is now owned by the Episcopal Parish of St. Bernard de Clairvaux. It stands on the grounds of a former plant nursery, so many ornamentals remained to serve as the basis for a graceful formal garden. The tour and gift shop hours are 10 a.m. to 5 p.m., Monday through Saturday and noon to 5 p.m. on Sunday.

The best beach in north Dade County is Haulover Boach at 10800 Collins Avenue/A1A. Although the beach has been re-nourished several times, the dunal vegetation and lack of condos give it a semi-natural appearance. The 177-acre beach park has lifeguards, surfing, a pier, fishing, marina, boating, nine-hole golf, picnicking, shelters, 20-station fitness course, and concessions. Beach walks are scheduled by the Metro Dade Parks and Recreation Department. The Metro Dade County beach is two to three miles east of Oleta River State Recreation Area.

Arch Creek Park
Miami/Dade County
Area: 8 acres
Trail Distance: .5 mile
Highlights: nature study, nature walk, guided walks, picnicking, shelters, nature center, museum, archaeological & historical site
Fee(s): interpretive programs

Arch Creek Park is small, but of special archaeological, botanical, and historical significance. The best place to start your nature walk is the pioneer-styled museum and nature center where excavated on-site Tequesta Indian and historical artifacts can be viewed. A naturalist on duty provides helpful information and answers any questions about the unique park. Naturalist-guided trail tours are given on Saturdays at 1 p.m.

The **Tequesta Nature Trail** begins just beyond the back door of the nature center and museum where a trail guide brochure is available. The self-guiding loop is wood chipped for comfortable walking and the trail itself was constructed by the Youth Conservation Corps. The hammock's flora is comprised of natives such as live oaks, paradise trees, sabal palms, Jamaican dogwoods, and satin leafs. The hammock is undergoing restoration and removal of non-native plants. A sizeable gumbo limbo is the largest tree in the park. A facsimile of a Tequesta Indian hut has been erected to show the temporary shelter of this semi-nomadic tribe. Archaeological evidence convincingly proves that a major Tequesta village occupied the site for 1,800 years from 500 B.C. to 1300 A.D. It is believed the Tequestas were the first Floridians to extract the "white bread" starch from the native coontie plant, a cycad, by crushing and leaching the otherwise toxic roots. Due to present day habitat destruction, the coontie is listed as a threatened species and is protected by law. American pioneers were also convinced of the value of the edible coontie root and established a coontie starch mill for the arrowroot industry in 1858-1859. They chose this location because of the natural limestone bridge over Arch Creek. Water was dammed to turn a waterwheel but the mill was not profitable and therefore was short-lived. The natural limestone arch bridge collapsed in 1973 (though it has now been restored), the same year the site was purchased by the state of Florida for preservation. Cross over the bridge to see the former coontie mill site and look along the east bank of Arch Creek to view the limestone caves. Lectures, archaeological digs, summer day camp, nature studies, and workshops are provided by the staff of the Metro Dade County Parks and Recreation Department. The county park's hours are from 9 a.m. to 5 p.m. daily.

To reach Arch Creek in North Miami from I-95, exit east onto 135th Street/S.R. 916 and drive to the entrance near the intersection with U.S. 1/Biscayne Boulevard. The address is 1855 N.E. 135th Street.

Simpson Park & Alice Wainwright Park
Miami/Dade County
Area: 29.5 acres
Trail Distance: 1 mile total
Highlights: nature study, nature walks, naturalist-guided walks, picnicking, shelters

Closedly situated, Simpson and Alice Wainwright Parks are nature-oriented facilities owned and administered by the City of Miami. Both parks preserve remnants of the former Brickell tropical hammock, which fronted Biscayne Bay from the Miami River south to Coconut Grove. Five miles long and half a mile wide, this was the largest of the estimated 500 hammocks in Dade County in the early years of settlement.

Simpson Park is named for naturalist-author Charles Torrey Simpson, author of *In the Lower Florida Wilds*. In 1915, city officials set aside five acres, removed the native undergrowth and replanted it with exotic plant material, making it more appealing to visit. It was then called Jungle Park. Appalled at the real estate development and subsequent removal of Brickell hammock, Simpson persuaded the authorities to replant the hammock with the original native plants. It was done, and Jungle Park became known as Simpson Park in 1927. Three acres were added in 1940 and a year later the Charles Torrey Simpson Memorial Garden Center was constructed.

Present-day Simpson Park has a naturalist on duty to guide visitors (reservations requested) through the preserve's meandering trails. The woodland paths are self-guiding and fine tropical tree specimens are labelled. The Miami oolitic limestone is well exposed. The broadleaf evergreen tree roots spread out and cling tenaciously to the pitted limestone surface, deriving life-giving nutrients and water. The most representative tree of the hammock is the red stopper, which produces a durable wood that was used for arrows by the original native inhabitants. *Licaria triandra* is the rarest tree. There are outstanding specimens of pigeon plum, mastic, strangler fig, satin leaf, gumbo limbo, crabwood, and other tropicals.

Unfortunately, the prized hammock is now in decline due to vandalism. Young understory trees are being destroyed by off-trail wanderings, threatening future regeneration of the eight-acre forest. Concerned friends of the hammock will need to organize to save it from further deterioration and oblivion.

To reach Simpson Park, just south of the Miami River and U.S. 41, exit U.S. 1 on S.W. 15th Road and go west to South Miami Avenue. Turn south and proceed two blocks to 17th Road, where you turn right/west. The address is 55 S.W. 17th Road. The park hours are 8 a.m. to sunset daily.

Approximately 15 blocks south and then east of Simpson Park is the **Alice Wainwright Park**. Officially dedicated in 1974, the hardwood hammock and picnic area are bordered by the Rickenbacker Causeway, Biscayne Bay, and residential neighborhoods. The park is named for a former Miami Vice-Mayor, who was an ardent conservationist. The urban parkland will always be maintained as a natural area under terms of a formal agreement that led to its acquisition. Outstanding evidence of the 50-mile-long Atlantic Coastal Ridge, the highest and oldest terrain in southern Florida, is well exposed along the southeast bayfront. Two miles further south along Bayshore Drive, a similar outcrop is called "Silver Bluff," formerly a conspicuous landmark to sailors several miles from shore. Unmarked nature trails meander through the hammock. Not quite as impressive as the Simpson Park hammocks, it is believed the Wainwright hammock was cleared at one time (1830-35), and the size of the present trees verify that belief. The preponderance of certain tree species, such as poisonwood, gives further evidence of a young, immature hammock. The park's 21.5 acres of bayfront shoreline are a fine area for picknicking. But vandalism has also taken its toll here, not only on plants but on the observation shelters.

To reach Alice Wainwright Park from Simpson Park, take South Miami Avenue to 32nd Road and turn left/east. Proceed for one block and go left/north onto Brickell Avenue. Shaded parking is available along Brickell Avenue. The park is just north of Vizcaya Museum and Gardens and the Museum of Science & Transit Planetarium. The park hours are 8 a.m. to sunset daily.

Vizcaya Museum & Gardens

Miami/Dade County
Area: 30 acres
Trail Distance: .6 miles
Highlights: nature study, garden and hammock walk, mansion museum tour, picnicking, cafe, gift shop, guided garden tours, programs, special events
Fee(s): entrance, special private function rental, photo location rental

Vizcaya

The Vizcaya Museum and Gardens were constructed in the early part of the 20th century by James Deering of the International Harvester Corporation as a winter home. Mr. Deering referred to his 16th century, Italian Renaissance-styled villa and formal gardens as "Vizcaya," a Basque word meaning "elevated place." Today's Vizcaya is a museum of European decorative arts (1500-1830), housed in 34 decorated rooms of the villa, and a horticultural showpiece with its 10 acres of native and exotic botanicals. Vizcaya is owned and operated by the Metropolitan Dade County Parks and Recreation Department.

The formal gardens adjoin the villa off the overlooking South Terrace. Columbian native Diego Suarez planned the gardens as a spacious outdoor room, with several smaller rooms "walled in" by vegetation and garden structures. The design style is a mixture of 16th century Renaissance Italian and 17th century French baroque. Amidst the trimmed hedges and tree-lined allées are cave-like grottoes, reflecting pools, sparkling fountains, artful sculptures, vase-shaped balustrades, decorative urns, and life-like statuary. This is not one, but many gardens: the central Forest Plaza, Fountain Garden, Maze Garden, Theater Garden, Secret Garden, Pergola Garden, and the Ellis A. Gimbel Garden for the Blind. The Mount, Casino, Tea House and Peacock Bridge are other special features.

The labeled **Hammock Trail** winds a short distance through a coastal tropical hardwood hammock of gumbo limbo, pigeon plum, and other trees and plants from the Vizcaya entrance to streetside at South Miami Avenue. It was Mr. Deering's wish that the hammock be preserved. Across the avenue is the former Vizcaya Farm Village.

To reach Vizcaya Museum and Gardens from I-95 and U.S. 1 in downtown Miami, exit 32nd Road east to South Miami Avenue and turn left. The entrance to Vizcaya is at 3251 South Miami Avenue, across from the Museum of Science & Space Transit Planetarium. The hours are 9:30 a.m. to 5 p.m. daily, except Christmas. The Gardens close at 5:30 p.m.

Museum Of Science & Space Transit Planetarium
Miami/Dade County
Highlights: science museum, wildlife center, planetarium, observatory, education programs, classes, museum shop, membership
Fee(s): entrance

The private, non-profit Museum of Science & Transit Planetarium is helping Miami residents and visitors to explore the many wonders of science and mysteries of the universe. More than 100 science gallery exhibits are "hands-on" and invite exploring. A simulated Florida coral reef, dioramas of the Everglades and Kissimmee Prairie are among the numerous exhibits. The health-conscious, Body-in-Action exhibit allows visitors to test themselves on an array of computerized exercise machines and instruments. The Natural History Collection Gallery has a library, exhibits, and many drawers filled with colorful minerals, geodes, butterflies, insects, and Florida tree snails. There is even an active bee hive. Outside the back door, the Wildlife Center maintains a large collection of reptiles, amphibians, and marine aquariums, a bird of prey aviary, a breeding program for woodstorks, and a full-time wildlife veterinary rehabilitation, education and research center.

The Space Transit Planetarium, adjoining the Science Museum, has a 65-foot dome, making it one of the world's largest dome planetariums. The PBS television series "Star Hustler," hosted by Jack F. Horkheimer, the Planetarium director, originated here. Quad sound, multi-media, film, holography, and laser shows are presented daily and nightly. The Weintraub Observatory allows free viewing of the heavens, weather permitting, Thursday through Sunday, 7:30 p.m. to 10 p.m. Special travelling exhibitions appear on a regular basis at the museum. Demonstrations and educational programs are held throughout the year. The Computer Learning Center features user-friendly robots, and classes in programming and graphic arts.

The Museum of Science & Space Transit Planetarium is near Coconut Grove, off U.S. 1. Follow the directional signs to the complex at 3280 South Miami, across from the Vizcaya Museum and Gardens. The hours are 10 a.m. to 6 p.m. daily, closed Christmas Day.

Planet Ocean
Miami/Dade County
Highlights: museum, educational programs, gift & book shop, concessions, membership
Fee(s): entrance

The Planet Ocean experience is a combination of theme park, museum, and classroom, all contained in a 10,000-square-foot indoor space. Founded in 1953, Planet Ocean was created and is operated by the World Headquarters for the International Oceanographic Foundation, a non-profit organization. The nearly 100 imaginative and challenging "hands on" exhibits focus on the watery world which occupies three-fourths of our planet's surface. A few of the exhibits include a submarine to explore, an indoor hurricane to experience, Morse Code to send and decipher, an iceberg to touch, a giant globe that asks you questions, and a meandering, circulating model of the Gulf Stream. There are seven theme areas that invite participation. And there are 12 theaters that run continously. Visitors are free to choose what they want to see. The best place to start your tour is the first theater on your left as you enter, which features the award-winning film, "The Unlikely Planet" (14 minutes). The average visit is three hours, but it would be easy to spend the day here.

Planet Ocean is at 3979 Rickenbacker Causeway on Virginia Key, between Miami and Key Biscayne, across from the Miami Seaquarium. From I-95 and U.S. 1. exit west onto the Rickenbacker Causeway (toll). Hours are 10 a.m. to 6 p.m. The box office closes at 4:30.

Miami Seaquarium is a theme park that features live animal shows, including Lolita the killer whale, dolphins (home of the original Flipper), Salty the sea lion, manatees (first ones born in captivity), and sharks. The gigantic seaquarium is one big tropical aquarium, the largest in southern Florida. There is also Lost Island, Show Queen Island Cruise, a monorail, concessions, and a gift shop. The Miami Seaquarium hours are 9:30 a.m. to 5 p.m. all year. Plan your visit for weekdays, since weekends tend to be crowded.

Fairchild Tropical Garden
Miami/Dade County
Area: 83 acres
Trail Distance: 3 miles
Highlights: botanical garden, guided walking tours, tram tours, amphitheatre, Palm Museum, Montgomery Library & Bookstore, concessions, special events, membership
Fee(s): entrance, tram tours

Fairchild Tropical Garden is the premier botanical garden in southern Florida. The garden actually began in 1938, when Colonel Robert H. Montgomery donated land and named the garden after his friend, plant explorer and author, Dr. David Fairchild. From that inception over a half-century ago, the garden has now become the largest tropical botanical "living museum" in the continental United States. Ideally, you should begin the garden tour in the morning, since there are numerous plant collections to view. Designed by landscape architect, William Lyman Phillips, the oldest area of plantings is near the upland front of the property. Palms are a specialty of the Fairchild and some 500 species are scattered throughout the garden, the largest collection in the continental United States. The cycad collection is also one of the world's largest. Additional collections include aroids, bromeliads, salt resistant plants, ground covers, tropical flowering trees, shrubs, especially hibiscus, and vines. Collections east of the overlooks at Pandamus Lake and Bailey Palm Glade in the lowland lakes area include Bahamian plants, Everglades plants, and a mangrove preserve. Although the tram tours visit each area, if you want to explore the collections at leisure, some amount of walking will be required. Special areas of the garden include the Rare Plant House, The Rain Forest, Moos Memorial Sunken Garden, Arid Rock Gardens, Garden Club of America Amphitheatre, and the Palm Products Museum, located at the Montgomery Library and Bookstore. A map of the garden is available with ticket purchase. A *Catalog of Plants*, listing many of the species in the garden by common and scientific names, is available at the bookstore. Seasonal guided walking tours are conducted, while tram tours board at the garden entrance. The Fairchild Tropical Garden, a non-profit educational and scientific institution, is operated in cooperation with the Metro Dade County Parks and Recreation Department. The garden is open daily 9:30 a.m. to 4:30 p.m., except Christmas Day.

To the immediate north of the Fairchild Tropical Garden is **Matheson Hammock Park**, a Metro Dade County Park. Picnicking facilities are available along the west edge of the park, near Old Cutler Road. West, across the Old Cutler Road, is the hammock portion of the park where unmarked nature trails interweave throuoh the forest. Tropical West Indian tree specimens are as impressive here as they are at Simpson Park near downtown Miami to the north. The park hours are 8 a.m. to sunset daily.

To reach Fairchild Tropical Garden at 10901 Old Cutler Road, and Matheson Hammock Park at 9610 Old Cutler Road, in Coral Gables, from U.S. 1 in Kendall, go east on North Kendall Drive/88th Street to Old Cutler Road and turn south. Proceed approximately 3/4 of a mile to the park and garden entrance on the east side of the road. Note: Fairchild Tropical Garden and Matheson Hammock Park were damaged by Hurricane Andrew, though Fairchild has since been largely restored to its former condition. You are advised to check with them directly for up-to-date information on conditions at each park.

U.S. Subtropical Horticulture Research Station
Miami/Dade County
Area: 210 acres
Trail Distance: .8 mile
Highlights: agricultural & landscape plants, horticultural information

The U.S. Department of Agriculture, Agricultural Research Service, administers the Subtropical Horticulture Research Station, sometimes called the Plant Introduction Station. This is one of eight, spread throughout the nation in different climatic zones. Since 1923, the Chapman Field station has introduced subtropical food and ornamental plants, distributed seed and plants for research, developed cultivars, conducted agricultural and market quality research, and quarantine treatment research with fruit flies. Visitors are welcome to walk the .8 mile, self-guiding loop that encircles the grounds. Should the visitor center be closed, directional signs will guide you to the U.S.D.A., ARS office at Building 22. Tour guide information containing a tour map may be borrowed from the office. Tag number, scientific and common names, block location, plant origin and general comments are given for 277 identified plants. The trail follows service roads. Palms, ornamentals, fruit, miscellaneous plants, mangos, avocados and sugar cane are covered on the tour. Southern Florida homeowners will find the plant list a useful reference to plants they may want to cultivate. But the station is not a tour garden or show garden in the usual sense. It is a research station and the national repository for certain tropical economic plants such as avocados, mangos, coffee, and sugar cane.

To reach the Research Station from U.S. 1, go east on S.W. 120th Street and south on Old Cutler Road to the entrance at Chapman Field Park, where the highway divides. Turn left and bear right along the fence to the main gate.

For a closer look at Dade County agriculture, a fee-charged **Agricultural Guided Tour** (unrelated to the above Research Station)is available to the public. It begins at the State Farmers Market on Krome Avenue/S.R. 27/S.R. 997 in Florida City from December 1 to April 1. The informative three-hour lecture tour is taken by bus throughout the farming areas of south Dade County. The tour begins at 9 a.m. and 1:30 p.m. Monday through Friday. For more information, write or call: Farm Tours, #32 Gateway Estates, Florida City 111034 (407) 248-6798.

Old Cutler Hammock Nature Center
Miami/Dade County
Area: 29 acres
Trail Distance: .5 mile
Highlights: nature study, nature trail, naturalist, interpretive programs, nature center, outdoor classroom, picnicking, canal fishing, campfire circle, astronomical observing platform

The Old Cutler Hammock Nature Center is one of Metro Dade County Park and Recreation Department's newest acquisitions. Opened in 1980, the compact acreage features a modern building that shelters the nature center, naturalist office, and restrooms. A native tree arboretum of 60 labeled species thrives on the surrounding grounds. A tropical hardwood hammock is the dominant plant community, while other areas of the park include a pine flatwoods and a relic pond apple slough. Of noteworthy interest is a U.S. national champion strangler fig (Ficus aurea), found growing in the adjoining hammock.

The **Old Cutler Nature Trail** was constructed by the Youth Conservation Corps when the park was first opened. Located at the backside of the nature center, the loop trail enters the hardwood hammock where Miami oolitic outcrops and sinkholes are highly evident. There are 20 interpretive stations corresponding to a trail guide available from the nature center. In addition to the hammock, the trail passes through a disturbed exotic area of cane grass and follows alongside a canal and residential neighborhood.

The Old Cutler Hammock Nature Center is at 17555 S. W. 79th Avenue, half a mile west from the Old Cutler Road. To reach the nature center from U.S. 1 in the City of Perrine, drive east on Richmond Drive/S.W. 168th Street to Old Cutler Road and turn south. Proceed south on Old Cutler Road to 176th Street, turn west/right and drive to the park entrance. The nature center is open daily from dawn to dusk. Free astronomy programs are conducted on Saturday evenings.

Miami MetroZoo
Miami/Dade County
Area: 280 acres
Trail Distance: 2 miles
Highlights: zoological gardens, monorail, amphitheatre, daily shows, concessions, restaurants, gift shop, special events, membership
Fee(s): entrance, monorail

Opened in 1981, the Miami MetroZoo is where 2,800 uncaged animals roam free in zoogeographic regions. Arranged by the continents of Asia, Eurasia, Europe, and Africa, the only separation between the animals and the visitor is an unobtrusive moat. Pictographs or visual interpretive symbols identify the animal's common and scientific names, origin, habitat, wild diet, activity time and survival status. There are three different shows featured three times daily: the Wildlife Amphitheatre Show, Asian Elephant Show (includes rides), and the Facts and Feeding Demonstrations, displaying three types of bears. Other programs include Zoo Close-Ups, held Friday and Saturday, and concerts. Besides providing recreation and education, the Miami Metrozoo is also a leader in wildlife conservation and research.

A wide, self-guiding path loops past the myriad of exotic wildlife that now make their home beneath the slash pine woodland of west Dade County. In addition to foot travel, the air-conditioned Zoofari Monorail encircles the zoo and even rides through the aviary. A tram ride is also available with advanced reservations.

Plains, jungles, steppes, and forests are some of the habitats found within the four continents. Two rare white tigers (only 110 in the world), are displayed at the Asian Siamese Temple. The Wings of Asia, a 1.5-acre, 65-foot-high aviary of 300 southeast Asian birds, is a major feature of the zoo. There are members of the gorilla family, Malayan tapirs and sun bears,, orangutans, Indian and black rhinoceros, European brown bears, pygmy hippopotamus, chimpanzees, African elephants and giraffes. Future African exhibits will include lions, cheetahs, impalas, and Arabian oryx.

From U.S. 1, take S.W. 152nd Street west three miles to the Metro-Zoo entrance. From the Florida Turnpike, take the S. W. 152nd Street exit west. Follow the directional signs. The MetroZoo address is 12400 S.W. 152nd Street or Coral Reef Drive and S.W. 124th Avenue. The hours are 10 a.m. to 5:30 p.m. daily. The ticket booth closes at 4 p.m.

Castellow Hammock Nature Center
Goulds/Dade County
Area: 60 acres
Trail Distance: 1 mile
Highlights: nature study, nature trail, nature center, naturalist, native plant arboretum, picnicking, shelter, field trips, interpretive programs, special naturalist services.
Fee(s): shelter reservations, field trips & other programs

Named in memory of James S. Castellow, citrus farmer who originally filed a homestead claim to the property in 1900, Castellow

Gumbo limbo, Castellow

Hammock Nature Center is a Metro Dade County environmental education facility that was established in 1974.

The front 10 acres is a suburban park-like setting where visitors can park, picnic under shady live oaks and view the labeled native plants of the arboretum. The nearby nature center separates the front acreage from the 50-acre pineland hammock. Displays of live animals and natural history collections of plants, bones, tree snails, butterflies and bird nests fill the nature center. Just outside the back door is a bird feeder that attracts colorful, seed-eating painted and indigo buntings from October to April. Pause for a worthwhile moment to view these brilliant finches. A naturalist is on duty to inform and answer any questions about the natural history of the park. Bird and plant checklists for Castellow Hammock are available on request, including a trail guide to the numbered posts along the path.

The **Castellow Hammock Trail** is a one-mile, partial loop with 22 interpretive stations, beginning and ending behind the nature center. At first, the trail passes through a perimeter of limestone slash pineland before entering the mature, tropical hardwood hammock. Three national champions listed on the Registry of Big Trees are identified along the trail: *Tetrazygia bicolor*, a 40-foot-tall, tree-like shrub with a restricted south Dade County range (at Station 8), a 90-foot wild tamarind (*Lysiloma latisiliquum*) at Station 12, and a 115-foot mastic tree (*Mastichodendron foetidissimum*) at Station 13. Other large trees include the paradise tree, strangler fig, gumbo limbo, pigeon plum, and live oak. Miami oolitic limestone outcrops and solution holes are a natural feature of the hammock floor. Twenty-nine species of ferns thrive in the high humidity of the broadleaf evergreen forest. At hammock's end, the trail loops back and reconnects to the original main trail.

Note: Castellow Hammock was severely damaged by Hurricane Andrew. The hammock's trees were ravaged with snapped trunks, and stripped and mangled vegetation. The nature center was also destroyed. The facility is planned to be reopened in 1994.

To reach Castellow Hammock at 22301 S.W. 162nd Avenue from U.S. 1 in Goulds, drive west on Hainlin Mill Drive/S.W. 216 Street, approximately five miles, to the intersection of S.W. 162nd Avenue. Turn south/left on S.W. 162nd Avenue and drive about half a mile to the park entrance on the east/left side of the road. The park is open to visitors from dawn to dusk. The nature center is staffed from 9 a.m. to 4 p.m. daily.

Three other nature-oriented parks with short nature trails in southern Dade County are **Larry and Penny Thompson Memorial Park** at 12401 S.W. 184th Street, south of the Miami MetroZoo; **Navy Wells**, a 250-acre pineland preserve on S.R. 27, south of Florida City, enroute to Everglades National Park; and 110-acre **Camp Owaissa** (weekdays, winter months only, if camp is unoccupied) at 17001 S.W. 264th Street/Bauer Road, four miles northeast of Homestead.

Preston B. Bird And Mary Heinlein Fruit And Spice Park

Homestead/Dade County
Area: 20 acres
Trail Distance: 1 mile
Highlights: nature study, nature walk, botanical garden, historic sites, horticultural services, tours, fruit and book store, classes & workshops, special events
Fee(s): tours, classes, special events

Described as a "botanical garden that emphasizes economic and edible plants," the 20-acre Fruit and Spice Park has more than 500 varieties of plants from around the world that thrive in this fertile corner of southeast Florida. In addition to fruit and spices, the park has a one-acre demonstration herb and vegetable garden, vineyard, nut trees, and a fenced-off, but viewable poisonous plant area. The public is not only allowed to look, but can taste the fallen fruit and collect seeds. An excellent guide book to the park's plant life is available from the Redland Fruit store (10 am. to 5 p.m.) for a nominal fee. Guided tours are conducted for a fee on Saturdays and Sundays at 1 p.m. and 3 p.m.

Dade County acquired the already cultivated orchard land for a tropical fruit park in 1944. Mary Heinlein, who owned a nursery with her husband, was the first person who applied for the park superintendent position. Mary had previously campaigned with Preston B. Bird, who was running for the office of County Commissioner. Preston promised, if elected, he would establish a county park for the display of tropical fruit. He was subsequently elected, fulfilled his campaign pledge, and appointed Mary the first park superintendent. Many of the trees visitors see today came from Mary Heinlein's nursery.

The park has been declared part of the Redland Historic District and historic buildings are located on the grounds, including the Bauer-Mitchell House, the oldest house in south Dade County.

To reach the Fruit and Spice Park, located five miles northwest of downtown Homestead, drive north on Krome Avenue/S.W. 177th Avenue/S.R. 27, four miles to Coconut Palm Drive/S.W. 248th Street and turn west. Proceed one mile on S.W. 248th Street to the park at the intersection with Redland Road/S.W. 187th Avenue. Telephone: (305) 247 5727. Park hours are 10 a.m. to 5 daily.

Note: the park was badly damaged by Hurricane Andrew, having lost about half its trees. Much remains to be seen, however, and educational programs have been beefed up since the hurricane.

Cities & Suburbs

Southwest Florida

The Pinellas Trail

Pinellas County
Area: 343 acres
Trail Distance: 47 miles (completed 1995)
Highlights: walking, biking, jogging, handicapped acessible, birdwatching, picnicking, playgrounds, access to several city & county parks

The Pinellas Trail is being developed as part of Florida's Rails-to-Trails Program and was acquired in cooperation with the Florida Department of Transportation and Pinellas County government. Once completed, the Trail will be the longest linear park in the eastern United States. The 151-foot-wide paved asphalt path is built along an abandoned railroad right-of-way that last carried a train in 1987. Government and concerned citizens acted quickly to obtain the former transportation route. By October 1993 more than 34 continuous miles had been completed and opened to walkers. People on foot or on bicycles can enjoy the Trail from Tarpon Springs south to St. Petersburg (34th Street and 7th Avenue). The final Northeast Extension from Tarpon Springs to near Oldsmar is 12 miles and is scheduled to be completed soon.

Access points for the park are numerous and parking, restrooms, benches, water fountains and trail maps have been provided thanks to the efforts of The Pinellas Trail, Inc., a member-supported non-profit community support organization whose purpose is to promote the value of the Trail. Habitats along the way vary from highly urban to seemingly remote waterways and hammocks. The Trail connects and runs adjacent to many existing parks such as Taylor, Ridgewood, Heritage and Seminole City Parks. Over 80,000 people enjoy the path monthly. The urban greenway is open only during daylight bours. For further information please contact the Pinellas County Park Department at 631 Chestnut Street, Clearwater, Florida 34616; telephone (813) 462-3347.

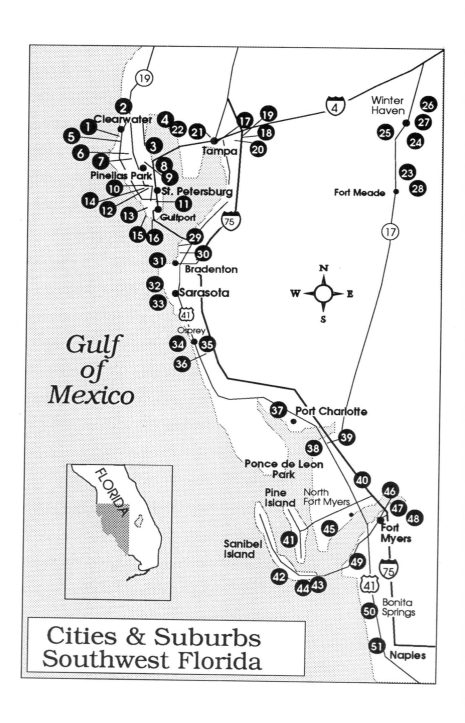

Cities & Suburbs
Southwest Florida

Gulf
of
Mexico

Clearwater
Pinellas Park
St. Petersburg
Gulfport
Tampa
Bradenton
Sarasota
Osprey
Winter Haven
Fort Meade
Port Charlotte
Ponce de Leon Park
Pine Island
North Fort Myers
Sanibel Island
Fort Myers
Bonita Springs
Naples
FLORIDA

1. Pinellas Trail
2. A.L. Anderson Park
3. John Chesnut Sr. Park
4. Phillippe Park
5. Hammock Park
6. Moccasin Lake Nature Park
7. Heritage Park
8. Taylor Park
9. Suncoast Botanical Garden
10. Sawgrass Lake Park
11. The Science Center of Pinellas County/St. Petersburg J. C. Planetarium
12. Lake Seminole Park
13. War Veteran's Memorial Park
14. Sunken Gardens
15. Boyd Hill Nature Park
16. St. Petersburg Bayfront Area
17. Lake Park
18. Lettuce Lake
19. Eureka Springs
20. University of South Florida Botanical Garden
21. Tampa's Nature Places
22. Upper Tampa Bay County Park
23. Ft. Meade Outdoor Recreation Park
24. Saddle Lake County Park
25. Florida Cypress Gardens
26. Street Nature Center & Sanctuary
27. Bok Tower Gardens
28. Babson Park Audubon Nature Center
29. De Soto National Memorial
30. Madira Bickel State Archaeological Site
31. South Florida Museum & Bishop Planetarium
32. Ringling Museum Grounds
33. Marie Selby Botanical Gardens
34. Spanish Point at the Oaks
35. Oscar Scherer State Recreation Area
36. Venice Fitness Trail at Pinebrook Park
37. Kiwanis Park
38. Juan Ponce De Leon Historic Park
39. Charlotte Harbor Environmental Center
40. Octagon Wildlife Sanctuary
41. St. James Creek Trail
42. J.N. "Ding" Darling National Wildlife Refuge
43. Frank Bailey Tract/J.N. "Ding" Darling National Wildlife Refuge
44. Sanibel-Captiva Conservation Foundation
45. Four Mile Cove Ecology Park
46. Edison Winter Home
47 The Nature Center of Lee County
48. Six Mile Cypress Slough Preserve
49. Lakes Park
50. Everglades Wonder Gardens
51. The Conservancy Big Cypress Nature Center

Boardwalk along Lake Tarpon

A. L. Anderson Park

Tarpon Springs/Pinellas County
Area: 128 acres
Trail Distance: 478 ft. boardwalk & footpath
Highlights: nature study, nature walk, picnicking, shelters, grills, playground, fishing, boat ramp, restrooms

Founded in 1966, the A. L. Anderson Pinellas County Park is situated along the shoreline of Salmons Bay and Lake Tarpon. The rolling, hilly terrain and the natural, wooded parkland setting overlook these freshwater bodies, making the day-use recreational tract an enjoyable place to picnic and walk. A short nature trail has been developed along the cypress tree-lined shore of Salmons Bay.

To reach A. L. Anderson Park from the Sunshine Skyway Bridge, drive north on U.S. 19 to Tarpon Springs. The park entrance will be on the east side of the road between Klosterman Road and West Tarpon Avenue, about a half-mile past the St. Petersburg and Tarpon Springs Junior College campus. The park's hours are from 7 a.m. to dark.

John Chesnut Sr. Park
Palm Harbor/Pinellas County
Area: 255 acres
Trail Distance: 6,808 ft. boardwalk & footpath
Highlights: nature study, nature trails, swimming, fishing, picnicking, shelters, boat ramp, canoe trail, softball field, playfields, playground, pier, windmill, observation tower, wildlife preserve, bathhouse, restrooms

This is an exceptional place to enjoy a high quality outdoor experience on the edge of a suburban setting. Dedicated in 1979, this modern scenic park is one of the newest acquisitions in the Pinellas County Park system. Situated on the east shore of Lake Tarpon, the largest freshwater lake in the county, John Chesnut Park is an active recreational facility in a passive woodsy environment. Two separate boardwalks and footpath trails, each over a half-mile long, wind through the park. The **North Loop** begins and ends immediately south of the weir and interior lake in the north portion of the property, where plenty of parking is available. A second trail to North Loop begins across the main park road from the windmill, where more parking is found. The trail alternates between sections of boardwalk and footpath through the pine flatwoods and hammock. The main focal point is the lookout platform overlooking Lake Tarpon. The **South Loop Trail** begins near the South Loop picnic area where parking is plentiful. The boardwalk follows the cypresslined lakeshore, then becomes a footpath which skirts the north bank of Brooker Creek, before returning to the parking area. A short trail spur leads to a 30-foot observation tower from the parking area along the 750-foot boat channel and launching ramp. The South Loop Trail is handicapped-designed.

To reach John Chesnut Sr. park from the Sunshine Skyway Bridge/U.S. 19, drive north on 19 to Tampa Road/S.R. 584 and head east. Continue on Tampa Road/S.R. 584 to East Lake Road and proceed north across Brooker Creek to the park entrance on the west/left side of the road. The address is 2200 East Lake Road. The park hours are from 7 a.m. to dark.

Phillippe Park
Safety Harbor/Pinellas County
Area: 122 acres
Highlights: nature study, historic site, picnicking, shelters, fishing, swimming, boat ramp, softball field, playground, restrooms

Rich in historical significance, Phillipe Park was the first county park established in Pinellas County. Overlooking Safety Harbor Bay, the large grove of live oaks beckons the visitor to explore the surrounding rolling wooded landscape.

The park is named for Count Odet Phillipe, a native of Lyon, France, who settled here in 1842. A surgeon for the French Armed Forces under Napoleon, Phillipe founded a plantation, St. Helena, and was the first to adapt the grapefruit to Florida culture. Several original trees are still growing today. Phillipe is buried in the park on a shady knoll.

Prior to European settlement, the Safety Harbor Site, as it became known to archeologists, was the main village of the prehistoric Tocobago Indians (1400-1700), who built the large ceremonial mound near the center of the park and along the shore. Burial mounds did exist throughout the park, but have since been excavated. Projectile points, pottery, stone, shell, and bone tools were found by excavators. The ceremonial mound is listed on the National Register of Historic Landmarks.

To reach Phillipe Park from the Sunshine Skyway Bridge/U.S. 19, drive north on 19 to S.R. 588 east to Safety Harbor's Main Street. Turn north at Phillipe Parkway/S.R. 590. The park entrance is at 2355 Bayshore Drive. Phillipe Park is open from 7 a.m. to sunset.

Hammock Park
Dunedin/Pinellas County
Area: 85 acres
Trail Distance: 5 miles total
Highlights: nature study, nature walk, observation platform, picnicking, shelters, playground, restrooms.
Fee(s): donation for trail brochure, group picnic rental

Hammock Park is a predominantly live oak-sabal palm hammock forest that encompasses 75 acres. (The remainder of the park to the north is ballfields, swimming pool, nature center and adminstrative park offices).

Hammocks are an uncommon natural habitat in high, dry, and sandy Pinellas County (or "pine" county). Six habitats are found in this botanical preserve: disturbed sites, mangrove-saltgrass, oak-pineland, hardwoods, bayheads and sand pine-scrub oak. Seven trails are interspersed throughout the forest: Sugarberry (.5 mile), Cross Trail (.2 mile), Live Oak (.5 mile), Palm Trail (.75 mile), Gopher Tortoise Trail (1 mile), Fern Trail (1 mile), and Cedar Trail (.5 mile) which is accessible to handicapped persons. Three-hundred and twenty plant species and over 125 bird species have been identified at the preserve.

The **Dunedin Nature Center** is located south of Michigan Boulevard on Ed Eckert Drive. The center has visitation hours from 3 p.m. to 4:30 p.m., Monday through Friday. You may see and touch a Gopher Tortoise, "Big Red" the rabbit, "Oppi" the opossum, "Pumpkin" the Red Rat snake, "J.P." the ferret, "Rascal" the skunk, and many more animals. Observing the educational displays and specimens preserved in formaldehyde helps visitors understand Florida's delicate environment.

To reach Hammock Park in Dunedin, go north on Broadway/Bayshore Blvd./Alt. U.S. 19 from downtown to Michigan Blvd. and then right/east. Continue on Michigan Blvd. to Ed Eckert Drive and turn right/south to the park. The park hours are from 8 a.m. to 8 p.m.

Creek bridge, Hammock Park

Moccasin Lake Nature Park
Clearwater/Pinellas County
Area: 50 acres
Trail Distance: 1 mile
Highlights: nature study, nature walk, interpretive center, picnicking, shelter, classrooms & laboratory, alternative energy exhibits, guided tours
Fee(s): entrance

Moccasin Lake Nature Park is one of the increasingly rare natural remnants or "green islands" that dot the developing landscape of Pinellas County. Encounters with various Florida ecosystems, and an on-site examination of the alternative energy systems that will eventually sustain the park without reliance on outside utilities, are some of the park's offerings.

The nature trails expose the day visitor to upland hardwoods, wetlands, five-acre Moccasin Lake, a floodplain, cypress and maple swamps, pine flatwoods, meadow and scrub oak habitats. Most of the native plant and animal life of the central Pinellas County peninsula is found within the park boundary. Future plans call for additional trails and boardwalks, educational materials, additional exhibits and displays, an observation tower and the transformation of the park into a wildlife sanctuary.

To reach Moccasin Lake Nature Center from the Sunshine Skyway Bridge/U.S. 19, drive north on 19 to the city of Clearwater and turn east onto Drew Street. Continue on Drew Street to Fairwood Avenue, turn north and drive to Park Trail. Turn west at Park Trail and proceed to the park entrance at the end of the road. The park is open 9 a.m. to 5 p.m. Tuesday through Friday and 10 a.m. to 6 p.m. Saturday and Sunday. Summer hours are the same (except 11:30 a.m. to 7:30 p.m. on Wednesday from June 1st to September 1). The park is closed Thanksgiving, Christmas, and New Year's Day.

Heritage Park
Largo/Pinellas County
Area: 21 acres
Highlights: historical interpretive walks, museum, historic sites, special events, membership
Fee(s): donation

The 21-acre Heritage Park is like a walk down memory lane. Sitting amidst the towering slash pines is a late 19th- and early 20th-century Pinellas County "village." A train depot, loghouse, barn, homes, cottages, bandstand, pavilion, church and Victorian home, called the "Seven Gables," comprise the village community. A modern historical museum traces the social and natural history of Pinellas County from pioneer days, with numerous exhibits and displays.

All visitors register at the museum, situated at the center of this outdoor historical park. Tour guides in dress of the period escort visitors through homes and other buildings, or you can stroll the brick pathways on your own. Available from the museum is printed literature describing the history of the structures. A map of the native plants used by pioneers for food, medicine, dye, and other practical purposes is available upon request. A Garden For The Blind is located near the Seven Gables Victorian mansion. Near the Lowe Barn is a sugar mill, and sugar "cane" garden, which is demonstrated during the October Country Jubilee.

To reach Heritage Park from I-275, take the Ulmerton Road/S.R. 688 exit westbound to the city of Largo and drive to 125th Street, just past Ridgecrest Park. Turn south on 125th Street to the Heritage Park entrance on the east side of the street. The hours are Tuesday to Saturday 10 a.m. to 4 p.m.

Taylor Park
Largo/Pinellas County
Area: 128 acres
Trail Distance: 1.8 mile
Highlights: walking & exercies trail, picnicking,shelters, fishing, boat ramp, playground, softball field, restrooms

Although the 53-acre reservoir is no longer utilized as a freshwater supply to surrounding residents, the impounded waters serve as aquatic habitat for many birds and other wildlife. The remaining 75 acres of land that border the reservoir are predominantly pine woods that cast welcome shade on picnic shelters and playgrounds. Primarily neighborhood-oriented, the park is a large, open green space. A 1.8-mile walking and exercise trail skirts the edges of the upper north end of the lake. Herons, galinules, cormorants and other birdlife, as well as fishermen, are frequently sighted seeking a meal.

To reach Taylor Park from I-275, take the Ulmerton Road/S.R. 688 exit west to Ridge Road and turn north. Continue on Ridge Road to 8th Avenue and turn west to the park entrance on the south side of the road. As for all Pinellas County parks, the hours are from 7 a.m. to dark. Taylor Park is an access point for the 47-mile Pinellas Trail.

Suncoast Botanical Garden
Largo/Pinellas County
Area: 60 acres
Trail Distance: 1.5 miles
Highlights: nature study, garden trails, botanic gardens, special events, membership

Suncoast Botanical Garden is a 60-acre, subtropical garden created to serve as a horticultural center for Pinellas County. Currently under development, the botanical oasis features several theme gardens to display and promote ornamentals and useful plants for Florida yards and parks.

Two nature footpaths encircle the garden grounds: South Trail and North Trail. **South Trail** leads through an open meadow filled with cycads, azaleas, magnolias, and palms. Lake Mildred, a small

North Trail

freshwater pond, is a fine place to rest and meditate on the green surroundings. The **North Trail** passes by picturesque areas: herb gardens, memory gardens, collections of bamboos, bald cypress, hollies and cactus. A short trail spur leads to the West Garden and the open meadow of native flowers. Other areas under development include Fern Glade, Meditation Pool, Flowering Tree Lane, Vine Pagoda, Rose and Hibiscus Gardens. In addition, greenhouses, propagation areas, and demonstration gardens are planned attractions.

All trails begin at the Garden House and parking area. The Garden House is used for meetings, workshops, youth study groups and plant shows. It is also the temporary location of the library, herbarium, plant museum, and offices until the Horticultural Hall can be constructed.

To reach Suncoast Botanical Garden from I-275, take the Gandy Boulevard/S.R. 694 exit west to the city of Seminole and Ridge Road, where you turn north. Turn north on 125th Street and the Garden will be on the west side of the street at 10410 125th Street North. The hours are from sunrise to sunset.

Sawgrass Lake Park
St. Petersburg/Pinellas County
Area: 390 acres
Trail Distance: 1.5 miles total
Highlights: nature study, nature walks, visitors center, museum, poisonous plant arboretum, picnicking, group tours, environmental education center, restrooms

Sawgrass Lake Park and Anderson Environmental Education Center is an excellent example of cooperative multiple-use of one facility. The Southwest Florida Water Management District owns the land and provides flood control. The Pinellas County School Board makes use of the site by allowing school children to visit the its outdoor classroom to study environmental education. Pinellas County Park Department administers public tours of the park. All three agencies work closely together to put forth the goal of public and environmental awareness.

The 390 acres of red maple swamp, aquatic habitat and oak hammocks provide natural surroundings easily viewed from the trails. The half-mile **Sawgrass Boardwalk Trail** begins near the visitors

Sawgrass Lake Tower

center and crosses over the flood control channel linking Sawgrass Lake. At the boardwalk trail fork, go left through floodplain red maple forest to the observation tower overlooking Sawgrass Lake. Skeet trap shooting across the lake may be distracting and unnerving. The trail loops back to the boardwalk "T" fork. Going left is the **Maple Leaf Trail**, while right leads back to the visitors center, the original route. The Maple Leaf Trail follows the winding boardwalk through the seasonally flooded landscape of swamp forest to arrive at an "L" trail fork. Going straight eventually leads to a loop footpath through a live oak-sabal palm hammock. Benches and an outdoor education pavilion are found underneath the spreading boughs of the large live oaks. The hammock is a fine place to rest and meditate before walking back to the "L" trail fork.

Continuing your hike, the boardwalk goes left on reaching the "L" and winds through more swamp forest to a trail "T" fork. Either fork will lead to the flood canal. Follow the canal service road to the right towards Arrow Lake and Poisonous Plant Arboretum. Many potentially poisonous ornamental and native plants are displayed. Complete your hike to the canal crossing and the visitors center. A self-guiding booklet is available for the boardwalk trails that corresponds to numbered stations. Checklists of wildlife and other publications are also available.

To reach Sawgrass Lake and Anderson Environmental Education Center from the Sunshine Skyway Bridge/U.S. 19, drive north on 19 to 62nd Avenue and turn east. Continue on 62nd Avenue east to 25th Street on the north side of the road just before the I-275 overpass. Turn north on 25th Street and proceed directly to the park entrance at 7400 25th Street North at the street's end. Access is also possible from I-275 via 54th Avenue or Gandy Boulevard.

There is no access from I-275 at 62nd Avenue north. The park opens at 7 a.m. and closes at dark daily.

The Science Center Of Pinellas County/
St. Petersburg Junior College Planetarium
St. Petersburg/Pinellas County
Highlights: nature study, gardens, museum, environmental education, field trips, gift shop, membership, planetarium, observatory

This is a private, non-profit educational institution supported entirely by the Pinellas County community. Established in 1959, the Science Center provides a variety of natural science activities for Pinellas County school children, adult residents, and visitors – such as the classroom extension program, field studies, a mobile outreach program, and workshops. Science Center membership is the best way to realize the many benefits.

For the first-time visitor, the natural history and discovery exhibits and the unique nature trail are enjoyable experiences that get you acquainted with the Center. Numerous exhibits and displays interpret Florida's floral and faunal life. Next door is the Discovery Wing where learning about nature is derived from "hands-on" sensory experiences.

Between the two museum wings is the circular nature trail known as the Walk-of-States and White Gardens. Within the formally landscaped garden are 50 sidewalk sections by artist Attilio Puglisi. Puglisi used vitreous tile and created the outline of the 50 United States, each including the state bird, flower and capital, all in the official state colors. There is even a representative rock that was shipped to Florida from each individual state. The bridge across the pond walk depicts in mosiac tile Ponce de Leon, Florida's Five Flags, Chief Osceola, Andrew Jackson, and other portraits.

To reach the Science Center of Pinellas County from I-275 at St. Petersburg, take the 22nd Avenue North exit westbound to the Center, at 7701 22nd Avenue North. The Science Center is open 9 a.m. to 4 p.m. Monday through Friday.

A few miles southeast of the Science Center is the planetarium and observatory of St. Petersburg Junior College, where Friday evening programs are provided free of charge during the college year as a community service.

The **planetarium** is a sky theatre under a 7.3-meter domed ceiling projector screen. A planetarium projector provides a simulated star field with planets and moon. The observatory, weather permitting, is open for telescope viewing after the hourly planetarium shows at 7 and 8 p.m. Both the planetarium and the observatory are in the Natural Science Building at Room 205.

To reach St. Petersburg Junior College from I-275, take 22nd Avenue North westbound to A19A/66th Street and turn south to 8th Avenue North. Turn west on 8th Avenue North two blocks to 69th Street and turn south. The parking lot is on the east side of the street directly behind the Natural Science Building.

Lake Seminole Park
Seminole/Pinellas County
Area: 255 acres
Trail Distance: 2.5 miles total
Highlights: nature study, nature and bicycle trail, picnicking, shelters, fishing, boat ramp, softball field, playground, restrooms

Established in 1968, Lake Seminole Park is an active day-use facility of Pinellas County Park Department. Activities surround two smaller man-made lakes, where picnic shelters, playground, and nearby boat ramp provides access to Lake Seminole. Although basically a "picnickers park," a two-mile paved pedestrian and bicycle path loops through a maturing pine-palm-oak forest at the north of the park, along with a half-mile unmarked nature footpath.

To reach Lake Seminole Park from I-275, take the Gandy Boulevard/S.R. 694 exit west to the park entrance on the north side of the highway prior to crossing the Lake Seminole Bridge. The park opens at 7 a.m. and closes at sunset.

War Veterans Memorial Park
Bay Pines/Pinellas County
Area: 122 acres
Highlights: nature study, historical site, memorial, sundial, picnicking, shelters, bicycling, swimming, fishing, boat ramp, playground, restrooms

Dedicated publicly in 1973, War Veterans Memorial Park is a Pinellas County day facility. The park was created from land donated by the Federal Government in 1963. Fringed by mangroves growing along the shores of Boca Ciega Bay, the park has an interior of slash pine flatwoods conducive to picnicking, bicycling, or just wandering about. Bay vistas are restricted by vegetation except in the southwest section of the shore. A 24-hour lighted boat ramp provides public access to the bay, Long and Cross Bayous, and the Gulf of Mexico via Johns Pass.

The focal point of the park is the Memorial Center and Lagoon. Surrounded by the flags of the armed forces is an impressive sundial. This large instrument is accurate to within a minute and was engineered exactly for this location. Instructions for its use are inscribed at the top of the analemma, a graduated scale shaped like a figure 8 which shows the sun's declination and the equation of time for each day of the year. A brochure is available at the sundial and War Memorial Plaza.

To reach the War Veterans Memorial Park from I-275 at St. Petersburg, take 38th Avenue North, exit westbound to Alt. 19 S.R. 595, and continue west across the Seminole Bridge. Across the bridge, turn south at the park entrance, 9600 Bay Pines Boulevard. The park hours are from 7 a.m. to sunset.

Sunken Gardens
St. Petersburg/Pinellas County
Area: 6 acres
Trail Distance: 1 mile
Highlights: nature study, botanical & zoological gardens, gift shop
Fee(s): entrance

Nestled near downtown St. Petersburg amid busy office buildings and old neighborhoods, is the Eden-like Sunken Gardens. Founded in 1903 by George Turner Sr., Sunken Gardens is the oldest such family-owned landmark in Florida. The gardens began as a small commercial grove of exotic fruit trees planted after the existing shallow lake and sinkhole were drained, revealing a rich cross-section of fertile soils. Mr. Turner's love of horticulture resulted in the gardens expansion, and by 1935 the gardens were a flourishing attraction.

Today, there are thousands of varieties of exotic flowers and plants representing every tropical region of the world. The Orchid Arbor contains over 1,000 orchids, many rare and endangered. Wildlife are encountered along the trail in enclosures blending harmoniously with the colorful gardens, including a walk-through aviary of exotic birds. Visually-pleasing bridges span natural lagoons and pass cascading waterfalls. Sealed off from the urban bustle by a natural wall of dense, forest-like vegetation, this peaceable kingdom is a delightful experience.

To reach Sunken Gardens from the Sunshine Skyway Bridge U.S. 19, go north to 22nd Avenue and turn east. Continue your drive on 22nd Avenue east to 4th Street and turn south to Sunken Gardens parking lot. The gardens are open daily 9 a.m. to 5:30 p.m.

Boyd Hill Nature Park
St. Petersburg/Pinellas County
Area: 216 acres
Trail Distance: 6 miles total
Highlights: nature study, nature walks, nature centers picnicking, shelters, playground, bicycling, guided tours, library, programs, annual events
Fee(s): entrance

Boyd Hill Nature Park was recognized for its uniqueness and natural beauty when it won a national award for landscaping and preservation in 1980. A model for park planners to emulate, this island of urban nature is surrounded by a sea of development. Six different loop trails have been designated, each representing a distinct Florida ecosystem: Oak-Pine Hammock, Swamp Woodlands, Willow Marsh, Lake Maggiore, Scrub Oak, and Pine Flatwoods. Each paved or boardwalk trail varies in length from half a mile to a mile and the loops average 15 minutes walking time. Checklists on the birds, vertebrates, and plants of the park are available at the trail entrance and nature center to enhance your walk. Along the trails, well-designed interpretive markers identify the flora and fauna of each community. Water fountains, shaded shelters, and benches make the walks more comfortable. The trails are handicapped-accessible. A half-day's outing is recommended to enjoy the trails, nature center and picnic grounds. Bicycle paths also loop through the park for weekday bikers.

Boyd Hill Nature Park can be reached from the Sunshine Skyway Bridge U.S. 19, by driving north to 54th Avenue South and turning east. Continue on 54th Avenue South to Highland Avenue, turn north and drive to the intersection of Country Club Way. Go left or west and follow Country Club Way to the park entrance at 1101 Country Club Way South. The park is located at the southwest shore of Lake Maggiore. It is open from 9 a.m. to 5 p.m. seven days a week, but closed Thanksgiving and Christmas. During daylight savings time periods, the park is open from 9 a. m. to 8 p. m. on Tuesdays and Fridays.

St. Petersburg Bayfront Area
St. Petersburg/Pinellas County
Highlights: pier, museums, parks, swimming, arboretum, fishing
Fees: museum entrance, rentals

Stretching for nearly two miles along the shoreline of Tampa Bay at St. Petersburg is a green belt of parks and cultural attractions. From Wylie Park at the north to the Bayfront Center in the south, the city's waterfront abounds with the sights and sounds of a mixture of subdued nature and urban culture.

You may want to begin your walk north of the Pier, at the two-acre **Gizella Kopsick Palm Arboretum** located at North Shore Beach

Posing, St. Petersburg Bayfront

Park. Over 200 native and exotic palms represent 45 species from around the world. A map brochure identifying these members of the palm family by their scientific and common names and origins may be obtained from the St. Petersburg Park Department of Leisure Services or the Chamber of Commerce Pier office, south of the beach park.

The **St. Petersburg Historical Museum** located at the land's end of the Pier (335 2nd Avenue N.E.) is the second largest historical museum in Florida. Natural history buffs will enjoy one of the largest shell collections in the United States and Native Indian artifacts include a 400-year-old cypress canoe, with over 10,000 other exhibits.

The landmark **Pier**, completed and opened in 1973, is the seventh municipal pier constructed at the St. Petersburg bayfront over the past century. Take a stroll out to the end for the vistas from the observation deck overlooking Tampa Bay and St. Petersburg. The free **Pier Aquarium** on the second floor is where visitors can see hundreds of native and tropical fish, sharks, and invertebrates. There is a "Shark Wall," shark tanks and hands-on exhibits from the nearby **Great Explorations Museum**. Get information from the Chamber of Commerce information desk regarding other bayfront attractions. The Pier's baithouse is a second home to the many pelicans you can observe close-up as they wait for feeding time. The fishing is good from the Pier and it has a sea-going atmosphere. To the immediate south of the Pier is the **City Marina and South Yacht Basin**, the moorage for hundreds of beautiful boats.

Among other points of interest at the bayfront: the **Museum of Fine Arts, Salvador Dali Museum, Al Lang Baseball Stadium, Cultural Bayfront Center, Straub Park, Pioneer Park** and **Kids and Kubs**.

To reach St. Petersburg Bayfront Area from I-275, exit either I-375 or I-175 downtown and drive east towards the bayfront. From U.S.19/Eisenhower Boulevard go east on Central Avenue. The Bayfront is located along Bayshore Drive. Parking is available on the Pier and in the parks. The Pier is open daily at 10 a.m. (Sundays 11 a.m.). Aquarium hours: 10 a.m.-8 p.m., Sunday 12-6, Tuesday 1-8 p.m. For more information call (813) 821-6164.

Lake Park
Lutz/Hillsborough County
Area: 600 acres
Trail Distance: 2 miles of service roads
Highlights: nature study, picnicking, playground, bicycle motocross trail, motorized dirt bike track, fishing, boat ramp, canoeing, archery range, group camp, special events, restrooms

Lake Park contains woodlands and five natural lakes, of which Starvation and Cooper Lakes are the largest. Largely undeveloped, the park is the well field source of freshwater for the city of St. Petersburg. Although close to the Tampa metropolitan area, Lake Park seems rural. Trails for walkers have not been established but there are dirt service roads to explore the park's scenic lakes, pine flatwoods, cypress swamps and hardwood hammocks. Numerous special events are held here. Four rodeos are sponsored annually, with a minimum of two horseshows a month, dog shows, and a holiday bluegrass festival.

To reach Lake Park from I-75 in north Tampa, take the Busch Boulevard 580 exit west to Dale Mabry Highway/S.R. 597 and head north. The park is located on the west side of the highway at 17302 North Dale Mabry Road and Van Dyke Road. The park can also be reached from I-275 by taking the Dale Mabry Highway exit north to the park entrance. Lake Park is open from sunrise to sunset.

Lettuce Lake
Temple Terrace/Hillsborough County
Area: 240 acres
Trail Distance: 8,500 ft. total
Highlights: nature study, nature trails, exercise course, bicycling trail, picnicking, shelters, nature center, fishing, playfield, observation tower, restrooms

A suburban Hillsborough County Park, Lettuce Lake was opened publicly in 1982 and offers high quality recreation for day visitors. Bordered on the north and west by the Hillsborough River, over half of the park's habitat is floodplain cypress and hardwood swamp forest, with the rest hardwood hammock and pine flatwoods. Over 300 species of plants have been identified.

The name Lettuce Lake refers to the formerly dense, inedible colonies of floating, lettuce-like exotic plants of the Araceae family, related to such northern wildflowers as skunk cabbage, Jack-in-the-pulpit, and green dragon. Cold winters have nearly eliminated the plant beds. Not really a lake, this is actually a quiet, shallow, finger-shaped backwater of the Hillsborough River. In times of high water, it serves as a cutoff or channel for the excess runoff.

Directly behind the visitor center, a 3,500-foot boardwalk meanders along the margins of this oxbow "lake," the Hillsborough River and adjacent floodplain swamp. A 35-foot-high observation tower adjoins the boardwalk at the confluence of Lettuce Lake and the Hillsborough River. There is a boardwalk guidebook available at the visitors center, which identifies the most conspicuous plants and interprets the ecology of the floodplain. A 5,000-foot mulched nature trail loops and winds through the upland habitat communities of pine flatwoods and hardwood hammock. The nature walk intercepts the 1.3-mile paved pedestrian and bicycle path that encircles the land area of the park and includes a fitness course which is specially modified for wheelchair use. A cypress dome is accessible on the path via a boardwalk spur. Besides preserving natural Florida, the park has available several large picnic areas with tables and shelters and a large grassy playfield, ideal for softball or other space-requiring recreational pursuits.

To reach Lettuce Lake County Park from I-75 business route in north Tampa, exit east on Fletcher Avenue/S.R. 582A. Head east past the University of South Florida campus. The park entrance is on the left side of the highway after crossing the Hillsborough River. From I-75 in east Tampa take the Fletcher Avenue exit and the park is half a mile west on the right. The park opens at 8 a. m. and closes at sunset year round.

Eureka Springs
Mango/Hillsborough County
Area: 38 acres
Trail Distance: 2,360 ft. total
Highlights: nature study, nature trail, botanical gardens, greenhouse, picnicking, restrooms

Formal developed gardens and informal natural forest blend together to form Eureka Springs County Park. After three decades of labor and love to create this botanical paradise of rare and unusual plantings, Albert Greenberg donated the tract to Hillsborough County. Exotic species of plants are interspersed with the native plants along the trail. Barbados cherry, bananas, creeping figs, bamboo, white-flowering ginger, sweet orange, elephant ear, and queen palm are some of the plants to be seen. A self-guiding booklet is available for the 1,700-foot boardwalk trail. The springs rarely flow now due to the lowering of the water table by construction of a nearby canal, but they were once used for baptisms by local churches and for the first tropical fish farm in Florida.

A brief 660-foot nature trail leads through a bald cypress forest and hardwood swamp. Sweet bay magnolia, dahoon holly, laurel oak, wild coffee, red maple, red bay, various ferns, black tupelo, and buttonbush are but a few members of the native forest.

The maintained landscaped grounds directly south of the entrance building include a greenhouse, display gardens, screened pavilion, and a small pond encircled by winding paths. The picnic grounds are north of the parking area in a wooded oak clearing. Additional information may be obtained from the park rangers at the entrance building.

To reach Eureka Springs County Park from I-4, east of Tampa, take Exit 6D, the first exit east of U.S. 301 exit, and bear right onto Eureka Springs Road. This can be an easy-to-miss exit. The park hours are from 8 a.m. to 6 daily. The park is closed Christmas Day.

University Of South Florida Botanical Garden
Tampa/Hillsborough County
Area: 6 acres
Trail Distance: .5 mile
Highlights: nature study, conservatory greenhouse, gardens, October plant sale, arranged guided tours

Within the six green acres of the University of South Florida's facility, you will discover a wide variety of subtropical and tropical plant life. The botanical garden serves as a teaching and research center for the biology department. The garden is open to the public and encourages public participation and support. The collection of plants from around the world, acquired since 1969, reflects the desire to have a diverse educational resource, at the same time, enriching the range of cultivated plant materials available to the Tampa Bay Area.

The best time to visit the garden is from April through December, but there are plants in colorful bloom all year. A self-guiding trail leads the day visitor along, past a variety of theme gardens. The Temperate Garden, Desert Garden, Palm Garden, Rainforest Area, Ginger Collection, Gymnosperm Garden, Canopy Area, Research Plot Garden, and a Tropical Plant Conservatory are some of the major collections. Rare species as well as common landscape plants are labeled with their scientific and common names, as well as country of origin. In addition, a pamphlet describing the interesting plants in each area has been prepared and is available upon request from the garden staff. Volunteers to help at the garden are welcomed. Visiting hours are from 8 a.m. to 5 p.m. Monday through Friday.

To reach the University of South Florida Botanical Garden from Business I-275 at north Tampa, take the Fowler Avenue/S.R. 582 exit east to 30th Street and turn north. Turn east at the first right, Oak Drive. The garden entrance is at the intersection of Oak and Pine Drive. From I-75 exit west on Fowler Avenue/S.R. 582 and proceed to the campus. Follow 30th Street to Oak and Pine Drives.

Tampa's Natural Places
Tampa/Hillsborough County
Highlights: nature study, outdoor recreation, cultural sites
Fee(s): entrance

Tampa, like most major cities, has a variety of outdoor recreational and cultural places to visit. Urban nature, a world removed from its wilderness counterpart, is there amidst the development and takes on many diverse forms.

There are three history-rich Tampa parks worthy of a visit: Plant Park, Ballast Point Park, and Picnic Island. **Plant Park**, located at the University of Tampa campus near downtown Tampa, borders the Hillsborough River. Thriving in the park is a spreading live oak beneath whose boughs Spanish conquistador Hernando de Soto, negotiated with the Indians of the area in 1539. In more recent times railroad magnate Henry B. Plant, who opened Tampa to expansion, carried out a huge landscaping scheme for his elegant Tampa Bay Resort Hotel, now Plant Hall of the University of Tampa. The park still retains many of the original 150 varieties of plants established by H. B. Plant, and the park is named in his honor. A walking tour of the 92-acre campus is recommended for those who care to explore further.

Ballast Point Park, in south Tampa, juts out into Hillsborough Bay and affords excellent views of the Tampa skyline. The park was formerly called Jules Verne Park. In his book, *From the Earth to the Moon and Round the Moon,* Jules Verne selected Tampa as the site for the first moon shot 100 years ago. An exotic Oriental pavilion was built earlier in the century, but was razed in later years. Today a pier extends out into the bay allowing for saltwater fishing and strolling.

Picnic Island Park is situated on the southwest side of the Interbay Peninsula and is probably the most "natural" and largest of Tampa City parks. Formerly a mangrove island before being dredged, Picnic Island was a training camp for U.S. soldiers before their embarcation for Cuba during the Spanish-American War of 1898. It was also a resort, with parks, dance pavilions, and a bathing beach for soldiers during their off-duty hours. Today, Picnic Island is hemmed in between MacDill Air Force Base and heavy industry, but manages to retain its semi-natural qualities. Picnicking is

Lowry Park resident

popular here along with fishing and swimming. One of the city's two municipal beaches is also on the island.

Florida's second largest theme park, **Busch Gardens**, has more than 500 rare and endangered animals and over 2,500 exotic birds roaming freely in an African setting. Open daily, 9:30 a.m. to 6 p.m., Busch Gardens is at 3000 Busch Boulevard in northeast Tampa, two miles east of I-275.

Lowry Park features a recently constructed modern zoo. The Lowry Park Zoo is upgrading both the natural environments for its animal inhabitants and the facilities for visitors. Animals from all five continents are represented. Picnic facilities and other park amenities are available. The Lowry Park and Zoological Gardens can be reached from I-275 by exiting at Sligh Boulevard west to North Boulevard.

The Museum of Science and Industry focuses on the scientific and technological. The visitor will discover the force of hurricane winds or create a thunderstorm along with other hands-on learning experiences. **The Hillsborough Historical County Museum** is also housed here and provides a glimpse of the area's historic roots. The museum is in north Tampa, east of the University of South Florida on Fowler Avenue. Take Fowler Avenue west from I-75 or east from I-275.

A smaller natural history museum owned by the county is at 1101 East River Cove, three blocks east of Nebraska Avenue in north Tampa along the Hillsborough River and next to the county park office. Indian collections, carvings, bird nest collection, rocks and minerals and other displays of interest are found here. Guided tours are available to school groups and others by appointment. The hours are from 10 a.m. to 4 p.m. Tuesday and Thursday and 1 p.m. to 4 p.m. on Sunday.

Other Tampa City Parks With Nature Trails

- **Copeland Park.** 11001 N. 15th Street, four acres.
- **ELAPP Forty-Eight Park.** 6400 S.MacDill Avenue, 102 acres.
- **Gandy Park.** W. Gandy Boulevard, 103 acres.
- **McKay Bay Nature Park.** 34th Street at McKay Bay, 74 acres.
- **Takomah Trail Park.** 10009 Takomah Trail, six acres.

Upper Tampa Bay County Park
East Oldsmar/Hillsborough County
Area: 596 acres
Trail Distance: 1.8 miles total
Highlights: nature study, nature walks, visitor nature center, interpretive displays, picnicking, shelters, fishing, canoe launch, playground, group camping, restrooms

Located on the northern shoreline of Upper Tampa Bay, this naturally-preserved peninsular park includes a variety of habitats: oak hammocks, wet prairie, salt barrens, seagrass beds, mangrove swamp forest, and salt marshes. It was a wild food habitat preferred by prehistoric Native Americans 4,000 years ago, as shown by the discarded shellfish mounds found throughout the park.

A major environmental study center is operated jointly with Hillsborough Community College at the park and is open to the public and special interest groups. In addition, Hillsborough Community College and the environmental study center conducts pre-arranged group programs at Cockroach Bay on the southeastern shore of Tampa Bay, south of Ruskin, where several miles of nature trails and extensive boardwalk exists.

Three nature walks are found in Upper Tampa Bay Park. Directly south of the visitor nature center and canoe launch area, a short 1,940-foot trail and boardwalk encircles a salt marsh and mangrove swamp. High tides flood the area, with the result that plants and animals here survive under extremely harsh conditions.

A second walk passes through slash pine and saw palmetto flatwoods, looping past two shallow freshwater seasonal ponds. The 2,980-foot trail also skirts the bay and has open views of the wildlife which thrive in the mangrove swamp. The walk begins near the family and group picnic ground.

A third trail leads from the pine flatwoods four feet down to sea level and Mobbly Bay via a 4,150-foot loop boardwalk. Salt barrens, devoid of most vegetation, are a common feature on this wooden trail along a mangrove lined shore, with open views of the developed bay towards Oldsmar. The trail is popular with environmental study groups.

To reach Upper Tampa Bay County Park from I-275 business route in central Tampa, take the West Hillsborough Avenue/S.R. 580 exit west towards Oldsmar, Pinellas County line. Before reaching the county line, exit south on the obscure Double Branch Road. Follow the directional signs. The park entrance is at the end of Double Branch Road. The park opens at 8 a.m. and closes at dark year round. It is closed on Christmas Day.

Ft. Meade Outdoor Recreation Park

Ft. Meade/Polk County
Area: 110 acres
Trail Distance: 1 mile round trip
Highlights: nature study, nature walk, picnicking, pavilions, fishing, boat ramp, canoeing, bandshell, showers, tent camping, restrooms

The 110-acre city park borders the Peace River. Donated by a local phosphate company to the city of Ft. Meade, it is a place to rest, picnic, or view the river's natural beauty. A river nature trail has been established along the east bank, beginning near the boat ramp. The trail curves gracefully with the river, where live oaks draped in Spanish moss prosper on the lush flood plain. Bald cypress, willow, sweet gum, and hackberry are also plentiful. The 67-mile Peace River canoe trail begins here; the furthermost upstream point of public access.

The Seminole Indians called the Peace River, "Tallachopka-hatchee." The name was derived from the word, "Tallachopko," meaning the edible portion of wild peas which were and are found in abundance along the stream banks. "Hatchee" means water. Historically, Ft. Meade is the site of the last skirmish of the Seminole Indian Wars.

To reach Ft. Meade Outdoor Recreation Park from I-4, exit S.R. 98 south and drive approximately 25 miles to Ft. Meade. From I-75 at Punta Gorda, go north on U.S. 17 about 65 miles; and from U.S. 27 near Frostproof, go west 17 miles on U.S. 98. At the center of town, turn east on East Broadway or S.R. 98. The park lies on the east bank of the Peace River and the entrance is on the south side of the road.

Consider visiting **Patterson Park** while in Ft. Meade. A short self-guiding and paved nature walk leads out on a landscaped "finger" into a man-made lake. Picnic facilities, gazebos, fishing piers and benches line the walk in this city park. Patterson Park is located on the north side of Ft. Meade along U.S. 17/98.

Saddle Lake County Park
Lakeland/Polk County
Area: 734 acres
Trail Distance: 3.2 miles total
Highlights: nature study, nature trails, swimming, fishing, picnicking, shelters, boat ramps, canoeing, playground, baseball field, target range, camping, restrooms
Fee(s): camping

The man-created "moonscape" of Saddle Creek was transformed into a county park after phosphate mining ceased. An amazing variety of birdlife and other wildlife are at home here in the several small ponds and lakes, including anhingas, herons, cormorants, ibis, egrets, gulls, ard numerous duck species.

The nature walks begin near the observation tower not far from the campground. A short .2-mile loop trail passes through a cypress swamp where several huge cypress stumps remain from earlier logging. A longer 1.5-mile trail follows a phosphate spoil bank ridge where good views of lakes and swamp forest appear on both sides. Birdlife is plentiful in this remote area of the park. The trail ends abruptly at the shore of a lake. Retrace your steps back to the observation tower trailhead.

To reach Saddle Creek, a Polk County Park, from I-4 exit take S.R. 98 southbound at Lakeland to S.R. 92 near the center of town. Head east on S.R. 92 for about six miles to Saddle Creek Park which will be on the north side of town. The nature walk area closes at 6 p. m.

Future Polk Coutity parklands that will include nature trails are Carter Road Park north of Mulberry and the state property along Bowlegs Creek south of Ft. Meade.

Florida Cypress Gardens
Winter Haven/Polk County
Area: 223 acres
Highlights: botanical gardens, theme gardens, live shows, restaurants, gift shops
Fee(s): entrance

Cypress Gardens first began nearly half a century ago on the southeast shore of Lake Eloise, where Richard Pope decided to create a botanical garden. From 16 obscure acres of reclaimed cypress swampland, a garden was transformed into what is today an internationally recognized family-oriented theme park. Aside from the commercial aspects of the park, the botanical and zoological gardens are excellent. Cypress Gardens has more tropical and subtropical plants grown under natural conditions than any other botanical garden in the world. A main trail meanders through the gardens, where more than 8,000 varieties of exotic and rare plants are well-labeled with their common and scientific names and place of origin. Colorful flowers from around the world are in bloom year round. Highlights of the walk include a Floral Clock, Big Lagoon and Gazebo, Esther Williams Florida Pool, statues of St. Fiacre, patron saint of gardeners and St. Francis of Assisi, Oriental Gardens, an Island Area and Aquarama Pool. A butterfly conservatory, "Wings of Wonder," has recently opened.

The Gardens of the World area features six theme gardens with floral displays: The Netherlands, Mediterranean Region, Italy, Greece, Ireland and the southern United States. An All-American Rose Garden is located near the Dutch Windmill. Designated by

Cypress Gardens

the All American Rose Selection Committee as the only official rose garden in Florida, it is one of 27 nationwide for testing and cultivating annual All-American Rose winners.

The Living Forest or Animal Forest is home for exotic and endangered animal species from around the world. Over 400 animals reside in this well-designed zoological park where they live in natural habitats similar to their own native regions. Educational and entertaining areas include Critter Encounters, Fly-Free Aviary, Cypress Point Pier, Hug Haven, Gator Show and a Bird Show.

To reach Cypress Gardens from I-4, take the Lakeland Memorial Boulevard exit south at Winter Haven and follow the directional signs. The Gardens are located three miles southeast of Winter Haven on S.R. 540. Cypress Gardens is open year around from 8 a.m. to sunset.

Street Nature Center & Sanctuary
Winter Haven/Polk County
Area: 30 acres
Trail Distance: 0.5 mile
Highlights: nature study, nature walk, museum, Audubon Society activities

The Street Nature Center, affiliated with the Florida Audubon Society, was the gift of Norman and Luella Street who lived on the property from 1921 to 1970. Overlooking Lake Ned, the rustic home is now the nature center and living quarters of the resident manager. Guided tours, a small museum, and a classroom are available. The **Norton Agey Nature Trail** is a self-guided walk through a once-formal botanical garden established by the Streets, which contained hundreds of exotic plant species. Due to Mr. Street's failing health in later years, the cultivated garden was allowed to return to nature. Many of the exotic and native plants and animals are identified in the trail guide brochure. The walk is a lesson in man's impact on the environment, plant succession and ecological balance. An unmarked loop trail circles the old orange grove.

To reach the Street Nature Center take U.S. 27 to S.R. 540 west near Waverly, north of Lake Wales. Drive approximately four miles to Lakefox Road, turn north and follow the road to where it curves and becomes Cypress Gardens Road. Look for Lameraux Road and turn north towards Lake Ned. The address is 115 Lameraux Road. The hours of the center are from 8 a.m. to 5 p.m. Wednesday through Sunday; closed Mondays and Tuesdays.

Bok Tower Gardens
Lake Wales/Polk County
Area: 128 acres
Trail Distance: 2 miles
Highlights: nature study, nature trails, visitors center museum, carillon, picnicking, concessions, gift shop

Bok Tower Gardens is the result of the deep love Edward Bok felt for the United States and his desire to make the world a more beautiful place to live. A Dutch immigrant, Mr. Bok arrived in America in his youth and in his later years became a successful author and publisher. Inspired by his grandparents' ideals and philosophy, he wanted to make his dreams come true. In 1922, with a personal fortune amassed, he selected and purchased 295-foot-high Iron Mountain, the highest elevation in peninsular Florida, and hired architect Milton Medary to design a "singing" tower and landscape architect, Frederick Law Olmsted, to design the surrounding upland grounds. By 1929, the tower and gardens were completed and dedicated on behalf of Edward Bok by President Calvin Coolidge "as a gift to the American people." His dream realized, Mr. Bok passed away in 1930 and was buried in the lawn between the tower's brass door and the moat.

Today, the visitor to the gardens will still find the original dream of Edward Bok alive. The gardens retain their beauty, along with a serene peacefulness. The 53-bell carillon rings out every half-hour and daily recitals occur at 3 in the afternoon. Thousands of native and exotic flowering plants line the winding walkways. The open vistas inspire and invite contemplation. The garden is a sanctuary from the harried world, a religious experience. Iron Mountain was and is considered a sacred place to the Seminole Indians.

The nature walkways have names such as North Walk, Mockingbird Trail, Sword Fern Path, and Pine Ridge Nature Preserve Walk. Walks led by a naturalist are available at certain times.Over 100 bird species have been sighted in this sanctuary. Special niches in the gardens include Window-By-The-Pond, Exedra (a semi-circular place for conversation in ancient Greece and Rome), a Lily

Garden, Sundial, Japanese Lantern, Live Oak Grove, St. Francis statue and bird feeder, and Reflection Pool. The public is restricted from entering the tower. Picnicking is permitted only in the picnic area near the parking, where tables are provided.

The gardens are a special place to meditate and find inner strength to face a complex world. On a sign posted near the trail to the Pine Ridge Nature Reserve is a quotation by John Burroughs, the American naturalist-author, summarizing the Bok Tower Gardens experience: "I come here to find myself, it is so easy to get lost in the world."

To reach Bok Tower Gardens, take U.S. 27 to S.R. 60 east to Lake Wales. Turn east on S.R. 60 to Alt. 27 and exit north. Go north through Lake Wales to Burns Avenue or Highway 17A and turn east. Drive just over a mile to the gardens entrance on the north side of the road. The gardens are open 8 a.m. to 5:30 p.m. every day of the year and everyone is welcome.

Babson Park Audubon Nature Center
Babson Park/Polk County
Area: 25 acres
Trail Distance: 1 mile
Highlights: nature center, museum, gift shop, guided tours, nature study, nature walk

The Babson Park Audubon Nature Center occupies a high point on the northeast shore of Crooked Lake, formerly known as Caloosa Lake. The nature center and the self-guiding **Caloosa Nature Trail**, illustrates the relationship of the plants and animals bordering the lake. Nearly 100 species of birds have been observed on the property.

The trail begins near the Center and first passes through a virgin remnant of the once-extensive, longleaf pine-turkey oak scrub forest which, before the arrival of the citrus agri-business, covered Polk County and the central Florida Ridge Region. As the trail descends to the beach, other habitats can be observed, such as the old lake "pond" bottom and a scrub oak thicket. Walking on, the lower beach habitat and ecological role is examined in the trail guide booklet available from the Center. The trail loops back through an upland community and turkey oak habitat. Take time to look at the exhibts and browse the available gifts at the Center.

The nature center is open 1 p.m. to 5 p.m. Tuesday through Sunday and is closed Monday. The trail is open from sunrise to sunset. Summer hours are 10 a.m. to 12 p.m. Monday through Friday.

De Soto National Memorial
Bradenton/Manatee County
Area: 25 acres
Trail Distance: 0.5 mile
Highlights: nature study, nature walk, historical site, fishing, visitors' center, museum, theatre, living history demonstration, gift shop

At the mouth of Tampa Bay, nearly 25 acres of mostly mangrove swamp forest bordering the Manatee River has been a national memorial since 1949. It commemorates the 1539 landing of the Spanish explorer Hernando de Soto in Florida. Although small in size, De Soto National Memorial is a historically rich and rewarding experience.

During your visit try to imagine you were one of the members of De Soto's expedition. De Soto, "The Knight of Santiago," and his

Gumbo limbos, De Soto National Memorial

force of over 600 men were the first major European explorers of what is now the southern United States. Seeking glory and gold, his greed and ruthlessness provoked the Native American tribes. Indian attacks were relentless and constant. Four years and 4,000 miles later, De Soto perished in the forest and was buried by his remaining followers in the Mississippi River. He never realized that the real riches were in the forest and streams. The four journals written about the expedition ironically helped to stimulate English colonization in the 17th century.

As you walk along the half-mile nature trail and encounter the plant and animal life – epiphytes, mangroves, strangler figs, cacti, yucca, seagrape, herons, lizards, and possibly a manatee – imagine how the Indians relied on the natural resources to sustain them. From December through April, the modern day explorer will take pleasure in the living history demonstration by park rangers, reenacting life in the Spanish camp and Indian village of Ucita.

The visitors center includes a museum with displays of Spanish artifacts. A theatre within the center runs a movie documentary, *The Exploration of De Soto 1539-1543: The Legacy of the Legend*. The gumbo limbo trees in front of the visitors center are outstanding specimens in size and beauty.

To reach De Soto National Memorial from I-75, take the S.R. 64 exit 42 west to and through Bradenton, where it becomes Manatee Avenue. From Manatee Avenue, turn north at 75th Street West. Drive to the end of the road to the memorial entrance and parking lot. The hours of the memorial are from 8 a.m. to 5:30 p.m.

Madira Bickel State Archaeological Site
Terra Ceia/Manatee County
Area: 10 acres
Trail Distance: .1 mile
Highlights: archaeological study, picnicking

One of the numerous mounds prehistoric Indians constructed along the southwest coast of Florida, the Madira Bickel Mound, was the first to be dedicated as a state archaeological site. Located on Terra Ceia Island ("Heavenly Land"), the ceremonial temple mound is believed to have been constructed somewhere between 1450 and 1650 A.D. by Timucan Indians during the Safety Harbor

Steps to Madira Bickel Mound

Period. The mound measures 100 X 170 feet at its base and 20 feet in height. A short trail leads up its western side.

Madira Bickel Mound is but a small portion of the original extensive Timucan village. Along the shores of Miguel Bay, northwest of the mound, an enormous shell midden was located, but most of it was removed for construction of the early roads in Manatee County. About 100 feet north of the mound is a small burial mound which has been partially removed by archaeologists, but has been primarily used for road building material. The long side faces a flat plaza where games and ceremonies were likely held.

Archaeological excavations have identified at least three periods of Indian occupancy. During the first period, when mound building begun, life was simple. The main interests were subsistence hunting and fishing. Kitchen midden mounds along the shore of the bay were likely begun about 2,000 years ago, as they start below the waterline. The second phase, the Weedon Island Period (700 A.D. to 1300 A.D.), produced the most artistic pottery discovered in Florida. During the third phase, known as the Safety Harbor Period, villages were larger and agriculture rose to prominence. In summary, the Bickel Mound Site contains evidence of prehistoric Indian life and culture as it gradually rose from simplicity and subsistence through artistic heights to religious expression in the building of temple and burial mounds. The preservation of the site was achieved through the efforts and financing of Karl and Madira Bickel, who donated the mounds to the state of Florida.

If you want to explore Florida Indian history further, the **Crystal River State Archaeolopical Site** is one of the most important Pre-Columbian sites in the state. Trails lead from the visitor center to the temple and burial mounds. The site is located northwest of Crystal River, Florida off U.S. 19/98.

To reach Madira Bickel Mound site from I-75, take the U.S. 301 exit 43 west to Ellenton, past the Gamble Plantation, where more information may be obtained about the mounds. Proceed to the Tamiami Trail/U.S. 41 and turn north. Then turn northwest on U.S. 19/I-275 from the Tamiami Trail/U.S.41 towards the direction of the Sunshine Skyway Bridge and St. Petersburg. Turn west at Bayshore Drive about two miles before the Sunshine Skyway Bridge and drive west about two miles. Follow the directional signs beginning at the community of Terra Ceia.

South Florida Museum and Bishop Planetarium
Bradenton/Manatee County
Highlights: nature study, museum, manatee watching, courtyard, observatory, planetarium, gift shop

The South Florida Museum is a vast natural and social history experience under one roof. Under the direction of Dr. W. D. Sugg, the museum was approved as a non-profit corporation in 1946. The first objects purchased were the Calusan and Timucan Indian relics of Montague Tallant: the most complete and varied collection of regional Indian artifacts in southwest Florida. Soon thereafter, outstanding collections of minerals, fossils, shells, and wildlife were added and displayed in imaginative and educational exhibits.

Since 1950, the manatee, "Baby Snoots," has been a member of the museum family and even has his own room and bath. Born in captivity, "Snooty" is very friendly and easy to view close up, especially at mealtime in the Aquarium Room. For many visitors, it may be the only opportunity to see a live manatee, whose ancestors were common in Florida waters less than a century ago. Today, there are estimated to be only 1,000 manatees in the state.

Other varied exhibits include the 16th century Hernando de Soto Plaza, Home and Chapel, the Medical Room Exhibit, Early American Collection, Confederate and Civil War Room, House of Dolls, Period Rooms, Guns and Exotic Weapons Collection, South Pacific Room, Sugg Commemorative Garden and, finally, a Titan Missile.

In the north wing of the museum is the **Bishop Planetarium**. The planetarium is equipped with a computer-controlled projector and extensive special effects systems. Starshows are periodically changed to include a variety of topics, such as UFOs, astrology, science fiction, and the space program. The Laser Fantasies Lightshow, a laser light and sound experience, is presented each weekend in the planetarium, the second largest in the state after the one in Miami. The observatory is located on the museum roof. A 12.5-inch reflecting telescope allows views of the outdoor sky several evenings a month, weather permitting.

The South Florida Museum and Bishop Planetarium are at 201 10th Street West in downtown Bradenton on Tamiami Trail/Business U.S. 41. From I-75, take S.R. 64 exit 42 west to Bradenton and Business U.S. 41. Turn north on U.S. 41 and proceed one block to the museum, just before the Manatee River bridge crossing. Plenty of museum and street parking is available.The museum is open Tuesday to Friday from 10 a.m. to 5 p.m. and Saturday and Sunday from 1 p.m. to 5 p.m. Closed Mondays.

Ringling Museum Grounds
Sarasota/Sarasota County
Area: 38 acres
Highlights: nature walk, botanic garden, art and circus museums, Ringling Mansion
Fee(s): museum entrance

For many visitors here, the exquisite landscape architecture of the formal Italian gardens is as memorable as the museum itself. Hundreds of exotic trees, shrubs, and flowers were planted on the grounds, along the shores of Sarasota Bay, under the supervision of John and Mable Ringling. The Ringlings left future generations a living subtropical floral exhibit in addition to their numerous art works. The majority of the 200 varieties of plants are labeled and identified, but a tree map is available from the Art Museum front desk at a minimal cost. The map includes a listing of the collection of palms and large tree specimens such as banyan, monkey puzzle and bunya bunya. The Rose Garden includes over 150 hybrids of tea rose bushes. The Secret Garden is a quiet corner of the lawn overlooking Sarasota Bay – a congenial place to sit and admire the formal surroundings. Numerous mature trees dot the grounds. Statues adorn the garden everywhere, adding charm and beauty.

If you are interested in touring the Art and Circus Museums, Asolo Theater, and the "Ca'd'Zan" mansion, one ticket purchase will admit you to all. Administered by the state of Florida, the museums, theater, and mansion hours are from 9 a.m. to 7 p.m. weekdays, Saturdays 9 a.m. to 5 p.m., and Sundays 11 a.m. to 6 p.m. The Ringling Museum grounds are open to the public free of charge during museum hours. They are located three miles north of Sarsota on Tamiami Trail/U.S. 41. To reach the Ringling Museum from I-75, take the University Parkway or County Line Road/S.R. 610 west to U.S. 301 and turn south to the junction of De Soto Road, where you turn west. The museum entrance is at the end of De Soto Road West, across Tamiami Trail/U.S. 41.

Other Nature Parks in the Sarasota Area

- **Arlington Park.** 2650 Waldemere Street, 20 acres.
- **Fruitville Road Park.** Northeast of Fruitville & Beneva Roads, five acres.
- **Phillippi Estate Park.** 5500 S. Tamiami Trail, 60 acres.
- **Twin Lakes Park.** 6700 Clark Road, 123 acres.
- Beach parks with nature trails include: **North Lido, South Lido, Siesta, Casperson** and **Indian Mound Parks.**

Marie Selby Botanical Gardens
Sarasota/Sarasota County
Area: 10 public acres
Trail Distance: .5 mile
Highlights: nature study, nature walk, botanic gardens, art museum, plant shop, book & gift shop, special plant sales & events, guided tours, display greenhouse, membership
Fee(s): entrance fee

Situated on a peninsula at Sarasota's "Window-to-the-Sea" bayfront, the Marie Selby Botanical Gardens are a lush, elegant green subtropical world. The late Marie Selby's love of plants led to the establishment of the garden's nucleus in the 1920s. Today the botanical gardens are world-renowned for their spectacular collection of exotic tropical flora and are the only gardens specializing in epiphytes, such as orchids and bromeliads.

There are several established gardens. A tropical and subtropical food demonstration garden grows a large variety of edible plants such as cassava, papaya, fig, taro, edible hibiscus, pineapple, and charya. Florida's finest display of hibiscus is found in the Hibiscus Collection. A quarter-acre succulent garden includes species from around the world and there is a fine bamboo garden.

The one main loop takes you along past these botanical treasures and includes sweeping vistas of Sarasota Bay. The Tropical Display House simulates a rain forest with waterfalls and many beautiful flowers, especially orchids. On the pathway to the Museum of Botany and the Arts, housed in the Christy Payne mansion, you will see native ornamentals that were originally planted by the Selby family. Housed in the other buildings is an active research staff that studies endangered plants of the disappearing tropical forests, the international Orchid Identification Center and Bromeliad Identification Center and the Eric Young Micropropagation Center, that is researching the cloning of rare plants.

You may want to include a walk to the city's nearby 10-acre Island Park and marina about two blocks north of Selby Gardens along the bayfront. A commercial "Fisherman's Wharf" atmosphere has been created with sea shops, restaurants, boat dockage, and even a ski school. There are many tropical landscape plants to enjoy in this maritime setting.

To reach Marie Selby Botanical Gardens from I-75, take the Fruitville Road/S.R. 780 exit 39 west to Main Street in downtown Sarasota, then proceed to the junction of U.S. 301 and turn south. Go right at U.S. 41/Tamiami Trail and look for the Selby Gardens sign just before South Palm Avenue. The address is 800 South Palm Avenue. Selby Gardens is open from 10 a.m. to 5 p.m. every day of the year except Christmas.

Spanish Point At The Oaks
Osprey/Sarasota County
Area: 30 acres
Trail Distance: 1.5 miles
Highlights: historic walks, museum, special events, gift shop, membership
Fee(s): entrance

Spanish Point at the Oaks is a unique archaeological, historic, and natural science preservation site overlooking Little Sarasota Bay and currently undergoing restoration by the Gulf Coast Heritage Association. The visitor to this history-rich location will discover along the footpaths and roads evidence of three separate eras of human occupancy: prehistoric and historic Indians, mid-19th century pioneers, and early 20th century habitation by one of America's elite families. It was the first site in Sarasota County to be included in the National Register of Historic Places.

Archaeologically, Spanish Point is one of the best preserved prehistoric Indian villages on the Gulf coast. Excavations continually yield new information about the early occupants. A rare Archaic period shell midden mound dated 2100 B.C. contains the first fiber-tempered pottery produced in the United States. Additional evidence suggests prehistoric Native Americans were here until the Late Weeden Island Period of 1100 A.D., after which the area was gradually settled by Calusa Indians. The entire point, the highest elevation in Sarasota County, was built up by the early residents from sea shells. After several centuries elasped, pioneer settlers John Green Webb and his family arrived in Florida from New York in 1867. They built several dwellings and kept the farm land intact, not disturbing the mounds. The Guptill House and the pioneer cemetery are physical testimony to their former presence. Mr. Webb named the site Spanish Point.

In the early 1900's, Mrs. Potter Palmer, widow of Chicago entrepreneur Potter Palmer, acquired the land from the Webbs. She continued in keeping the grounds intact, but modified an existing hunting lodge for her own occupancy, and named it The Oaks. Mrs. Palmer was extremely interested in tropical horticulture and landscaping and she built many structures and gardens. In 1980, Mrs. Palmer's heirs deeded the property to the Gulf Coast Heritage Association, a non-profit corporation.

To reach Spanish Point at The Oaks from I-75, exit 37 Clark Road/Stickney Point Road west and drive to Tamiami Trail/U.S. 41. Turn south on Tamiami Trail/U.S. 41 and proceed about two miles to the north edge of Osprey. Turn in at the entrance on the east side of the highway at 500 Tamiami Trail. The hours are from 10 a.m. to 3 p.m. Tuesday through Sunday (closed Mondays).

Oscar Scherer State Recreation Area
Osprey/Sarasota County
Area: 462 acres
Trail Distance: 1 mile
Highlights: nature study, nature walk, picnicking,, shelters, swimming, canoeing, bicycling, fresh & saltwater fishing, camping, guided ranger walks, restrooms
Fee(s): entrance and camping

Leaving behind the congestion of the nearby cities of Venice and Sarasota, you may breathe a welcome sigh of relief as you enter the gates of Oscar Scherer State Recreation Area. The park is fairly undisturbed with the exception of an occasional marl pit or evidence of scars on the slash pines tapped for turpentine in the early years of this century. In 1957, the land was given to the state of Florida by Elsa Scherer Burrows, in honor of her father, who came to love the land during his winter sojourns.

A one-mile linear marked nature trail follows the north bank of South Creek. A variety of plant and animal communities thrive in the tract. The scrubby pine flatwoods community is composed of myrtle oak, sand live oak, Chapman's oak, palmetto, sabal palm, wire grass, and slash pine. This type of ecosystem has become increasingly rare in south Florida in recent years due to over-development. The threatened Florida scrub jay is at home in this plant community, along with the sand skink, black racer, and gopher tortoise.

Sawgrass, cattail, and maiden cane are major plant components of the freshwater marsh. The grass-sedge-rush association is highly productive for wildlife such as the marsh rabbit, wood stork, alligator, wading birds, waterfowl, turtles, and snakes. Additional plant and animal communities you may encounter in your exploration of the park on foot include the salt marsh spartina grass, juncus rush, egrets, diamond back terrapins, otter and raccoon, mangrove swamp (red, white, and black mangroves), coon oysters, land crab, mullet, and the submerged aquatic habitats (arrowheads, water lilies, water hyacinth, aquatic insects and an occasional manatee).

The State Recreation Area is located along the banks of South Creek, two miles south of Osprey, and six miles north of Venice. To reach Oscar Scherer SRA from I-75, take exit 37 Clark Road/S.R. 72 and Stickney Point Road in south Sarasota west to Tamiami Trail/U.S. 41. Turn south on Tamiami Trail and drive through Osprey to the park entrance on the east side of the highway. In addition, the 1-75 Venice exits 34 and 35 to Venice Farms Road and Venice Avenue west to Tamiami Trail/Venice Bypass north will take you through Nokomis and Laurel to the park entrance. The park opens at 8 a.m. and closes at sunset. Enjoy a day or overnight outing in this green island sanctuary in the midst of an ever-urbanizing landscape.

Venice Fitness Trail At Pinebrook Park
Venice/Sarasota County
Area: 5 acres
Trail Distance: 1.6 miles
Highlights: nature study, nature walk, exercise course, tennis, picnicking, restrooms

Designed and constructed by local governmental and community agencies, the 1.6-mile Venice Fitness Trail is a combined exercise and nature walk set in natural surroundings. The trail has 20 exercise stations evenly spaced through the pine flatwoods, abandoned open fields, and along Curry Creek tributary. The well-wooded City of Venice parkland is a sanctuary for various wildlife. The loop trail begins and ends near the parking lot where two lighted tennis courts, picnic shelters, and restrooms have been provided.

Pinebrook Park can be reached from I-75 at Jacaranda Avenue exit 34 or Everglades Boulevard exit 35 to Venice Farms Road, then to Venice Avenue. Continue west on Venice Avenue about 4.5 miles from the I-75 Jacaranda Avenue exit or two miles from Everglades Boulevard exit to Pinebrook Road on the north side of the highway and turn north. Drive past Venice Well Field Recreational Complex, the source of the City of Venice water supply, to the entrance and parking lot of Pinebrook Park on the east side of the road.

Kiwanis Park
Port Charlotte/Charlotte County
Area: 31.5 acres
Trail Distance: 3/4 mile
Highlights: nature study, nature walk, picnicking, shelters, jogging fitness trail, observation deck, playground, lake fishing, restrooms

Surviving suburbanization, this green island has many large specimens of live and laurel oaks, slash pine, and sabal palms, with an understory of saw palmetto. Vegetation bordering the man-made Horseshoe Lake and wetlands includes cattails, sea myrtle, coastal plain willow, broom sedge, and various showy wildflowers. Twenty-seven species of birds have been sighted, including the endangered wood stork. The 20-station Norwegian-style mulched jogging/fitness trail doubles as a nature walk as it winds through the native vegetation along the 3/4-mile course. An observation deck and bridge provide a better opportunity to view wildlife and access to the picnic facilities on the center island in two-acre Horseshoe Lake. Future plans include a nature center and more trails.

To reach Kiwanis Park from I-75, exit west on the Port Charlotte Road on the north bank of the Peace River. Drive to Tamiami Trail/ U.S. 41, turn north and proceed 2.5 miles to Midway Boulevard, then turn west and drive one mile to the park.

Additional nature-oriented parklands in the Port Charlotte area include **Salyers Park** at Quesada and Saylers Streets and the **Port Charlotte Beach Complex** at 4500 Harbor Boulevard, which is also the main headquarters of the Charlotte County Recreation and Parks Department.

Juan Ponce De Leon Historic Park
Punta Gorda/Charlotte County
Harbor Frontage: 810 ft.
Area: 16 acres
Trail Distance: 3/4 mile total
Highlights: nature study, nature walks, historic site, wildlife center, picnicking, shelters, boat ramp, fishing, restrooms

Facing Charlotte Harbor, gateway to the Gulf of Mexico, this small but history-rich city park will take you back to the beginnings of the 16th century. It is thought to be near this point that Ponce de Leon landed in 1521 to establish the first plantation colony for Spain. Prior to his attempted settlement, Ponce de Leon was the first to enter Florida, near St. Augustine in 1513, after failing to locate Bimini Island and the legendary "fountain of youth." He named the land "La Florida" because it had beautiful views of many cool woodlands and, moreover, because its discovery coincided with the Catholic Feast of Flowers.

When he returned on the second voyage to Florida in 1521 to establish America's first colony, Ponce de Leon had two ships, 200 colonists, priests, 50 horses, livestock, and farm implements. The expedition landed at the Bahia del Espiritu or the "Bay of the Holy Spirit," now Charlotte Harbor, and started building a permanent camp.

The colony lasted six months before finally collapsing under a fierce attack by the Calusa Indians, which killed several Spaniards and wounded Ponce de Leon himself. The colonists boarded their ships and sailed for Cuba, where Ponce de Leon died. It was 20 years later that Hernando de Soto landed near Tampa Bay.

On the park's south boundary is a 1,000-foot boardwalk nature trail which passes through the mangrove swamp forest. The three species of mangroves are identified along the loop walk, as are the types of herons. On the property's west side the 3,000-foot **Indian Trail** encircles midden shell mounds and Calusa Indian holding canals used for shellfish and canoes. The park also features the **Peace River Wildlife Center**. With an excellent staff of volunteers, the wildlife center has been highly successful at rehabilitating and releasing injured creatures back to the wild. The park has been declared a bird sanctuary.

To reach Juan Ponce de Leon Park from I-75, take the S.R.17/35 exit west to Punta Gorda, the first exit south of the Peace River. The highway becomes West Marion Punta Gorda. Continue on west Marion through town to the park entrance. The park hours are from daybreak to sunset.

Charlotte Harbor Environmental Center
Punta Gorda/Charlotte County
Area: 3,000 acres
Trail Distance: 3 trails totalling 2.3 miles
Highlights: hiking, nature center, nature study, picnicking, canoe launch, restrooms

The Charlotte Harbor Environmental Center occupies the land fringe of the Alligator Creek addition to the Charlotte Harbor Aquatic Preserve; one of eight aquatic preserves in southwest Florida. The center serves as an outdoor environmental education center for Charlotte County and all interested individuals.

The three nature trails begin and end at the parking area adjacent to the temporary visitor's center, meeting room, screened in picnic area, and restrooms. Please check in and out at the visitor's center. A trail map is provided.

Trail 1 is a .8-mile loop hike through pine and palmetto flatwoods. Woody and herbaceous plants are identified along the way. Special areas include a black needle marsh, two man-made ponds, and Alligator Creek where you can picnic or launch a canoe. **Trail 2** (.57) and **Trail 3** (.9) begin and end along the entrance drive near the visitor's center. These two pine and palmetto paths intermesh with each other to provide a solid nature hike.

The center's hours of operation are 8 a.m. to 3 p.m., Monday to Friday. Volunteers lead guided tours Tuesday, Thursday, and Saturday beginning at 9 a.m. Charlotte Harbor Environmental Center is about 4.5 miles south of Punta Gorda on Burnt Store Road. From I-75 exit west on S.R. 80 into Punta Gorda, then on to U.S. 41. Go south on U.S. 41/Tamiami Trail on the outskirts of Punta Gorda to Burnt Store Road and turn south/left. The center is about 1.5 miles south of the intersection at 10941 Burnt Store Road.

Octagon Wildlife Sanctuary
Punta Gorda/Charlotte County
Area: 10 acres
Trail Distance: 1 mile of walking paths
Highlights: nature walk, wildlife observation
Fee(s): entrance donation

If you wonder where aged animals go after spending their younger years in zoos and circuses, Octagon Wildlife Sanctuary is one such place. The non-profit sanctuary is a sort of "old folks home" for retired exhibition animals. The site also serves as a rehabilitation center.

Visitors will discover a menagerie of native and predominately exotic animals contained within a mix of wire and pole cages. There are felines, bears, and primates to view here, but keep in mind that this is not a zoo so much as a haven for unfortunate creatures who otherwise would probably have been destroyed. The rows of contained animals serve an educational purpose for school children as well as for the general public.

To reach Octagon from I-75 in North Fort Myers, exit 26 east on Bayshore Drive/S.R. 78. Drive 3.5 miles to S.R. 31 and turn north. Proceed five miles on S.R. 31 and turn left/west on Horseshoe Road. Drive 0.3 mile to the entrance parking lot. The hours are 9 a.m. to 5 p.m. daily. The telephone number is (813) 543-1130.

Enroute you may want to visit **ECHO Gardens**, a subtropical and tropical edible plant nursery just north of Bayshore Drive. ECHO also serves the world, especially the Third World, by providing seed and plants for food. Guided tours are given of the grounds and nursery while guides explain the humanitarian mission of helping the starving people of the world. The garden, on Durrance Road just off Bayshore Road/S.R. 78, is open for tours on Tuesdays, Fridays and Saturdays at 10 a.m. Group tours are by appointment. ECHO is an acronym for Educational Concerns for Hunger Organization. You can buy edible plants from the nursery Monday through Saturday from 9 a.m. to noon.

St. James Creek Trail
St. James/Lee County
Area: 150 acres
Trail Distance: 0.5 mile one-way
Highlights: nature walk, nature study

Currently the St. James Creek Trail is the only publicly accessible walking path on Pine Island thanks to the Calusa Land Trust. A former shell road, the linear path is walled in by mangroves and wetlands with an occasional vista. Large melaleuca trees provide shade along the normally dry path. Herons and other aquatic birds are commonly sighted. The trail terminates at a mangrove "island" or shell spoil spit where vistas of the open waters of St. James Creek and Matlacha Pass are splendid. You must return the way you came.

The trail property is owned and managed by the Calusa Land Trust whose mission is to protect the coastal wetlands of Charlotte Harbor, Pine Island Sound, and the Matlacha Aquatic Preserve. The local Pine Island group has acquired and preserved over 700 acres since 1976. Their seven holdings include Calusa Indian mounds, hardwood hammocks, eagle nesting sites, and wetlands.

To reach the St. James Creek walking trail on Pine Island from I-75 exit S.R. 78/Bayshore Road west in North Fort Myers. Continue west on Bayshore Road to U.S. 41/Tamiami Trail where Bayshore becomes Pine Island Road/S.R. 78. Proceed west on Pine Island Road/S.R. 78 across Matlacha Pass and the village to Pine Island Center and C.R. 767/Stringfellow Road. Turn left/south and drive about seven miles towards St. James City and Laratonda Road.

Turn left/east on Laratonda Road and proceed about a half-mile to the trailhead on the left/east side of the road, where there is road-shoulder parking for five or so vehicles.

While on Pine Island, consider visiting the **Museum of the Islands,** which features the natural and social history of the area. The museum is at the corner of Sesame Drive and Russell Road next to the Pine Island library in Phillips Park at Pine Island Center. It is open daily during the winter season and on weekends during the summer. The telephone number is (813) 283-1525.

J. N. "Ding" Darling National Wildlife Refuge
Sanibel Island/Lee County
Area: 5,014 acres
Trail Distance: 5.3 miles total
Highlights: nature study, nature trails, bicycling, canoeing, fishing, limited crabbing
Fee(s): entrance, canoe rental

Composed primarily of mangrove estuary wilderness, with smaller parcels of island upland, the J. N. "Ding" Darling National Wildlife Refuge is a birder's paradise. The refuge borders San Carlos Bay and the Pine Island Sound, on the "backside" of the subtropical barrier island, not far from the thriving center of Sanibel's commercial and residential areas.

Established in 1945 as the Sanibel National Wildlife Refuge, the sanctuary was re-named in honor of Jay Norwood Darling, a Pulitzer Prize winning political cartoonist and avid conservationist, who helped establish 180 similar wildlife refuges throughout the United States. Darling accepted the position of head of the U.S. Biological Survey, forerunner of the U.S. Fish and Wildlife Service, when approached by President F. D. Roosevelt, and was very successful in bringing leadership to the cause of proper wildlife management. "Ding," as he was affectionately known by many, maintained a winter residence on nearby Captiva Island.

The first stop of your visit, before embarking on the five-mile one-way, self-guiding drive through the refuge, should be the visitor center at the entrance to the drive. Exhibits, publications, audio visual programs, and staff will inform you of the wildlife, habitats, and other aspects of the refuge. Over 290 varieties of resident and migratory birds can be seen here, including migratory ducks, the rare roseate spoonbill, brown pelicans and the Everglades kite. A booklet is available for a minimal fee to enhance and interpret your drive through the refuge. As you drive along, you will learn about the upland vegetation, wading birds, waterfowl, mangrove ecology, mosquito control, and estuarine cycle of life.

Those who enjoy walking will discover an elevated dike roadway that runs four linear miles through the refuge. The **Indigo Trail** begins near the visitor center, where you can park. Just beyond the entrance fee booth, the trail heads west for about two

Shell Mound Trail Boardwalk

miles before arriving at an "L" trail junction. Go right across the dike road spur to the observation tower and the main wildlife drive. Either retrace your steps or follow the wildlife drive back to the visitor center. Inquire at the visitor center desk for more details.

A second trail, **Shell Mound Trail,** is near the end of the wildlife drive. This 1/3-mile boardwalk and footpath loops through a tropical hammock. Many West Indian plant species thrive here, including wild key limes. Please remember that no collecting of plants is permitted.

For canoeists, the well-marked two-mile Commodore Creek Canoe Trail is located along the western edge of Tarpon Bay. The trail weaves through red mangrove wetlands and muddy tidal flats. Canoes can be rented at the marina at the end of Tarpon Bay Road.

Offshore from Captiva Island and separated by the Roosevelt Channel, is Buck Key, named for the white-tail deer that inhabit the island. Also part of the refuge properties, Buck Key has four miles of canoe and walking trails which pass through former Indian burial and shell mounds and desert-like environs. Inquire at the visitor center for information regarding canoe rentals for this day excursion. Additional properties connected to the Refuge include the Bailey and Perry Tracts.

To reach J. N. "Ding" Darling National Wildlife Refuge from I-75 at Ft. Myers, exit west at Daniels Road, and drive right on Six Mile Cypress Road across U.S. 41/Tamiami Road. Go left on Summerlin Road and proceed to the Sanibel Causeway toll bridge ($3.00 round trip). After crossing the causeway, turn right at the four-way stop onto Periwinkle Drive and proceed to the three-way stop at Tarpon Bay Road. Turn right and continue a short way to a second three-way stop and Sanibel-Captiva Road. Turn left and proceed to the refuge entrance about 2.5 miles further. The refuge is open from sunup to sunset.

Frank Bailey Tract/
J. N. "Ding" Darling National Wildlife Refuge
Sanibel Island/Lee County
Area: 100 acres
Trail Distance: 2 miles
Highlights: nature study, hiking

The 100-acre Frank Bailey Tract was the first National Wildlife Refuge on Sanibel Island. This freshwater wetland was originally leased from pioneer Frank P. Bailey but was purchased by the U.S.

White ibis, Frank Bailey Tract

Fish and Wildlife Service in 1952 for $50 an acre. Captiva resident J.N. Darling financed the establishment of a now-defunct observation tower and flowing well to attract wildlife. The U.S. Fish and Wildlife Service dredged several ponds to provide and encourage birds and other fauna to visit the site. Ospreys nest atop installed pole platforms at the north edge of the property near Island Bay Road. There are two miles of dike trails, boardwalks, and footpaths laced throughout the tract.

Cordgrass Trail is an easy half-mile trail that loops Ani Pond. The

Canal Trail is a 1.2-mile loop alongside Ani Pond, Mangrove Head Pond, and Airplane Canal, a former landing area for pontoon aircraft. Visitors may see herons, egrets, alligators, and other wildlife that frequent the ponds, especially at sunrise and sunset.

To reach Frank Bailey Tract from I-75 at Fort Myers take the Daniels Road exit west, which becomes Six Mile Cypress Road and cross U.S. 41. Go left on Summerlin Road, which takes you to Sanibel Causeway toll bridge. After crossing the causeway turn right/west on Periwinkle Way at the first four-way stop. Continue west on Periwinkle Way to Tarpon Bay Road at a three-way "T" stop. Turn left/south and proceed to the tract entrance and parking area on the right side of Tarpon Bay Road. A second parking and access area is at Smith Pond on Island Bay Road. Just before reaching the main entrance on Tarpon Bay Road turn right on Island Bay Road and drive half a mile to the marked parking area. If you continue south on Tarpon Bay Road you will arrive at Tarpon Bay Beach.

Sanibel-Captiva Conservation Foundation
Sanibel Island/Lee County
Area: 247 acres
Trail Distance: 4.2 miles total
Highlights: nature study, nature trails, visitor center, exhibits, observation tower, herbarium, library, nature shop, native plant nursery, lecture series, guided tours

Founded in 1967, the Sanibel-Captiva Conservation Foundation encompasses 247 undisturbed acres of spartina grass wetland marshes, sandy sabal palm ridges, and a section of the freshwater "Sanibel River" which forms the preserve's southern boundary. The members of the Foundation are very active in preserving the natural systems of the encompassing islands through land acquisition, public education, environmental activism, and conservation.

Directly behind the nature center, housing the library, nature shop, bookstore, interpretive displays, and restrooms, are over four miles of nature walks on 10 separately-named loop trails that pass through marshlands, ridge vegetation and along the winding Sanibel River. At the Sanibel River is the Betty Mattheissen Observation Memorial Tower, which provides birds-eye views of the surrounding property. Osprey are seen nesting nearby on established pole platforms.

The trails are as follows:

- **Booth Courtenay Trail:** .55 mile. Leads to Buckthorn Grove and air plant collection.
- **Elisha Camp Trail:** .30 mile. Usually dry. A trail guide, "Walk in the Wetlands," is available.
- **Sabal Palm Trail:** .47 mile. An all-weather ridge trail leading to the "Alligator Hole" and gopher tortoise habitat.
- **Center Road:** .32 mile. A dry wide path over swales leading to the Betty Mattheissen Observation Tower and Sanibel River.
- **Purslane Trail:** .12 mile. Occasionally wet trail crossing several other trails.
- **West River Trail:** .45 mile. Wet, but interesting. Alongside the Sanibel River.
- **Upper Ridge Trail:** .47 mile. Alternates between low and wet and high and dry.
- **Fern Trail:** .35 mile. Damp to wet. Good habitat for Cordgrass and leather ferns.
- **East River Trail:** .86 mile. Longest trail. Sand and boardwalk combination. Follows the river to overlook.
- **Middle Ridge Trail:** .26 mile. Usually dry. Diverse vegetation.

Trail conditions are posted on the boardwalk at the entrance to the trails. Watch for poison ivy. While here, take time to browse the native plant nursery next to the parking lot where the plants are for sale.

To reach Sanibel-Captiva Conservation Foundation from I-75 at Ft. Myers, take exit 21, Daniels Road, to Summerlin Road. Proceed left to the Sanibel Causeway ($3 round trip). Turn right onto Periwinkle Way at the four-way stop and go west to Tarpon Bay Road at the three-way stop. Head north to the junction of the Sanibel-Captiva Road, at the second three-way stop. Go left to the entrance of the Foundation, one mile west from Tarpon Bay Road at 3333 Sanibel-Captiva Road. The hours are from 9:30 a.m. to 4:30 p.m., Monday through Saturday, Thanksgiving to May, Monday through Friday from June to Thanksgiving.

Four Mile Cove Ecology Park
Cape Coral/Lee County
Trail Distance: 1 mile
Highlights: nature study, nature walk, observation tower, canoe trail, restrooms
Fee(s): seasonal canoe rental

Administered by the city of Cape Coral, the Four Mile "Eco" Park features a 3,700-foot boardwalk and 1,500-foot footpath that loops through three distinct habitats: black juncus rush marsh, mangrove swamp forest, and melaleuca-Australian pine woodland. Bordering the Caloosahatchee River, the park's atmosphere is currently one of tranquility, "far removed" from nearby Del Prado Boulevard, the "main street' of Cape Coral. A new river bridge to connect with Ft. Myers is to be constructed near here, however, so the peacefulness may not last.

The walk begins by the parking area. An interpretive shelter station includes a map and general information to orient you to the park. As you walk out onto the long boardwalk, you will be passing over and through a large stand of black rush marshland, one of the largest remaining in southwest Florida. The conspicuous plant life is labeled by wooden markers. Red, black and white mangroves, leather ferns, and black rush predominate. Near midpoint is the observation pier deck and canoe launch dock, with benches to rest and view the estuary.

Continue on the boardwalk towards the river through more rush areas and mangrove forest to the observation tower. Outstanding red mangroves specimens thrive in the river bottoms. The 32-foot tower is at the river's edge and offers views of the surrounding Ft. Myers and Cape Coral area just above the tree tops. Weekend summer canoe rentals are available at the riverside concession shed and pier near the observation tower. A canoe trail has been laid out, with three rain shelters at selected sites in Four Mile Cove, allowing canoeists to dock. Continue your walk on the footpath through a "down-under" forest of Australian pines or "beefwood" and Australian "cajeputs" or melaleuca. Both of these exotic trees have crowded and shaded out the existing native vegetation in places, but the shaded forest is sublime and peaceful. The trail loop ends at the parking lot where you began.

Four Mile Cove Ecology (or "Eco" Park) can be reached from I-75 in North Fort Myers by exiting west at Bayshore Road/S.R. 78. Go west on Bayshore across the Tamiami Trail/U.S. 41 where Bayshore Road becomes Pine Island Road. Continue to Del Prado Boulevard at the east edge of Cape Coral and turn south. Follow Del Prado Boulevard about three miles to S.E. 24th Street and turn east/left towards the river. Drive to the park entrance on the left side of the street. Parking is available for about 40 cars. The park is open from sunrise to 7 p.m.

Edison Winter Home
Ft. Myers/Lee County
Area: 14 acres
Highlights: botanical garden, museum, laboratory, Edison home, gift shop
Fee(s): entrance

Besides his numerous inventions, Thomas Alva Edison (1847-1931) developed one of the most extensive subtropical botanic gardens in the United States. A master horticulturist, Edison employed the various plant products and by-products from his practical, yet beautiful garden in scientific experiments.

The gardens contain more than 1,000 varieties of subtropical and tropical plants from around the world. Plant specialties include codiaeum and palms. A banyan tree brought from India by Harvey Firestone measures more than 400 feet in diameter, the largest in Florida and third largest in the world. Four national champion trees registered with the American Forestry Association are the largest of the species within the United States: a ligustrum or California privet, a Panama tree, a trumpet tree, and an African tulip tree.

Edison decided to buy the land after seeing giant bamboo growing along the shores of the Caloosahatchee River. Eventually, he would utilize the bamboo as electric light filaments. In other experiments, through hybridization, he arrived at a subspecies of goldenrod that served as a source of natural rubber. Edison was also responsible for the acquisition and planting of hundreds of stately Florida royal palms that line McGregor Boulevard in Ft. Myers today.

Continous tours of the gardens, his home, "Seminole Lodge," the museum and laboratory are conducted by guides. They explain the history of the two early prefabricated homes as well as telling of the many products and by-products produced from the unusual plants found in the garden.

Operated by the city of Ft. Myers, the Edison Winter Home is open Monday through Saturday from 9 a.m. to 5 p.m. Sunday hours are 12:30 p.m. to 4 p.m. The home is closed Christmas Day. To reach the Edison Winter Home exit west on Palm Beach Boulevard/S.R. 80 from I-75. Palm Beach Boulevard becomes First Street downtown. Continue on First Street to McGregor Boulevard and turn right, driving one block to the parking area on the left side of the boulevard. The address is 2350 McGregor Boulevard.

The Nature Center Of Lee County
Ft. Myers/Lee County
Area: 105 acres
Trail Distance: 5 miles
Highlights: nature study, nature walks, aviary, museum, planetarium, picnicking, special events, programs, gift shop, membership
Fee(s): entrance

A diversity of outdoor activities have been provided for the day visitor by the professional staff of this southwest Florida nature center. Two loop trails, each approximately a mile long, meander through the 105 acres of slash pine flatwoods and bald cypress swampland. A third, the Wildlands Trail, loops the perimeter of the property. The aviary trails begin at the nature center museum, planetarium, gift shop and offices where the visitor is oriented and can obtain a trail guide. The Audubon Society has erected an aviary that houses permanently injured birds. Specimens of Florida's poisonous snakes are on display in the museum.

Well-marked, the **Cypress Loop Trail** and the **Pine Loop Trail** wind through two different south Florida plant communities. The half-mile Cypress Loop Trail is mostly a well-constructed boardwalk that snakes around live oak, holly, and bald cypress groves with a variety of ferns as undergrowth. The wooden trail arrives mid-point at an observation platform overlooking a seasonal pond, mostly filled with swamp flag plants. Although the airport and freeway are nearby, the setting seems far removed from city surroundings. Veer left and follow the sign to Pine Loop Trail. Pine Loop frail is mostly a limestone and shell marl trail that passes along dry to seasonal wet pineland with numerous herbs, grasses, saw palmetto, and the dominant slash pine with an occasional red maple. The trail ends at the aviary.

The three-mile **Wildlands Trail** begins at station 28 on the northwest boardwalk section of Pine Loop Trail. Blue painted triangular blazes appear evenly-spaced along the wooded lowlands section of the trail. This one-mile section will be seasonably wet and tree stubs and cypress require careful walking. From the wooded section the trail emerges out onto a spoil bank alongside a drainage canal and across from a golf course. Follow the unmarked but obvious path back to the nature center.

To reach the Nature Center of Lee County from I-75 at Fort Myers, exit 22 west on Colonial Boulevard. From Colonial Boulevard drive west about a half-mile to the first stoplight and turn right/north onto Ortiz Avenue. The center entrance is about a quarter-mile on the left/west side of Ortiz Avenue. Parking for 50 vehicles is available. The museum and gift shop bours are 9 a.m. to 4 p.m. Tuesday through Saturday. Sunday hours are from 11 a.m. to 4:30 p.m. The planetarium has scheduled shows Wednesday through Sunday. The grounds are open until sunset.

Six Mile Cypress Slough Preserve
Ft. Myers/Lee County
Area: 2,000 acres
Trail Distance: 6,300 ft. of boardwalk
Highlights: nature walk, picnickings shelters, amphitheatre, photography blind, fishing, nature study, restrooms
Fee(s): entrance

This Lee County wetland park is easily accessible, with over a mile of elevated boardwalk that penetrates the heart of a slough. The nature walker is exposed to five distinct slough plant and animal communities: pine flatwoods, hardwood transition, flag pond, hammock, and cypress slough. Specific wetland areas within the slough include Ibis Marsh, Gator Lake, Wood Duck, Otter, and Pop Ash ponds. Throughout this pond cypress and mixed hardwood forested strand, a variety of orchids, ferns, mammals, birds, fish, insects, reptiles and amphibians make the wetland their home. Six Mile Cypress Slough is popular as an outdoor education site for area school groups.

Greatly reduced in size from what it once was, the nine-mile-long and half-mile-wide slough is like a slow moving stream whose waters flow southwest to join with Estero Bay. The place name has nothing to do with size but arises from the fact it was six miles east of Fort Myers. If you are adventuresome and don't mind getting wet, a loop trail passes through a stand of pond cypress across Penzance Road from the preserve's parking lot. The Six Mile Cypress Slough was purchased by Lee County and the South Florida Water Management District through the Save Our Rivers Program. Future plans include additional land purchases. A detailed boardwalk explorers' companion brochure is available that interprets the marked stations along the walk.

The preserve's hours are 8 a.m. to 5 p.m. To reach the preserve from I-75 exit 22 west on Colonial Boulevard and drive about one mile to the first stoplight and Six Mile Cypress Parkway. Turn left/south and drive about three miles to Penzance Road, where you turn left/east to the parking entrance. The preserve is easily spotted from the parkway. It can also be accessed from exit 21 west on Daniels Parkway to Six Mile Cypress Parkway going north two miles.

Lakes Park
Ft. Myers/Lee County
Area: 279 acres
Trail Distance: 3 miles total
Highlights: nature study, nature trail, vita course, swimming, lifeguards, picnicking, shelter, bicycling, fishing, boat marina, boat rental, amphitheatre, observation tower, playfield, concessions, restrooms, camping
Fees: entrance, boat rental, group shelter reservations

The Lakes Park, a Lee County facility, is a reclamation and recreational success story. The 279 acres now occupied by the water-oriented park were operated as a limestone rock excavation pit during the 1960's. It was abandoned, earth-torn and scarred, but melaleuca and Australian pines gained a foothold and became well-established in the disturbed area surrounding the man-made lakes. With foresight and funding, Lee County purchased the wasteland. Publicly dedicated in 1984, the once barren landscape was transformed into a highly active recreational parkland, set in a passive exotic woodland.

For the nature walker, there are three miles of paved trails including a two-mile fitness course with numerous exercise stations. An observation tower surveys the watery paradise and picnic grounds and a wide boardwalk spans an unnamed lake. On the opposite west shore, a loop trail passes through a remnant oak-palm hammock. For the fishermen, there are more than 150 acres of interlocking freshwater lakes stocked with bass and brim. Boats can be rented for fishing and pleasure at the marina. For the beach lover and swimmer, there is 900 feet of imported sugar sand. For the picnicker, there are 50 picnic tables with grills and 14 picnic shelter pavilions. For the camper, there is a 40-acre first-class camping area. There seems to be something for nearly every outdoor recreationist. Recent proposals include a botanic garden, plant clinic, aviary, children's petting zoo, and historic village.

To reach Lakes Park from I-75, take the Daniels Road exit west to Tamiami Trail/U.S. 41 and turn south. Continue south on Tamiami Trail to Gladiolus Drive/S.R. 865 and turn west. Drive directly to the park entrance at 14561 Gladiolus Drive. The park hours are from 10 a.m. to 6 p.m. during the winter months, and 10 a.m. to 8 p.m. during the summer, Thursday through Monday (10 a.m. to 6 p.m. Tuesday and Wednesday).

Everglades Wonder Gardens
Bonita Springs/Lee County
Area: 4.5 acres
Highlights: nature study, zoological and botanical garden, gift shop
Fee(s): entrance

The time-worn, slightly sensational, red and white signs advertising the Everglades Wonder Gardens line the roadsides of Collier and Lee Counties, giving notice to motorists seeking entertainment under the Florida sun. Despite the "Burma Shave" approach, this educational private zoo in the heart of Bonita Springs contains a nucleus of common and rare fauna indigenous to southern Florida, and particularly to the Everglades. The gardens have been in business for nearly 50 years and many of the animals were actually captured in the wild.

Either with a guide or on your own, you will see many animals that are difficult or almost impossible to view in the wild. Rare inhabitants include the Florida black bear, Florida panther, and saltwater

American crocodile

Florida crocodiles. Successful breeding programs are in progress for the Florida panther and the Florida crocodile. Other natives within this Everglade microcosm are the bobcat, southern bald eagle, 30 species of snakes, alligators, roseate spoonbill, wild boar, white-tail deer, otters and numerous mammals, reptiles, and birds from other parts of the world. Be sure to bring a flash and high speed film if you plan to take photographs. The subtropical and tropical fruit tree collection produces heavy shade in the gardens. In the gift shop numerous natural history exhibits are on display.

To reach the Wonder Gardens from I-75, take the Bonita Springs exit west to the Tamiami Trail/U.S. 41 and turn north. Proceed through town. The gardens will be on the west side of the road just past the Imperial River Bridge. They are open 9 a.m. to 5 p.m. daily.

The Conservancy Big Cypress Nature Center
Naples/Collier County
Area: 13,5 acres
Trail Distance: 3 trails total 0.5 mile
Highlights: nature study, nature trail, aviary, museum, boat trips, education programs, gift shop, membership
The Big Cypress Nature Center is an outstanding environmental education facility centrally located in Naples. Established in 1959,

the nature center is an educational, scientific, cultural, and recreational institution dedicated to instilling in visitors an appreciation for the natural environments of south Florida.

Three short, well-maintained, self-guiding nature walks loop their way around hardwood hammock, pine flatwood, tidewater lagoon and along the mangrove-lined Gordon River. Along the trails are interpretive signs to enhance your outdoor experience. Boardwalks connect the trails and the handsome wooden buildings. There is a walkway to a gazebo which overlooks a tidal lagoon.

Besides nature walks, the center offers a natural history museum, aviary, guided boat trips (December through March), natural history library, wild animal hospital, family and children's programs, gift shop and bookstore, 350-seat auditorium, interpretive services, and various field trips. Information about the nature center and membership is available at the reception desk.

To reach the Big Cypress Nature Center from the Tamiami Trail/U.S. 41 in Naples, take the Goodlette Road/S.R. 851 north to 14th Avenue and turn east. The Nature Center entrance is at the end of 14th Avenue North on the left side of the street at 1450 Merrihue Drive. Hours are 9 a.m. to 5 p.m. Monday through Saturday.

Inland Florida

"The world of small wild things - be they plant or animal - needs a leisurely approach, the time to look carefully and closely at a spider web, at a leaf covered with hairs, at a vivid butterfly clinging to a flower."

Charlotte Orr Gantz, *A Naturalist in Southern Florida*

"For all such things were on earth before us, and will survive after us, and it is given to us to join ourselves with them and to be comforted."

Marjorie Kinnan Rawlings, *Cross Creek*

It was the uninhabited interior of 19th century southern Florida that the Seminole Indians fled to and where they made their stand against the American armies. This remote and seemingly hostile territory offered sanctuary to a people who had learned by trial and error the unique natural ways of the mysterious landscape. This was the world the American pioneers eventually claimed and whose lifestyle is so keenly described in Marjorie Kinnan Rawling's classic works, *The Yearling* and *Cross Creek*. Physically removed from the populated coastal regions, the present day southern Florida interior, or the "Other Florida," still offers areas of wildness and isolated wilderness to those who seek it along the miles of accessible foot trails.

The nature walks are as diverse as the various ecosystems they traverse. Temperate, subtropical, and tropical meet and mix in southern Florida, giving validity to the statement that Florida has more habitats, flora, and fauna than any other part of the continental United States. The inland region is geographically divided into southeast and southwest Florida by U.S. 27, running north and south through the interior's midsection.

Central Florida, north of Lake Okeechobee, offers outstanding areas of virgin hardwood hammocks, marshlands, prairies, and sandy pinelands at Highlands Hammock, Myakka River, and Kissimmee State parklands. The Hillsborough River valley features a string of parks along its upper reaches. Lithia Springs is a special place with its beautiful and warm spring waters. Several county park systems maintain excellent nature-oriented parks such as Morgan Park in DeSoto County, Harney Pond in Glades County, and Alderman's Ford in Hillsborough County. State nature preserves include Fakahatchee Strand. Several privately maintained preserves include the Audubon Society's Corkscrew Swamp Sanctuary, The Conservancy's Stephen F. Briggs Memorial, Florida Power and Light's Barley Barber Swamp, and The Nature Conservancy's Tiger Creek. Excellent day hikes are found at Collier-Seminole State Park and Jonathan Dickinson State Park. Florida Trail sections follow the wilderness of the Big Cypress, and the dike shores of Lake Okeechobee north. FTA membership is recommended and deemed necessary for private property crossings.

South of Lake Okeechobee lies the watery region of the Big Cypress Swamp and the Everglades. Bald and pond cypress dominate the swamplands of the Big Cypress National Preserve where trails meander along the higher ground of pine islands. The Everglades National Park is virtually a "river of grass" that separates the Atlantic coast from the western pinelands, grasslands, and marshes of the Big Cypress National Preserve. Both the Big Cypress and the Everglades National Parklands are most outstanding for their abundance and variety of wildlife and they provide the richest natural experiences in southern Florida.

Inland Florida has the added attraction of being off the beaten track. The best time of year to travel the area is during the winter months from December to March, when the daytime temperatures are 60-70° and the trails are normally drier. Heat, humidity, insects and water-covered trails during the late spring, summer, and fall months are overwhelming for most. In many of these areas you will encounter few people.

Among the recommended basic tips for hikers: always tell someone where you are going and when you plan to return; hike with a friend if possible; check the weather forecast; and wear proper clothing. Problems can happen unexpectedly: accidents, getting lost, a snake bite. The old Boy Scout motto still applies: Be Prepared. Weather will be the most important factor. Hot weather hiking will increase the risk of heat stroke and exhaustion, so bring plenty of water or water purification tablets. Wear a hat and sunscreen to protect the head and face, light colored cotton clothing, and avoid the hottest time of day. Be sure your footwear is comfortable. Day hikers will want to include in their day pack a knife, map, butane lighter, raingear, first aid, fruit and other high energy foods. Backpackers, of course, will want to include more items, such as sleeping gear, toilet articles, and other personal needs to make the overnights as enjoyable as possible. Trails will vary from well-maintained, wide, dry, and smooth to rarely maintained, narrow, wet, muddy, and rough.

The interior of southern Florida is by no means untouched by civilization. Agriculture and urban development have taken their toll of the primeval wilderness and the wildlife it once sheltered. Only remnants exist of the vast majestic pine forests, virgin cypress stands, swamplands and glades. Allow your walks through this special region of North America to stimulate your mind, body, and spirit.

Inland/Southeast

Bull Creek Wildlife Management Area
Holopaw/Osceola County
USGS Map(s): Deer Park 1:24,000
Trail Distance: 22 miles total
Highlights: hiking, nature study, primitive camping, seasonal hunting

The **Bull Creek Loop** section of the Florida Trail allows hikers to experience a variety of central Florida habitats along the orange-blazed (both ways) pathway. Sabal palm hammocks, cypress domes, floodplain, scrub oak, sand pine scrub, hardwood swamps, wet and dry prairies are encountered along old roads, firebreaks, and old railroad grade beds. The vast acreage was once exploited for timber, turpentine, and cattle grazing, so most of the trail was created by logging and farm industries. Today the Florida Game and Fresh Water Commission leases the wildlife management area from one owner, the St. Johns River Water Management District.

There are two trailhead access points. One is at Levee 73 which is 14.5 miles west of I-95 at Melbourne along U.S. 192/S.R. 500 on the left/south side of the highway, where parking is available just west

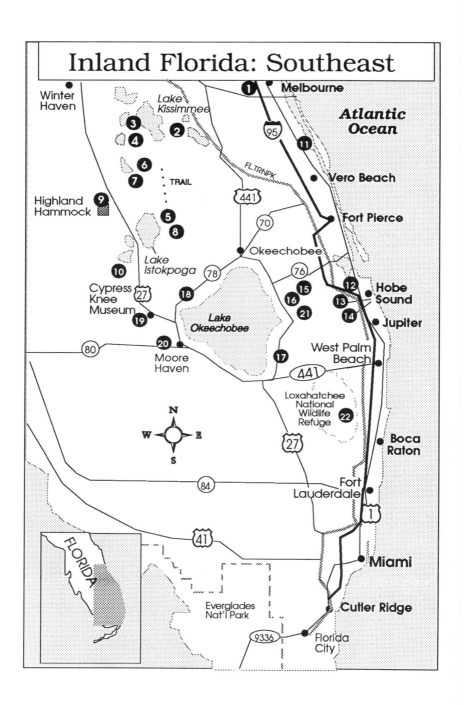

Inland Florida: Southeast

of the levee. Please register at the registration box. It is nearly 4.5 miles hike one-way to reach the **Crabgrass Road trail**, with second trail access via the levee southeast, then west across Crabgrass Creek and the floodplain, and then south along an old tram road. This route would be about nine miles longer than the Crabgrass Road access alone.

The second trailhead access route is from Crabgrass Road. To reach Crabgrass Road from I-95 exit west on U.S. 192/S.R. 500 and drive 19 miles (about 4.5 miles beyond Levee 73) to Crabgrass Road on the left/south side of the highway. Continue six miles south and east on Crabgrass Road (dirt road) to the dead end trailhead, parking, and hunter/hiker check station, where there is a registration bulletin board. Potable water is available at the primitive North camp site. A permit is required to camp, as is the case in nearly all wildlife management areas, and permits are available from the Florida Game and Fresh Water Commission, 1239 SW 10th Street, Ocala, Florida 32674; telephone (904) 732-1225. Include your date of visit, vehicle license number and choice of campsite. Trail hikers do not need to purchase the $25 WMA stamp to visit Bull Creek or any other WMA that has the Florida Trail passing through their property.

1. Bull Creek Wildlife Management Area
2. Prairie Lakes/Three Lakes Wildlife Management Area
3. Lake Kissimmee State Park
4. Tiger Creek Nature Preserve
5. Kissimmee River National Scenic Trail
6. Lake Arbuckle National Recreational Trail
7. Avon Park Bombing & Gunnery Range
8. Hickory Hammock/Florida Trail
9. Highlands Hammock State Park
10. Archbold Biological Station
11. Donald Macdonald Park/Dale Wimbrow Park
12. Hobe Sound Nature Center/National Wildlife Refuge
13. Jonathan Dickinson State Park
14. St. Lucie Lock and Dam
15. Barley Barber Swamp
16. Dupuis Reserve State Forest
17. Lake Okeechobee Dike/Levee Trail
18. Harney Pond Recreation Area
19. Cypress Knee Museum
20. Ortona Indian Mound Park
21. J.W. Corbett Wildlife Management Area
22. Arthur R. Marshall Loxahatchee National Wildlife Refuge

From the Crabgrass Road access and trailhead, the trail heads southeast 0.8 mile to join the 17-mile loop. The trail heads east and south on the loop road trail to join and rejoin with an old railroad bed that follows the west perimeter of the Bull Creek floodplain. A second permit-required campground, Little Scrub Camp, lies nine miles from the junction of Loop Road and Crabgrass Road and no water is available. The south portion of Bull Creek Trail is desert-like, with habitats of sand pine and oak scrub. The western section is prairie and pine flatwoods punctuated with cypress dome stands. Be prepared for wading during the rainy season, especially along the eastern section of the loop trail.

Prairie Lakes/Three Lakes Wildlife Management Area
Kenansville/Osceola County
USGS Maps: Kenansville, Lake Marian NE, Lake Marian NW, Lake Marian SW, 1:24,000
Area: 45,303 acres
Trail Distance: 3 trails total 37 miles
Highlights: hiking, nature study, fishing, seasonal hunting, primitive camping

Hikers will not need the $25 wildlife management stamp to enter and hike this vast reserve but, if camping overnight, you will need to obtain a camping permit from the FG&FWFC central Florida administrative office in Ocala (see Bull Creek Trail for address). Day hikers will enjoy the figure-eight loop trails that total some 10.5 miles or segments of the longer linear Florida Trail that runs northwest to southwest – a distance of 26.6 miles.

The Prairie Lakes Unit within the Three Lakes WMA comprises over 8,000 acres of low and flat prairie, pine flatwoods, marshes, cypress domes, and live oak-sabal palm hammocks. The preserve's landscape is shaped by seasonal flooding and drought, and peri- odically by fire. The marshes and wet prairies of the rainy summer season become the dry prairies of the normally dry winter months. Induced controlled burning maintains the distinct prairie flora and eliminates the takeover by hardwood plants. The sandhill crane, burrowing owl, and Audubon's caracara are at home in these open grasslands.

The Florida Trail Association has constructed two loop trails which total 10.5 miles, both of nearly equal distance. Both trails also have camping sites with outdoor pit toilets and pitcher pumps that will need to be primed to obtain the untreated water. Hiking here anytime is bound to be a near-solitary experience. Do expect to get your feet wet even during the dry winter season.

The **North Loop** passes through all the aforementioned habitats, especially wet and dry prairies. A primitive tent campsite exists at Parker Hammock. Backpackers should begin their hike at least two hours before sunset to establish camp. The South Loop is mostly hiking through shaded oak-palm bammocks. Backpackers heading to Dry Pond primitive campsite should begin their hike two hours before sunset. If the wind is just right, you can smell the waters of Lake Jackson and Lake Marian, but never see their shores on the **South Loop Trail**. Both trails are well marked with white blazes in both directions. Trail spurs to campsites are blazed in blue.

The Prairie Lakes Unit of Three Lakes WMA is located nine miles north of Kenansville, Florida on S.R. 523/Canoe Creek Road. Go north from S.R. 60 at Yeebaw Junction on U.S. 441 or south from St.

Parker Hammock Camp

Cloud on U.S. 192/441. The preserve's hours are from 8 a.m. to sunset.

For those who prefer a greater hiking challenge, the **Three Lakes Trail**, a non-looping 26.6-mile path, runs the entire length of the wildlife management area. From northwest to southwest, the trail traverses old roads, firelanes, jeep trails, spoil banks, railroad beds, under the toll road overpass, adjacent to and on an unimproved road (Williams Road), past U.S. 441 and connecting portions of the Prairie Lakes loop trails. Habitats encountered include: sabal palm and hardwood hammocks, wet and dry prairies, cypress domes, pinelands and palmetto scrub, and wetlands.

The northwest trailhead terminus is located along U.S. 441 approximately 1.5 miles north of the hunter check station or 8.3 miles north of Kenansville on the left side of the road across from Fontana Lane. The south trailhead terminus is an access road located at S.R. 60, 4.5 miles east of the Kissimmee River bridge, 14.5 miles west of Yeehaw Junction, Florida.

There are five evenly-spaced campsites along the 26.6-mile trail route. A camping permit is required. Designated backpack camp-

Cypress Dome

ing is not permitted during the hunting season. All water sources need to be purified.

Lake Kissimmee State Park
Lake Wales/Polk County
Area: 5,030 acres
Trail Distance: 13 miles total
Highlights: nature study, hiking, observation tower, picnicking, shelters, fishing, boat ramp, playground, 1876 frontier "cow camp," camping
Fees: entrance, camping

Lake Kissimmee State Park's 5,030 acres forms a portion of the headwaters of the Everglades. The park is nearly encircled by three lakes: Rosalie, Tiger, and Kissimmee. Within its boundaries the flat terrain of the Osceola Plain features seasonal ponds, swamps, floodplain prairies and marshes, live oak-sabal palm hammocks, and pine flatwoods. The diverse natural communities and habitats provide scenic variety to the outdoor experience.

Wildlife is abundant. Thirty-one different mammals have been sighted and recorded, including the marsh rabbit, longtail weasel, mink, gray fox, river otter, bobcat, white-tailed deer, bat, and the Florida panther. Largemouth bass, catfish, bluegill, sunfish, killifish, gar, bullfish, and warmouth are commonly found in the freshwater lakes. Sandhill cranes, scrub jays, pileated woodpeckers, vireos, warblers, hawks, wild turkeys, ospreys, bald eagles, and the very rare Audubon's caracara are but a few of the birds encountered along the trails. The Florida Trail Association in cooperation with the Department of Natural Resources has nearly 13 miles of trail on two loop walks: The **Buster Island Loop** and the **North Loop and Gobler Ridge Spur.**

Named after a Seminole Indian, Billy Buster, the Buster Loop (six to seven miles round trip) passes through three wilderness preserve habitats: dry prairie, pineland scrub, and live oak-sabal palm hammock. Bald eagles nest here in winter. Primitive camping is available at Buster Island Campground (three miles from trailhead), but you will need to bring your own water. In order to establish camp, it is recommended that you begin your hike three hours before sunset. The site is limited to 12 people. The same rules apply to Fallen Oak Campground (also three miles from trailhead) on North Loop Trail.

The North Loop Trail (five to nine miles round trip) is not as remote. The trail passes through more pinelands and pine flatwoods and you will cross the main park road four times. The Gobler Ridge Spur (2.2 miles round trip) leads to the shoreline of Lake Kissimmee through live oak-savannah grassland. Gobler Ridge is a name given to the sandy ridge along the shore of the lake and was created by storm winds and pounding wave action over the centuries. Both trails are blazed and easy to follow. U.S.G.S. quadrangle maps 1:24,000 include Lake Weohyakapka NE, and Hesperides.

Near the parking lot where the loop hiking trails begin, is the short **Flatwoods Pond Nature Trail**. The quarter-mile loop encircles a seasonal pond that is typical of the landscape. At the picnic grounds is an observation tower that provides clear views of Lake Kissimmee on the horizon.

A special feature of the park is the living history, 1876 frontier "cow camp," complete with scrub cows descended from the Spanish Andalusian cattle in a holding pen, a "cow hunter" dog, a horse equipped with McClellan saddle and a pot of strong, unfiltered

White tail deer, Lake Kissimmee State Park

coffee. The cow camp tours are provided on Saturday, Sunday, and holidays from 9:30 a.m. to 4:30.

To reach Lake Kissimmee State Park (about 14 miles northwest of the city of Lake Wales), take U.S. 27 to Lake Wales and head east on S.R. 60 about eight miles to Boy Scout Road. Turn north on Boy Scout Road and Barney Keene Road, then drive 3.7 miles to Camp Mack Road. Turn east and drive 5.6 miles to the park entrance on the south side of the road at 14248 Camp Mack Road. The park opens at 7 a.m. and closes at sunset daily.

Tiger Creek Nature Preserve
Lake Wales/Polk County
Area: 4,500 acres
Trail Distance: 12 miles
Highlights: nature study,hiking

Since 1968, The Nature Conservancy bas been acquiring land in the Tiger Creek area southeast of Lake Wales – the Ridge section of central Florida. One-third of all Florida's native tree and shrub varieties are found in the preserve. The sanctuary serves as a buffer for over eight miles of the pristine blackwater Tiger Creek which is home for 15 of the state's rarest species, such as the fleet-footed scrub lizard, the striking pygmy fringe tree, and the colorful flower called bonamia. In addition, the river otter, muskrat, armadillo, osprey, wood duck, opossum, raccoon, red and gray fox, white-tailed deer, and bobcat make their home here. The preserve is open to the public daily during daylight hours.

Several marked nature trails have been designated in the north and south sections of the preserve. To reach the north section from Lake Wales take U.S. 27 to S.R. 60 east. Go east on S.R. 60 and drive about 10 miles to Lake Walk-in-the-Water Road and turn south. Proceed three miles or so on Walk-in-the-Water Road to Wakeford Road. Turn east on Wakeford Road and drive to where the road dead ends. This is the entrance of Tiger Creek Preserve, where you can park.

Basically there are five interconnecting trails that loop through the north section, totalling about four miles. The **Cary Bok/Morrison Trail** is a half-mile loop walk that follows a sand pine ridge and descends to the spring-fed waters of Tiger Creek.

The Allston Jenkins Trail is a loop walk of about 1.5 miles that passes along the banks and floodplain of the tranquil stream. Follow The Nature Conservancy's markers that appear along the trail.

North and west of the Jenkins loop trail is the non-looping **Carter Hill Trail** that leads through Dry Pond and eventually the short interconnecting **Hammock Trail**, a total of about two miles round trip.

To reach the south portion of the preserve from Lake Wales take Alt. U.S. 27 south 3.5 miles to Babson Park Audubon Nature Center, just north of Webber College at North Crooked Lake Drive. A map of the preserve and additional information is available here. From the Audubon Nature Center go south 1.5 miles and turn east on Murray Road. Follow Murray Road 2.2 miles to Pfundstein Road. Go left on Pfundstein to the first utility pole on the left side of the road. Four trails start here. The **George R. Cooley Trail** is a 30-45-minute loop through a small hickory and oak scrub, a cut-throat grass seep, and on to a point on Patrick Creek. A short side trail dead ends in the hardwood swamp. The **Florida Trail**, **Patrick Creek Overlook** and the **Highlands Loop** actually begin further east a short distance at the first clay road to the left/north side of Pfundstein Road. The parking area is about 200 yards from the road going north. To access these trails follow through on the left side of the gate. Go downhill 100 feet and take a sharp left. Follow the orange blazes. Actually the Florida Trail and Patrick Creek Overlook are one. If you continue to follow the Florida Trail it will lead to Patrick Creek Overlook which is a 30-45 minute one-way hike. If you continue on the Florida Trail for 45-60 minutes you will reach Highland Loop Trail. The loop takes two hours. Allow four-six hours for the entire hike.

The Catfish Creek Preserve is also in the Lake Wales area. Although no trails are established, the property is open to the public. From Lake Wales go north on Alt. U.S. 27 to Lake Hamilton and turn right/east onto C.R. 542. Drive 8.2 miles on C.R. 542 to the junction with Firetower Road and turn right/south. Proceed 4.6 miles to a F.F.A. lodge and park. The preserve occupies the east shore of Lake Pierce.

The Nature Conservancy is a national conservation organization whose objective is the preservation and protection of environmentally significant land and the plants and animals that depend on it for survival. To achieve its goal, the Conservancy purchases lands using its revolving fund, which is then replenished through fund raising. It accepts gifts of land and retains and protects those lands in advance of governmental agencies' ability to do so. For further information contact The Nature Conservancy, 225 East Stuart Avenue, Lake Wales, Florida 33853; telephone (813) 675-1551.

Kissimmee River National Scenic Trail
Highlands & Polk Counties
USGS Maps: Ft. Kissimmee 1:24,000, Ft. Kissimmee NW 1:24,000, Lake Marian SW 1:24,000
Trail Distance: 30.8 miles
Highlights: biking, nature study, camping, seasonal hunting

The remote one-way hiking path follows the west bank of the Kissimmee River through a rich variety of natural habitats and historical sites. Nearly 20 miles of the trail passes tbrough some of the most beautiful oak hammock in Florida. Three historical sites are found along the route and include Old Fort Kissimmee, the ghost town of Kicco, headquarters of the Kissimmee Island Cattle Company, and the old Rattlesnake Hammock homestead of Owen Godwin, founder of Gatorland.

Twelve miles of the scenic trail passes through the Avon Park bombing range where camping and hiking restrictions do apply. Upon entering and leaving the property, sign in and out for your own protection. Do not hike solo through the bombing range and do not leave the blazed trail. During the general hunting season campsites are off-limits to hikers on the Air Force property (there are four campsites along the trail).

The south trailhead and parking terminus begins at the north dead end of Bluff Hammock Road just south of canal lock S65B. Bluff Hammock Road access is about a mile east of Lorida, Florida along U.S. 98 in Highlands County. From U.S. 98 and Bluff Hammock Road drive about four miles north to the trailhead where you may also camp (no permit required). The north trailhead access is adjacent to S.R. 60, 19 miles west of Yeebaw Junction and seven miles east of Indian River Estates, just west of the Kissimmee River bridge. It is suggested you drive from S.R. 60 about five miles south on the River Ranch Road to the Kicco Wildlife Management Area to park, and where free camping is permitted.

Significant sites enroute, north to south, include the following: S65 Lock & Spillway, Sheep Hammock, Wildcat Hammock, River Ranch Resort, Long Hammock, Daugherty Hammock, Rattlesnake Hammock, Kicco Site, Camp Hammock, Orange Hammock, Fort Kissimmee, Burnt Hammock, Hicks Slough and S65B Lock.

Lake Arbuckle National Recreational Trail, Avon Park Bombing & Gunnery Range
Avon Park/Polk and Highlands Counties
USGS Maps: Lake Arbuckle 1:24,000, Lake Arbuckle NE 1:24,000
Trail Distance: 15 miles
Highlights: hiking, nature study, picnicking, shelters, fishing, boat ramp, seasonal hunting

Hiking the Lake Arbuckle Loop is not recommended for those who prefer a free come-and-go arrangement. To hike this Florida Trail requires that you contact the Avon Park Bombing Range at (813) 452-4119 to determine if there are any restrictions on the day or days of your hike. Hunting season accounts for most restrictions. On the eve of your hike, final permission must be obtained from the Security Police, (813) 452-4195. Check with Security Police at Building 425 before entering and leaving. These restrictions are necessary because the bombing range is an active military training base and a popular hunting preserve. Don't be surprised to hear and see mock bombing runs during your hike.

Lake Arbuckle National Recreational Trail extends 15 miles within Avon Park Bombing Range, which is on S.R. 64, 10 miles east of the city of Avon Park in Highlands County. The Air Force gate on S.R. 64 at the south end of Lake Arbuckle is the only entrance and exit for the public. The trail passes through typical central Florida terrain: a mixture of pine-palmetto flatland, oak and hardwood hammock, a commercial pine forest, and marshy floodplain. Grazing cattle may be spotted along the way. Wildlife is abundantly visible if you walk quietly.

Proceeding clockwise from Camp Willingham campsite and parking area (the live oak grove also offers picnicking and restrooms), you will come upon the historic Fort Arbuckle site, now marked by a well with a hand pump. The mid-point campsite has a potable well and an old cattle dipping vat close by. Hikers should not pick up any devices for they may be explosives dropped from military training aircraft. The best portion of the hike may be the first three miles where the blazed trail passes through high and dry pinelands and oak groves. The remainder of the trail is subject to seasonal flooding.

There is a short nature trail enroute to Camp Willingham that leads to Lake Arbuckle. This is mostly boardwalk with labelled trees. Boats may put in on Lake Arbuckle just outside the entrance to the bombing range. Fishing and birding is excellent on this undeveloped natural lake.

Catwalk, Lake Arbuckle Loop

Hickory Hammock/Florida Trail
Lorida/Highlands County
U.S.G.S. Maps: Basinger NW 1:24,000
Trail Distance: 7.5 miles one-way
Highlights: hiking, nature study, backpacking, camping

The Hickory Hammock hiking trail is ideal for day use or over-night tent camping. Thanks to the trail blazing efforts of the Florida Trail Association, hikers may enjoy this large Save Our Rivers Tract that is administered by the South Florida Water Management District. The property is part of a vast acreage dedicated to restoring the natural flow of the nearby Kissimmee River.

The trailhead, parking, and registration box are located on the north side of U.S. 98 about halfway between Lorida and Cornwell, Florida, roughly 0.4 mile west of the Istokpoga Canal. A marked topographic map of the trail and property plus additional information is also available. The orange-blazed trail heads north across abandoned pasture studded with live oak and sabal palm. The shade of the trees is welcome even in winter and the leaf litter makes a fine soft trail surface. Birding is excellent due to the combination of open grassland and forest. A marked tent campsite is about two miles from the trailhead. Hickory Hammock is further north and west of an abandoned farm. The trail and hammock continue west to a small stream crossing.

After crossing the stream the trail becomes a straight path through an open cattle pasture for about two miles. The walking in this area is considered the most difficult of the entire hike as it heads towards Bluff Hammock Road and the end of the 7.5-mile trail. Hikers may want to consider returning to the original trailhead at the stream crossing since the rest of the trek becomes strenuous and monotonous. There is no trailhead parking at Bluff Hammock Road, only hiking access. Incidentally, at the north dead end of Bluff Hammock Road is the southern terminus of the 27-mile Florida National Scenic Trail. It follows the Kissimmee River north to terminate at S.R. 60 and the S-65 Lock and Spillway.

Hickory Hammock hiking trail lies between Sebring and Okeechobee, Florida on U.S. 98 and is accessed from U.S. 27 or S.R. 70.

Highlands Hammock State Park
Sebring/Highlands County
Area: 3,800 acres
Trail Distance: 3.3 miles total
Highlights: nature study, nature trails, interpretive center, playground, bicycling, tram tours, concessions, camping
Fees: entrance, bicycle rentals, tram tours, camping

Highlands Hammock State Park has the distinction of being the first state park in Florida, established in 1931. Preoccupied with the sincere desire to preserve an ancient oak-sabal hammock from agriculture, Margaret Shippen Roebling led the effort to establish the state park. The Civilian Conservation Corps developed the park for public use during the 1930's.

Nine separate short trails are interspersed and nearly interconnected through the park. The best place to begin your walk is the interpretive center, where you can park your car. The 2,929-foot **Wild Orange Trail** heads up on the south side of the concession building, opposite the interpretive center. Wild orange tree escapees from pioneer days will be spotted in the understory of the pristine bay forest. The path is wet in places. The trail does not loop, but arrives at the main park road and crosses to the Big Oak Trail.

The 975-foot **Big Oak Trail** harbors enormous live oaks that are over 1,000 years old. The interconnecting, 2,196-foot **Hickory Trail** features a fine stand of hardwoods that include basswood, sweetgum, laurel oak, pignut hickory, and mockernut hickory. There is a catwalk section. The Hickory Trail arrives at the main park road once again, crossing over to the **Fern Garden Trail**. This 1,641-foot trail is a circular or loop catwalk through a hardwood

Wild Orange Trail

swamp where many varieties of wild and domestic ferns thrive. The adjacent **Richard Lieber Memorial Trail** of 1,624 feet is named for the "Father of the Indiana Park System," who had visited Highlands Hammock during the 1930's and offered helpful advice. The trail enters a tranquil hardwood swamp via a catwalk to arrive at a rest point with benches. Retrace your steps and follow the trail spur back to the main park road. Continue west/left along the park road about 60 yards to the Young Hammock Trail.

The 2,954-foot **Young Hammock Trail** traverses a slash pine forest that, without the aid of fire, would gradually become a hardwood hammock. A trail brochure with information on the numbered stations is available at the trail head. Along the main park road, you will encounter the largest sabal palm in the state of Florida.

The **Cypress Swamp Trail** of 2,355 feet is probably the most popular walk of the park. Twenty interpretive markers line the catwalk, explaining the life of the cypress swamp and Little Charley Bowlegs Creek. Rest benches have been provided at intervals along the narrow catwalk which, like the park road, is one-way.

The **Ancient Hammock Trail** is 3,005 feet. This is probably the hammock that inspired Margaret Shippen Roebling to preserve

Hickory Trail

the park. A memorial to her is nearby along the park road. This is the finest example of virgin hardwood hammock in the state. Continue your walk on the park road to the "T" junction and the orange grove, then go right back to the Wild Orange Trail and the interpretive center parking area.

The newest walking path, the quarter-mile **Alden Altvater Trail**, loops through pine flatwoods. It is just north of the ranger entrance station, south of the recreation hall.

To reach Highlands Hammock State Park, take U.S. 27 to Sebring, Florida and turn west onto C.R. 634. The park entrance is three miles from the junction of U.S. 27 and C.R. 634 west. Plan to spend an entire day or camp overnight. The park hours are 8 a.m. to sunset throughout the year.

Archbold Biological Station
Lake Placid/Highlands County
Area: 4,250 acres
Trail Distance: half-mile nature trail; 20 miles of firelanes
Highlights: nature study, hiking. Permission required in advance before visitation.
Fee(s): donations requested for land acquisition fund

The Archbold Biological Station, a non-profit biological research institution, was founded by Richard Archbold in 1941. The staff, research associates, and visiting scientists from many prestigious universities and associations conduct research in the areas of vertebrate and invertebrate ecology, plant and aquatic ecology. The principal focus of the staff research program is the ecology of the Highlands area of southcentral Florida.

The biological station is on the south edge of the Lake Wales Ridge of Central Florida. The area contains a broad range of natural habitats such as the southern ridge sandhill association, sand pine scrub, scrubby flatwoods, low flatwoods, bay tree forests, and swales. Aquatic habitats on the main property include 90-acre Lake Annie, a small sinkhole pond, numerous seasonal ponds, and several ditches. The number of species so far recorded on the station property includes 13 fishes, 54 amphibians and reptiles, 142 birds, 36 mammals, 350 vascular plants and more than 1,500 insects and other invertebrates.

The first stop during your visit is the office, located at the south end of the building complex on the right or west side. A video presentation surveys the history and mission of the station. A self-guiding nature trail booklet is also available to further understanding of the surrounding natural communities. The marked nature trail loops through the Florida oak scrub directly behind the office, dining hall and parking area. In addition to the numbered interpretive stations that correspond to the booklet, numerous plants are identified by their common and scientific names. Of further interest is the firelane animal track area and the weather station. The area has recently been burned to stimulate and restore the plant communities. At least 20 miles of hikeable sandy firelanes weave through the woodlands dominated by oaks and pines. Permission must be obtained in advance if an individual or group wishes to visit the station. Please send inquiries to:

Executive Director
Archbold Biological Station Route #2
Box 180
Lake Placid, Florida 33852
Phone: (813) 465-2571

Archbold Biological Station is easily reached from U.S. 27 south of Lake Placid. Turn west on S.R. 70 at the junction with U.S. 27. Drive about a mile to Old State Road 8, then south two miles to the entrance on the west side of the road. Archbold Biological Station is a U.S. National Natural Landmark.

Donald Macdonald Park/Dale Wimbrow Park
Sebastian/Indian River County
Area: 113 acres total
Trail Distance: .5 mile total
Highlights: nature study, nature trail, picnicking, shelters, boat ramp, fishing, piers, camping
Fee(s): camping

These two nature-oriented county parks border each other along the east bank of Sebastian Creek in northern Indian River County. Seemingly out of the mainstream of human activity, both parks are well-wooded, though MacDonald Park is more developed, with camping faciltes and a nature trail.

Named for a former County Commissioner who was primarily responsible for the establishment of the facility, MacDonald Park is maintained by the Florida Division of Forestry. Day visitors may park just inside the park entrance near a small picnic area. The trailhead begins north of the entrance along a sandy road forking off to the west prior to the campground and boat dock roads. The truck-wide loop path skirts the campground sites as it passes through sand pine and scrub oak flatwoods in the direction of Sebastian Creek. At the road bend, the trail curves south alongside the edge of the mangrove swamp forest and over a wooden foot-bridge. Passing over and down spoil banks, the path heads east towards the highway to eventually reach the main park entrance. Unfortunately, the trail does not enter the adjacent bordering Dale Wimbrow Park.

Although there are no sweeping vistas of Sebastian Creek from the streambanks, there are two piers in Macdonald Park. These narrow wooden catwalk piers provide fine places to observe the ocean-bound stream and its wildlife. If interested in a private and quiet camping area, the 27 sites are naturally screened from each other by saw palmetto, scrub and live oaks, longleaf, slash and sand pines. Fortunately, the nearby Sebastian Municipal Airport is not too busy with disruptive air traffic.

South of MacDonald Park, approximately half a mile, is the undeveloped Dale Wimbrow Park. A boat ramp that grants access to Sebastian Creek (downstream to the Indian River, Sebastian Inlet, and the Atlantic Ocean) and a picnic ground with drinking water in the open understory of sand pines is available to day visitors. The park is named for an award-winning writer, who arrived in the area during the mid-1940's and began publication of the Indian River newspaper.

To reach Donald MacDonald and Dale Wimbrow Parks from I-95 exit east on S.R. 512, drive 3.5 miles to S.R. 505 and turn north. Proceed about two miles to Dale Wimbrow Park and 2.5 miles to

Donald Macdonald Park, located on the west side of the highway.

Hobe Sound Nature Center/
National Wildlife Refuge

Hobe Sound/Martin County
Area: 965 acres
Trail Distance: 0.25 mile
Highlights: nature study, nature trail, natural history museum, special programs, field trips

Established in 1969, Hobe Sound National Wildlife Refuge consists of two separate land parcels situated about six miles apart: the north Jupiter Island Beach tract and the Hobe Sound National Wildlife headquarters and nature interpretive center, The latter is off U.S. 1, two miles south of Hobe Sound and nearly two and half miles north of the Jonathan Dickinson State Park entrance.

One of the outstanding features is the **Sand Pine Scrub Nature Trail**, a self-guiding, 20-minute loop walk. The trail winds through the endangered sand pine scrub environment; 90% of this native sand pine community has been lost to development in south Florida. This sandy trail, thought to be an ancient shoreline, is well-marked as it traverses the hilly, forested dunes.

Windswept – Hobe Sound Nature Center

Trail leaflets are available at the trailhead adjacent to the nature center. Numbered posts correspond to the leaflet and identify plants, wildlife, and general ecology. The salt spray of the nearby Atlantic Ocean, along with persistent wind and fire, sculpted this grove of sand pine. The striking silver-white foliage of the saw palmetto, unique to the east coast from Hobe Sound south to Fort Lauderdale, is in sharp contrast to the normally green leaves. The trail is open to the public from sunrise to sunset.

In cooperation with the Hobe Sound Refuge, the Hobe Sound Nature Center, Inc. is privately funded and staffed. Special programs and field trips are conducted regularly. The Elizabeth Kirby Room, a small natural history museum, features displays and exhibits on the southern Florida coastal environment. There are five habitat dioramas, an 18-foot mural depicting local plant communities, and exhibits on shells, mangroves, sea turtles, manatees, and freshwater pond life. The hours of the center are from 9 a.m. to 11 a.m. and 1 p.m. to 3, Monday through Friday. The trail is open daily during the daylight hours.

To reach this site from I-95 in SE Martin County, exit at S.R. 708/Bridge Road east and drive to the junction with U.S. 1. Go south about two miles. The Nature Center will be on the east side of U.S. 1.

Jonathan Dickinson State Park
Hobe Sound/Martin County
Area: 10,284 acres
Trail Distance: 21 miles total
Highlights: nature study, nature trails, picnicking, shelters, bicycling, fishing, boat launch ramp, boat tour, campfire programs, guided ranger walks, conference building, family, youth, and primitive camping, concessions
Fee(s): entrance, canoe and rowboat rentals, boat tour, pavilion rental, bicycle rental, cabin rental, camping

Formerly a U.S. Army base before donation in 1947, Jonathan Dickinson State Park is a vast preserve of natural Florida. The park is named for the shipwrecked English Quaker who, with many others of the same faith, sailed from Port Royal, Jamaica in late August, 1696. Their intention was to settle in Pennsylvania. Nearly a month later the barkentine *Reformation* went aground off Jupiter Island. For two months the survivors struggled with the hostile elements and Indians before they eventually reached St. Augustine, 200 miles north. This fascinating account was written into a journal, *God's Protecting Providence*, by Dickinson. It reveals a great deal about the pre-settlement Florida landscape and the Indians who inhabited it.

There are three short nature trails and one long backpacking trail in the park. From the entrance station, follow the main park road in the direction of the Loxahatchee River, turning north on the first road right. This leads to "Hobe Mountain" parking area. The sandy, well-defined 684-foot trail (one-way), leads up to a 25-foot observation tower atop the 86-foot-high "mountain," one of the highest natural points in southeastern Florida. The overlook has several rewarding vistas of the Intracoastal Waterway, Atlantic Ocean, and the park's plant communities. Retrace your steps back to the parking area and drive to the riverfront along the main park road.

East of the concessions area, the unmarked 3,958-foot loop **River Trail** follows the east bank of the Loxahatchee (Indian word for "Turtle River"). The trail traverses tall slash pine woodland and a cypress swamp forest. The opposite shoreline is predominately mangrove. Many of the cypress trees are dying from the excessive saltwater intrusion. The Northwest Fork of the Loxahatchee River is a National Wild and Scenic River, an Aquatic Preserve and an official state-recognized manatee sanctuary.

The Kitching Creek and Wilson Creek trailhead is in the northwest corner of the parking area. The **Kitching Creek Trail** is an 8,238-foot loop path through pine flatwoods and wet prairie, to an overlook platform on Kitching Creek, a tributary of the Loxahatchee River. Available at the trailhead, a leaflet identifies and describes the plants, ecology, and effects of man upon the area. There are 25 numbered stations along the route. The shorter, half-hour loop, **Wilson Creek Trail**, spurs off Kitching Creek Trail, follows Wilson Creek southwest and rejoins the main trail, to return to the parking area.

Other riverfront activities include picnicking, canoe and row boat rentals, and a river cruise tour on the 30-passenger *Loxahatchee Queen*, heading upstream to the former home of Trapper Nelson.

Kitching Creek

The 9.3-mile one-way **Kitching Creek backcountry hiking trail** and the 9.4-mile **East Loop Trail** begin north of the entrance station parking area. Whether a day hiker or overnight camper, you should begin early in the day since it normally requires three to eight hours of hiking with gear to reach Scrub Jay or Kitching Creek primitive campsites. Even though there are two working water pumps you will have to treat the water. Expect ankle-deep to knee-deep wading in spots even during the ideal winter season. A detailed and informative trail map brochure is available at the entrance station. A bird and plant list is also available. The marked (both ways) white-blazed trail follows a beeline path north except for the optional quarter-mile trail spur to Hobe Mountain observation tower along a beach-like shady trail through a wind-swept sand pine scrub area. The trail passes the old north entrance station and curves west to Old Dixie Highway, then across the mainline Florida East Coast Railroad tracks.

After 5.3 miles, the trail reaches a well on the northwest side and a trail junction. The trail fork right/west continues on to Kitching Creek. The trail fork left/east returns to the entrance station trailhead and parking area via the East Loop Trail. Scrub Jay campsite is 0.3 mile down the East Loop Trail and about four miles back to the trailhead. This shorter loop segment makes an ideal distance for most day hikers.

Before reaching the final destination of Kitching Creek Camp the truck-wide mowed path passes along and through pine flatwoods, seasonal ponds, fire roads, wooden bridges, power lines, a canal, and cypress stands. The lighter-weight day hiker, if experienced, may hike the entire 18.6-mile round trip in one day. But the shorter trails are definitely rewarding.

Jonathan Dickinson State Park entrance is off U.S. 1 about six miles south of Hobe Sound, Florida and six miles north of Jupiter, Florida.

St. Lucie Lock And Dam
Stuart/Martin County
Area: 100 acres
Trail Distance: 1 mile
Highlights: nature study, nature walk, picnicking, shelters, fishing, boat launch ramp, camping
Fee(s): camping

Eight miles inland from the city of Stuart, the St. Lucie Lock and Dam was constructed in 1944 by the U.S. Army Corps of Engineers for navigational, flood control and recreational purposes. The lock and dam keeps the water level at a depth of eight feet on the 38-mile St. Lucie Canal – a sizeable segment of the 155-mile Okeechobee Waterway that flows across southern Florida from the St. Lucie Inlet west to Lake Okeechobee and on to Ft.Myers.

The St. Lucie Nature Trail lies directly north across the canal from the main recreational area. Obtain a trail guide brochure from the park attendent at the campground entrance, then proceed across the lock and dam catwalk to the opposite north shore. The well-maintained trail traverses a variety of south Florida habitats. A portion of the trail visits a nameless island via footbridges. The vegetation is transitional pine flatwoods, oak hammock, wetlands, and exotics in the disturbed areas. Wildlife is plentiful and includes the secretive river otter. There are 11 interpretive stops on the sandy woodland loop. Future plans include a new campground and additional trail development in this area of the north property.

To reach St. Lucie Lock and Dam from U.S. 1 in Stuart, turn onto S.R. 76 and go west. About one mile west of the Florida Turnpike overpass turn north on Locks Road. Follow Locks Road through the growing residential area to where it dead ends at the lock and dam. Additional camping is provided at Phipps Martin County Park, which is just east of the lock and dam entrance on a gravel spur road.

Barley Barber Swamp
Indiantown/Martin County
Area: 400 acres
Trail Distance: 5,800 ft.
Highlights: nature study, nature walk tour. Reservation required two to three days in advance.

Named after an early 20th century homesteader, the Barley Barber Swamp comprises one of the last undisturbed virgin bald cypress stands in southeast Florida. Preservation of the giant cypress trees, some over 500 years old, and the surrounding strand community is a major concern of the Florida Power and Light Company, the present owners.

Constructed in 1980, the elevated boardwalk is just over one mile long, and traverses the home of 16 species of mammals, 30 species of reptiles and amphibians, and over 120 species of birds, including the endangered wood stork and southern bald eagle. A 300- to 900-year-old, 16-foot-high Pre-Columbian Indian sand mound, believed to have been used as an inland trading place, is near the middle of the walk. Thirty-three numbered stations mark points of interest that correspond to the colorful guide booklet. Flora, animal life, general ecology, geology, physical features, and social history are touched on. The ranger guides will further enhance your visit by adding their own knowledge and answering any questions. The boardwalk is accessible to the handicapped, has rest points with benches, and has restroom facilities near mid-point.

Access to the sanctuary is by appointment only and the walk is supervised. For reservations to visit Barley Barber Swamp telephone the Environmental Coordinator at (305) 863-3646 from 8 a.m. weekdays or write Florida Power and Light Company, P. O. Box 14000, 700 Universe Boulevard, Juno Beach, Florida 33408. Reservations may be made for one person or for groups up to 25, no less than two to three days in advance. A directional how-to-get-there map will be mailed promptly including information about the natural area. The ranger guide naturalist will meet all parties at the marked entrance gate six miles northwest of Indiantown on S.R. 710. The tour requires two to three hours.

Dupuis Reserve State Forest

Port Mayaca/Martin & Palm Beach Counties
USGS Maps: Port Mayaca, Bryant 1:24,000
Area: 21,935 acres
Trail Distance: 4 loop trails total 15.5 miles
Highlights: hiking, nature study, bicycling, equestrian trails, picnicking, primitive camping, seasonal hunting
Fees: day use, camping

Day hikers and overnight backpackers will enjoy the four interconnecting trail loops that penetrate the state forest and wildlife management area lands of western Martin and Palm Beach counties. The usually dry winter months are the best time to hike, but the level landscape of pine flatwoods, sabal palm hammocks, ponds, wet prairies, and cypress domes retains water so the paths may be wet after a rain. The DuPuis Reserve was purchased by the South Florida Water Management District under the state's Save Our Rivers Program.

Trail parking, registration and the trailhead are found at Gate #2 adjacent to S.R. 76, three miles east of Port Mayaca and six miles west of Indiantown on the south side of the highway. Brown information road signs identify the site.

Fishing osprey, Barley Barber Swamp

The orange-blazed loop trails were established by the Florida Trail Association in cooperation with the administering land agencies. The trails are accessed by walking 0.7 mile south to the trail junction of Loop 1E (or East) and Loop 1W (or West). Trail distances for the four loop trails are: Loop 1 – 4.3 miles; Loop 2 – 6.8 miles; Loop 3 – 11.5 miles; Loop 4 – 15.5. miles.

The 16.3-mile **DuPuis Grade Road** is also open to walking but it is open to vehicles and bicycles as well. The DuPuis Grade Road is accessible from the Jim Lake Grade Road, the forest reserve administrative office or the south end of Loop 4. The primitive campground is just south of the 3W and 4W trail junction and a permit is required to camp. Permits may be obtained by calling (407) 924-8021 or (813) 763-2191. Bring your own water or be prepared to sterilize existing sources.

The loop trails are restricted to hikers only although horse trails intersect in Loop 1 and Loop 2. Wild feral hogs may be encountered and they do extensive rooting along the trails, but they fear humans. Day users may visit the property from sunrise to sunset. Gate #3 is the trailhead for equestrians. Gate #6 is the access for the administration center.

Lake Okeechobee Dike/Levee Trail

Glades, Hendry, Palm Beach, Martin & Okeechobee Counties
USGS Maps: Moore Haven, Clewiston North, Clewiston South, Lake Harbor, Belle Glade, Pahokee, Okeechobee 4SW, Okeechobee 4NW, Okeechobee, Okeechobee NW, Okeechobee SW, Fisheating Bay 1:24,000
Trail Distance: 107.8 miles
Highlights: hiking, nature study, picnicking, boating, boat launch ramps, fishing, camping, bicycling
Fee(s): camping

According to the natural resources office of the U.S. Army Corps of Engineers at Clewiston, the entire Herbert Hoover dike or levee that nearly encircles Lake Okeechobee is hikeable, except for the canal locks or areas with posted no trespassing signs. The Florida Trail Association considers 107.8 miles around the second largest freshwater lake in the continental United States hikeable, which includes some roadways. The dike is an essential link or "necklace" in the 1,300-mile (north to south) hiking trail now nearing completion.

Although the high, basically dry and level dike trail is easily walkable and provides access to the open expanse of interior southern Florida, the "trail" is actually a treeless service road and it requires a Zen-like state of mind to walk any distance on this monotonous and unvarying stretch. Therefore only short day hike segments are recommended. It is an ideal trail for urbanites who seek wide open spaces for a healthy change.

One suggested day hike is the 11- to 12-mile segment from the Alvin Ward Sr. Glades County park, just south of the lock in Moore Haven southeast to the Clewiston city park at the lakeside end of Francisco Street. This segment is fairly remote and removed from distracting highways and development. Parking is available at both public parks and a car shuttle is recommended. The elevated dike provides great vistas of the surrounding countryside and access to the wooded Australian pine shoreline. Birding can be terrific.

A second trail segment begins at Pahokee city lakeshore park (formerly Pahokee State Recreation Area). Hikers may walk north about four miles one-way to Canal Point, Florida and the West Palm Beach Canal or south 5.5 miles one-way to Paul Rardin roadside park. This southeast segment of the dike provides fine views of the open lake. The linear earthen ridge is like a "great divide" that separates the world of towns, highways, and fields from the "Okichubi" or "big water." The Herbert Hoover dike was constructed in the 1930's by the U.S. Army Corps of Engineers after the devastating hurricanes of 1926 and 1928 took the lives of over 2,000 people wbo lived along the south shore. Additional lakeside parks that provide access to the dike are John Stretch Park between Clewiston and South Bay along U.S. 27 and Fisheating Creek wayside park along S.R. 78 near Lakeport. (See also Harney Pond, below).

In addition, the five mile (one-way) Highlands-Okeechobee section of the Herbert Hoover dike (located on the east side of the Kissimmee River from Okee-tantie Recreation Area on S.R. 78 north to S65E structure) is also hikeable.

Harney Pond Recreation Area
Lakeport/Glades County
Area: 81 acres
Trail Distance: 1.5 miles
Highlights: nature study, nature walk, fishing, swimming, boat ramp, observation tower, picnicking, shelter

The Indians aptly named this huge freshwater body, "Okeechobee," meaning "big water," and indeed it is. After Lake Michigan, Lake Okeechobee is the second largest freshwater lake in the United States, measuring 40 miles long and 30 miles wide. Harney Pond boardwalk trail represents one of the few nature walks found along the west side of the lake. The Glades County Park Department, in cooperation with the Marine Institute, Inc., a non-profit educational organization that works with youth offenders, constructed the nature trail.

The land the nature trail and observation tower occupies was created by the digging of Harney Pond Canal. The spoils form a narrow finger of land that juts out into the lake, providing the visitor excellent views of the open watery expanse of Fisheating Bay all the way to the horizon. Birding is good, but the motorboats zooming in and out of Harney Pond Canal create a disturbance, especially on weekends. Common galinules, coots, herons, curlews, hawks, ducks, red-wing blackbirds and possibly an occasional Everglades kite or Audubon's caracara grace the peaceful surroundings. Spikerush, cattails, water-lily, sawgrass, wire cordgrass, breakrush, buttonbush, and willows are noticeable representatives of the plant kingdom. Fish include speck, crappie, bluegill, shellcracker, catfish, pickerel, bream, and the famous Florida largemouth bass, the official state freshwater fish.

The Recreation Area is just off S.R. 78 west, across the bridge at Lakeport and the Seminole Indian Reservation. Drive to the extreme end of Shell Road where you will find the picnic shelter, observation tower, and trailhead. Plenty of parking is available.

Cypress Knee Museum
Palmdale/Glades County
Area: 40 acres
Trail Distance: .75 mile
Highlights: nature study, boardwalk trail, museum, gift shop
Fee(s): entrance

Connoisseurs of native bald cypress, as well as the curious, will find much to learn about this conspicuous, swamp-loving conifer at this unique southern Florida attraction. The bald cypress is deciduous, losing its feathery foliage during the winter months (when it becomes "bald"). The function of its "knees" is uncertain. They may possibly help the lofty tree stand upright in the muddy swamp or enable the roots to breathe much like the black mangrove. Interestingly, no other tree grows knees and even the cypress will not form these woody projections in dry habitats.

Begin your visit at the museum, which features a collection of cypress knees resembling famous people and animals. The world's largest transplanted cypress tree occupies the center of the museum. Across U.S. 27 is the boardwalk or "catwalk" and sales room/gift shop. The narrow wooden catwalk meanders through bald cypress swamp, live oak-sabal palm hammock and a bayhead near the banks of Fisheating Creek. The "bay" found in this wet area is sweet bay, a native magnolia that has showy, white fragrant flowers in springtime. Etched on the cypress slab signs along the walk are tidbits of Florida Cracker humor by Tom Gaskins, who originated the bald cypress knee industry in 1934. Experiments with "shaping" the knees into bottles and other objects may be seen from the boardwalk. The salesroom, wood yard, boiler shed, factory and restrooms are located at the trailhead to the boardwalk.

Cypress Knee Museum is one mile south of Palmdale, Glades County near the junction of U.S. 27 and S.R. 29. The museum is open daily from 8 a.m. to sundown.

Ortona Indian Mound Park
Ortona/Glades County
Area: 131 acres
Trail Distance: 0.75 mile
Highlights: nature walk, nature study, picnicking, shelters, playground, lake, fishing, fishing piers

This park is named for the prehistoric habitation and ceremonial mounds that were discovered here. They are believed to have been constructed by the Caloosa about 1100-1200 A.D. The mounds are the main focus of the nature trail which includes 24 interpretive stops that relate to the ecology of the scrub oak, sabal palm, and wetland habitats.

The trail begins south of the parking near the park entrance and leads to a picnic shelter area. The wood chipped trail loops around the shaded palm-pine hammock and then heads towards the Indian mound interpretive site. A boardwalk leads out over part of a small mound and is near a 2.3-mile former Indian canoe canal that connected with the Caloosahatchee River to the south. The mound complex is the largest earthworks on the western edge of the Everglades. Ortona was a former site of interregional trade between inland and coastal tribes.

The trail next reaches the lakeshore and follows the shoreline to eventually loop back along the same path. The scrub woodland is one of the best sites to view Florida scrub jays and gopher tortoises. The trail culminates at the main picnic shelter, playground, and restroom.

The Park entrance is on a gravel road 15 miles west of Moore Haven, 0.2 mile north of S.R. 78 between a sand quarry and the Ortona Cemetery. A sign is posted along S.R. 78 just west of the Ortona Cemetery.

You may also want to visit the Army Corp of Engineers' Ortona Lock and view the coming and going of boats on the Caloosahatchee River. Ortona Lock is 2.8 miles west and south on Ortona Road/78A.

J. W. Corbett Wildlife Management Area
USGS Maps: West Palm Beach 2NW, West Palm Beach 2SW 1:24,000
Area: 57,892 acres
Trail Distance: 1.2-mile boardwalk/28-mile hiking trail
Highlights: biking, nature study, fishing, archery, seasonal hunting, youth camp, backcountry camping
Fee(s): WMA entry stamp required if not hiking

By far the most remote hiking experience in urban Palm Beach County is found in the sprawling semi-wilderness of the J. W. Corbett Wildlife Management Area. The vast acreage encompasses a variety of habitats including bald cypress sloughs, slash pine-palmetto flats, seasonally wet prairies, freshwater and sawgrass marshes, dry prairie grasslands, sabal palm hammocks and abandoned pastures and fields.
Because this is a state managed hunting area, periodically closed for hunting from August to January, the best time to hike is during

small game season from January to March,when there are few hunters on the property and the weather is ideal. Purchase of the $25 WMA entry stamp is not required for hikers of the boardwalk or the Florida Trail. However overnight backpackers will need to obtain a permit from the Everglades Regional Office, (800) 432-2046 or (407) 640-6100.

Recently the WMA has constructed the **Hungryland Boardwalk and Interpretive Trail** that loops 1.2 miles through pine flatwoods, hardwood hammock, freshwater marsh and cypress swamp. The trailhead begins half a mile from the gate entrance on the right/north side of Stumpers Grade Road. The Corbett Section of the Florida Trail also begins at the same location. The 14-mile (one-way) hiking trail is laid out for two to three overnight outings. White eye-level blazes appear on evenly spaced trees for trail direction each way. Two designated backpacking sites are located at the five mile and eleven mile points. It is best to bring your own water rather than treating available sources. Park your vehicle at the nearby check station for safekeeping.

The sandy trail follows next to and sometimes on Road 7 along a slash pine ridge (10 foot elevation) that is normally dry during the winter season. There will be several rutted-out holes to negotiate. After walking approximately five miles due west you will come upon the first campsite, Hammock Camp. Turn south at the junction of Road 7 and Road 9 and walk 3/4 mile to the camp, which is situated on a small sabal palm hammock island in the center of a shallow pond. Wading is the only access, but it is worth the wet effort.

Continuing on the trail from the camp junction approximately 1.5 miles is Hungryland Slough. Expect to get your feet wet as you road-wade through what is known as the "Hole-in-the-Wall," a "window" or pass on Road 7 through the bald cypress swamp. The terrain changes once more to pineland and palmetto nearing South Grade Road.

Turn right/north at South Grade and follow the road for 50 yards, then turn left/west. The trail follows an overgrown buggy trail through pineland until reaching a wet prairie opening and more wading; watch carefully for blazes. After 1.5 miles or less, the trail crosses a canal and connects with Road 3, traversing for one mile an abandoned tomato field before reaching another pine-shaded woodland section. Continue on Road 3 in a northwest direction for about half a mile before reaching a second canal, where the trail turns left/southwest and leads to Little Gopher Camp. The camp is in a fine stand of slash pine. The trail continues on to the west boundary of the WMA and the end of the marked trail. Retrace your steps back to the trailhead and the eastern terminus of the 14-mile trail.

To reach the south entrance of J. W. Corbett WMA from the Palm Beach area go northwest on S.R. 710/Beeline Highway to North-lake Boulevard and turn left/west. Proceed on Northlake Boulevard west eight miles to Seminole Pratt Whitney Road and turn right/north. Follow Seminole Pratt Whitney Road three miles to the south entrance on the left/west side of the road. The north gate check station entrance is further north and west on S.R. 710 at the junction with S.R. 706, on the south side of the highway. The area is open daily from dawn to dusk.

Arthur R. Marshall Loxahatchee National Wildlife Refuge

Palm Beach County
Area: 145,635 acres
Trail Distance: 7.2 miles total
Highlights: nature study, nature walks, interpretive center, fishing, boat launch ramp, canoeing trails, airboating, seasonal hunting, naturalist programs, natural history membership
Fee(s): entrance, airboat permit, guided airboat tours (at Central Area), fishing guides, boat rentals (at Hillsboro Recreation Area)

Nature walkers visit only a small portion of the seemingly boundless Everglades within the 221 square miles of the Loxahatchee National Wildlife Refuge. Since 1951, the U.S. Fish and Wildlife Service has managed the refuge for wildlife that inhabit the saw-grass marshes, wet prairies, sloughs, and tree islands. Levees, canals, water impoundments, and compartments have been constructed to provide habitat for the 150 species of birdlife. Raccoons, river otters, bobcats, white-tailed deer, rabbits, and alligators also inhabit the vast refuge. The main headquarters area includes the Wildlife Interpretive Center, Everglades Canoe Trail, a boat ramp, an airboat trail, a fishing area, and two nature trails.

The **Cypress Swamp Boardwalk** is a .4-mile self-guiding loop that begins and ends directly behind the Wildlife Interpretive Center. The 400-acre remnant bald cypress strand is reported to be the largest remaining in Palm Beach County. Depending on the season, the water level will vary from three feet to completely dry. Limpkins, pileated woodpeckers, northern flickers, redbellied woodpeckers, water moccasins and water snakes are some of the wildlife that inhabit the slough, according to the visitor's guide available at the Interpretive Center. Pond apple, coastal plain willow, wax myrtle, primrose willow,

Cypress Swamp Boardwalk

buttonbush, arrow arum, epiphytes, ferns and guava are identified plant life. The most striking and colorful feature of the slough is the abundant red lichen that thrives on the trunks of the bald cypress. Red lichen or "Baton Rouge" ("red stick") was well known to the French explorers.

Just west of the Interpretive Center, the well marked .8-mile **Marsh Nature Trail** follows an earthen dike around the perimeter of a rectangular-shaped freshwater impoundment marked #7. This area of intensively managed wetlands is planted with aquatic wildlife food plants such as Japanese millet to attract waterfowl. The best time to observe the birdlife is early morning, late afternoon, or early evening.

A 20-foot-high observation tower is located at the southwest corner of the impoundment. Visitors are welcome to hike around the dike levees of all 10 impoundments, about six miles, where water levels, plant life, and wildlife will vary. Besides these three nature walks, the 5.5-mile **Everglades Canoe Trail** loop, a 3 1/2-hour journey, is highly recommended. Contact the Wildlife Interpretive Center for further information.

The Center hours are 9 a.m. to 4 p.m., Monday through Friday and 9 a.m. to 4:30 on weekends. The Center is closed Christmas. Loxahatchee National Wildlife Refuge hours are generally sunrise to sunset daily. Exact times, which can vary, are posted at the entrances. To reach Headquarters entrance from I-95, exit onto Atlantic Avenue/S.R. 806 and proceed west under the Florida Turnpike to U.S. 441. The refuge entrance is three miles north of the intersection of S.R. 806/Delray West Road and U. S. 441 at Lee Road on the west side of the highway.

Although no nature trails exist, two other points of entry include the north access at Twenty-Mile Bend and the south access at Hillsboro Recreation Area. Twenty-Mile Bend includes a boat ramp and docks at the junction of U.S. 441 and U.S. 98. From I-95 in West Palm Beach, exit Southern Boulevard/S.R. 98 and drive west approximately 20 miles to the junction and Twenty-Mile Bend.

Hillsboro Recreation Area is reached from I-95 by exiting onto Hillsboro Boulevard/S.R. 810 in Deerfield Beach, Broward County, and driving west to U.S. 441. Turn north at 441, drive half a mile and turn west onto Lox Road/S.R. 827. Then proceed six miles to the recreation area. The area includes four public boat ramps, guided airboat tours, boat rentals, field fishing guides, concessions, and a fishing store.

Inland/Southwest

Hillsborough River State Park
Thonotosassa/Hillsborough County
Area: 3,002 acres
Trail Distance: 6 miles total
Highlights: nature study, nature trails, picnicking, shelters, fishing, canoe launch, swimming, camping, concessions, Ft. Foster Historic Site tours
Fee(s): entrance, boat & other rentals, camping, Ft. Foster tour

Hillsborough River State Park has been a popular park for outdoor enthusiasts and history buffs since the mid-1930's. Its scenic beauty of hardwood hammocks, pine flatwoods, cypress swamps, floodplain, grass ponds, reconstructed fort, and the lovely and historic Hillsborough River accounts for the park's ongoing appeal.

Three brief, easy trails are located near the river: Rapids Trail, River Trail and the Baynard Nature Trail. The half-mile Rapids Trail is the shortest of the three. It leads to the river from a parking area along the main park road. From the river bluff you will see the black waters of the Hillsborough River form rapids as they cascade over outcrops of Suwanee limestone boulders. Bass, bream, gar and catfish are common in the river and other wildlife is attracted to the stream's shores. The walk continues downstream to the one-mile River Trail. The forested path loops near the stream's edge back to the Rapids Trail and the parking lot. Two separate spurs lead to the picnic and concessions area. The floodplain forest is composed of bald cypress, pop ash, and red maple. The River Trail junctions with one of two suspension bridges in the park. This one leads over the river to the Baynard Nature Trail.

The Baynard Nature Trail is a mile-long loop trail through mature hardwood hammock and river floodplain of live oak, southern magnolia, hickory, cabbage sabal palm, sweetgum, American elm, American hornbeam, cypress, basswood and hackberry. The second foot bridge crosses the river and connects the boat dock and concessions area with the nearby picnic area. The self-guiding and interconnecting trails are easily hiked in one outing.

For those who would like a longer hiking experience, a white blazed (both ways) 3.4-mile Florida Trail loop begins across the river bridge from the concessions/recreation hall/picnic and parking area or can be accessed from the Baynard Nature Trail. The trail follows the Hillsborough River bank downstream, crossing the tributary creek four times on foot bridges. Curving northwest and north, the trail enters maturing palm hammocks. After 2.2 miles you reach the blue blazed 0.1 mile campsite trail. Campers will need to register with the park office and bring their own water. The trail continues for one more mile back to the trailhead, completing a comfortable day hike.

Across the highway at the park entrance, historic Ft. Foster (1836-1849) has been recently rebuilt following a fire. Park rangers act out the role of soldiers in the U.S. 2nd Artillery during the Second

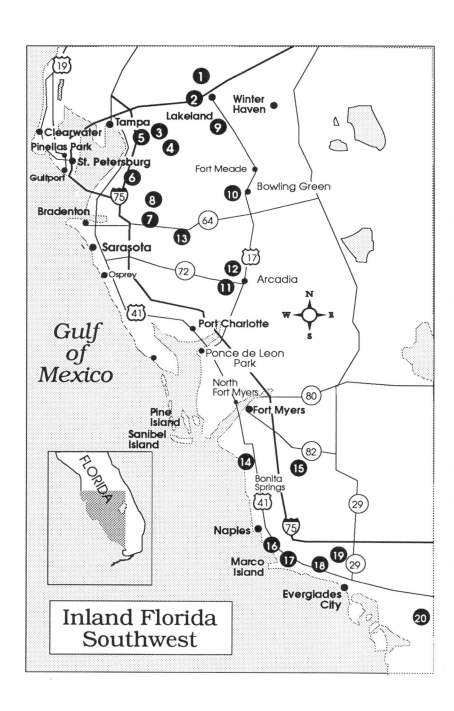

Inland Florida
Southwest

Seminole War. Tours are conducted on weekends and holidays. A shuttle van leaves hourly from 9 a.m. to 4 p.m., except at the noon hour.

To reach Hillsborough River State Park from I-75/93A, exit east onto S.R. 582/Fowler Avenue and drive east to U.S. 301/S.R. 41. Continue northeast to the park entrance. The state park is six miles south of Zephyr Hills and nine miles north of Thonotosassa. Hours are 8 a.m. to sunset year round.

Lower Hillsborough Wilderness Park
Hillsborough County
Area: 16,000 acres
Trail Distance: 12 miles total
Highlights: nature study, nature trails, bicycling, picnicking, shelters, fishing, boat launch ramp, canoeing, restrooms

The Lower Hillsborough Wilderness Park consists of five separate areas or sites seven miles northeast of the Tampa suburb of Temple Terrace: Flatwoods, Morris Bridge, Trout Creek, Dead River and Flint Creek. The Southwest Florida Water Management District purchased this vast natural acreage to serve as a flood detention area and as a source of freshwater for metropolitan Tampa. The recreational facilities are operated and maintained by Hillsborough County Park Department.

1. Hillsborough River State Park
2. Lower Hillsborough Wilderness Park
3. Edward Medard Park
4. Alderman's Ford County Park
5. Lithia Springs Park
6. Little Manatee River State Recreation Area
7. Lake Manatee State Recreation Area
8. Rye Wilderness Country Park
9. Bone Valley Museum
10. Paynes Creek State Historic Site
11. Morgan Park
12. De Soto Environmental Learning Laboratory
13. Myakka River State Park
14. Koreshan State Historic Site
15. Corkscrew Swamp Sanctuary
16. Stephen F. Briggs Nature Center
17. Collier Seminole State Park
18. Fakahatchee Strand State Preserve
19. Big Cypress National Preserve
20. Loop Road Interpretive Center

Flatwoods and Morris Bridge areas are close to each other on Morris Bridge Road/S.R. 579 along the Hillsborough River. A seven-mile paved loop road has been designated as a hiking trail at the Flatwoods Area. This roadway is closed to motorized vehicles. Drive into the park and leave your car at the picnic area near the closed gate where hiking signs have been placed. Downstream at the recently opened Morris Bridge area is a 6,000-foot boardwalk that winds through floodplain cypress-maple swamp forest. Both areas also offer picnicking and fishing; Morris Bridge has a boat ramp for access to the river. Further downstream the Trout Creek area is currently under development.

To reach Flatwoods, Morris Bridge, and Trout Creek areas from I-75, exit east on Fletcher Avenue/582A/Morris Road. Continue northeast on Morris Bridge Road about five miles to the sites on the west side of the highway.

Dead River and Flint Creek areas are further apart but are both located on U.S. 301 and along the Hillsborough River. Dead River area (Dead River Road and U.S. 301) is a four-mile hike round-trip on a shell road that leads to the confluence of Dead River and the Hillsborough River, site of the ranger's residence. The trail road passes through a dense oak-palm hammock and floodplain forest. Park your car at the gate entrance off the side of the trail service road. Dead River area is just downstream from Hillsborough River State Park. Youth camping is available at Dead River. Downriver, the Flint Creek site (Stacey Road and U.S. 301) has recently been developed with picnic facilities and a boat ramp. A 1,300-foot boardwalk winds through the Hillsborough River floodplain.

Both sites may be reached from I-75 and U.S. 301 north exit east of Tampa. Exit Fowler Avenue/S.R. 582 and drive east to U.S. 301. Go north on U.S. 301 about five miles to Flint Creek and 10 miles to the Dead River area. All sites are open from 8 a.m. to sunset.

Edward Medard Park
Hillsborough County
Area: 1,284 acres
Highlights: nature study, boardwalk, observation tower, swimming, fishing, boat ramp, picnicking, shelters, playground, camping, restrooms
Fee(s): camping

Bridge over calm waters, Edward Medard Park

Primarily a fisherman's park where bass fishing is popular, Edward Medard Park also offers picnicking, swimming, camping, and walking. Eight hundred acres of the park is Pleasant Grove Reservoir, a reclaimed phosphate mine that is maintained by the Southwest Florida Water Management District.

A boardwalk that doubles as a fishing pier leads out to a small island and an observation tower which provides views of the watery park. The "Sacred Hills" area near the picnic grounds are the slag hill deposits of phosphate diggings. These hills add interest to the park and several unmarked trails follow the "ridgeline." Campers will appreciate the wooded and shaded campground. A swimming area has been opened at the main picnic grounds.

To reach Edward Medard Park from I-4, take the S.R. 39 exit south at Plant City to S.R. 60 and turn west. Drive three miles west on S.R. 60 to Turkey Creek Road and turn south. The park entrance is two miles south on the east side of the road. The hours are from 6 a.m. to 10 p.m.

Alderman's Ford County Park

Hillsborough County
Area: 596 acres
Trail Distance: 4.5 miles total
Highlights: nature study, nature trail, bike trail, historic site, visitor center, fishing, boat ramp, canoeing, picnicking, shelters, playground, primitive camping

Alderman's Ford County Park has a colorful historic past. The historical marker near the visitor center reads "James Alderman was the first settler to homestead south of the Alafia River. Having found a shallow point in the stream, he made a crossing or ford for wagons and horses that came to be known as Alderman's Ford. Local folks enjoyed picnics and other gatherings near the ford during the latter part of the 19th century. A political rally was held on the site in 1902 and for more than 60 years thereafter, Democrat Party candiates of Hillsborough County traditionally began their campaigning at Alderman's Ford."

There are several nature trails that wind through a variety of habitats at the Hillsborough County Park. Directly behind the visitor center, across the bridge, begins a mulched quarter-mile loop trail that encircles and pentrates a dense oak-palm hammock. A two-mile pedestrian/bicycle asphalt-surfaced loop trail also begins near the visitor center and picnic area and offers scenic vistas of the Alafia River. Near the picnic area is an unpaved quarter-mile spur trail that passes along the floodplain forest of the Alafia River and connects the bike/hike trail to form a loop. Canoe access is provided across S.R. 39 near the manager's office. Canoe trips of 13 miles or more will take you to Lithia Springs County Park downstream.

At the base of the hill below the visitor center and picnic area, an 1,875-foot boardwalk meanders through an area of hardwood forest and swamp between the North and South Forks or Prongs of the Alafia River. A pavilion overlooks the confluence that forms the river. Cabbage palms, poison ivy, sweet gum, water locust, Virginia creeper, American elm, water hickory, wild citrus, summer grape, hornbean, buttonbush, bald cypress, and southern red cedar are a few of the plants identified along the walk by the guidebook.

Just beyond the boardwalk, over the South Prong, is a 1.5-mile loop hiking trail that ascends from the lowland swamp forest to the drier sandy elevation of slash pines and live oaks. Blazed painted markers appear on the trees allowing easy trail passage. Overnight backpackers will find 10 marked primitive campsites at the Oak Hammock and Pine Hill campground. Reservations must be made in advance and campers must obtain a permit at the park office.

To reach Alderman's Ford County Park from I-4, take the S.R. 39 exit south at Plant City. Drive about 10 miles south on S.R. 39 to the park entrance on the east side of the highway, just before the Alafia River bridge. The park opens at 8 a.m. and closes at sunset year round.

Lithia Springs Park
Hillsborough County
Area: 160 acres
Trail Distance: 200 yards
Highlights: nature study, nature walk, swimming, bathhouse, picnicking, shelters, playground, canoe launch ramp, camping, restrooms, concessions
Fee(s): entrance, camping

Lithia Springs Park is administered by the Hillsborough County Park Department and is one of their most popular regional parks. Its popularity is attributed to the naturally warm, year round 72° spring waters which are delightful for swimming. This spring discharges 24 million gallons of clear and clean mineral water daily from caverns beneath the surface. The turquoise color of the springs results from the depth of the clear reflecting water. The waters contain large amounts of calcium, magnesium bicarbonate, and lithium salts, hence the name. The springs are U-shaped and flow about 200 yards from their origin before entering the Alafia River. As a matter of interest, Florida has more springs than any other state.

A river nature trail has been established along the bank of the Alafia River, adjacent to the springs and beach area. The short meandering trail passes through river cypress floodplain and a small springs inlet near the picnic area. Interpretive guided walks and programs are available upon request.

A canoe launch is provided for river trips down the Alafia River to near Tampa Bay. You can also start your day-long river journey from Alderman's Ford County Park boat ramp, just upstream on S.R. 39.

To reach Lithia Springs County Park from I-4, take the U.S. 301 exit south to S.R. 60 and head east to Brandon. From Brandon take S.R. 640 southeast about six miles to Lithia Springs Road and turn right. The road dead ends at the park entrance. The park opens at 8 a.m. and closes at dusk year round.

Little Manatee River State Recreation Area
Wimauma/Hillsborough County
Area: 1,638 acres
Trail Distance: 10.5 miles total
Highlights: nature study, nature walks, picnicking, shelters, bridle trails, fishing, canoeing, canoe launch ramp, camping
Fee(s): entrance, camping, picnic shelter reservations

Rustic and seemingly remote, the Little Manatee River State Recreation Area is one of the newest state facilities in southern Florida. Five miles of the Little Manatee River's 40-mile meandering course to Tampa Bay flows through the park boundaries. Cool and moist floodplain forests of sabal palm and live oak thrive along the shores. Away from the river, well-drained white sandy soil support stands of sand pine with an undergrowth of scrub oaks, saw palmetto, wildflowers. Pileated woodpeckers, rufus-sided towhees and gopher tortoises are commonly seen in these increasingly rare environs.

A short quarter-mile loop nature trail skirts the south bank of the river near the picnic grounds. Dense growth of sabal palms and other moisture-loving vegetation provides a cool shady walk, even on the warmest days. The woodland path skirts a small backwater lake or bayou. Hikers may also traverse the two interconnecting horse trails that lead through the scrub pine forest away from the river. Day visitors may park at the spacious picnic area parking lot and walk southwest on the main park road to the trailhead of **Dude Lake Horse Trail**, a three-mile loop that joins with the one-mile **Mustang Horse Trail**.

Recently the 6.2-mile **Little Manatee River SRA hiking loop trail** was developed by the Florida Department of Natural Resources in cooperation with the Florida Trail Association. The trailhead and parking area is accessed east and north of the main park entrance along U.S. 301, a quarter-mile north of the Little Manatee River highway bridge on the left/west side of the road – about five miles south of the junction of U.S. 30 and S.R. 674. Day bikers and over-night backpackers must register at the entrance station on Lightfoot Road (3.25 miles) to obtain the lock combination number for the gate to the parking/trailhead area. Water is not available on the trail.

Little Manatee River

The white-blazed path follows the higher ground along the flood-plain of the Little Manatee River, crossing Cypress Creek and continuing on to the primitive campsite, which is about four miles distant. The oak-palm hammock campsite spur is blue blazed and 0.2 mile long. The trail continues through hardwood bammocks one mile and recrosses a second bridge over Cypress Creek. It is an additional 1.3 miles to the trailhead through sand pine scrub.

To reach Little Manatee River State Recreation Area in south Hillsborougb County from I-75, exit east at Moccassin Wallow Road and drive five miles to the intersection with U.S. 301. Go north on 301 about seven miles and turn west on Lightfoot Road, then proceed a short distance to the park entrance.

You can also exit from I-75 east onto S.R. 674/Ruskin-Wimauma Road and drive three miles to the junction with U.S. 301 at Sun City Center. Turn south on U.S. 301 and drive about six miles to Light-foot Road. Turn right/west and proceed to the park entrance on the right/north side of the highway. Follow the brown directional road signs. The park opens at 8 a.m. and closes at sunset year round, unless you are camping.

Lake Manatee State Recreation Area
Bradenton/Manatee County
Area: 556 acres
Trail Distance: no established trails
Highlights: nature study, swimming (lifeguard), picnicking, shelters, fishing, boat ramp, restrooms
Fee(s): entrance

Lake Manatee State Recreation Area consists of 556 acres of sand pine scrub, sandhills, pine flatwoods, and hammocks situated along three miles of the south shore of man-made Lake Manatee. The surrounding landscape is similar to what Majorie Rawlings described in her book, *The Yearling.* The sandhill scrub community is considered to be endangered due to over-development, logging, and agriculture. Very few such stands remain outside public lands.

Undesignated nature walks are found along the shoreline, woods, saw palmetto opens, and abandoned field lanes of old pastures. The sandhill woods are perhaps the most interesting areas. There are no established trails as yet, but some are planned.

The sandhills are low, rolling pine-clad prairies with "openings" filled by tree islands and grassy understory. The plant community supports longleaf pine, turkey oak, blue jack oak, wiregrass, laurel and live oak, saw palmetto, myrtle oak, sand live oak, Chapman's oak, rosemary, and rusty lyonia. Fox, squirrel, gopher tortoise, indigo snake, pine snake, fence lizard, quail, black racer, sand skinks, Florida mouse, bobcat, gray fox, and raccoon are some of the animals that are home here. Lake Manatee, the source of drinking water for the residents of Manatee County, is stocked with bass, bream, speckled perch, catfish, and bluegill, for lovers of freshwater fishing.

To reach Lake Manatee State Recreation Area from I-75, take S.R. 64 exit 42 east five miles to the park entrance on the north side of the highway. It opens at 8 a.m. and closes at sunset year round.

Rye Wilderness County Park
Rye/Manatee County
Area: 50 acres
Trail Distance: 3/4 mile
Highlights: nature walk, horse trail, picnicking, shelter, playground, canoe launch, ranger station, restrooms

Wilderness it is not, but secluded it is. This compact eastern Manatee County park offers enjoyable outdoor activities in a natural scenic setting along the north bank of Rye Creek. The well marked nature trail is a loop path that begins and ends near the park center, across the main park road from the picnic shelter, playground, and restrooms. The vehicle-wide path follows Rye Creek and loops back across the road to the park center. The mature sand pines are festooned with Spanish moss, with an understory of palmetto, oak and bayberry. The 1.5-mile horse trail can also be explored. The trail surface is a fine sugar sand. The park is open dawn to dusk.

To reach Rye Wilderness from I-75, exit 42 onto S.R. 64 east and drive 2.5 miles to Upper Manatee River Road, where you turn north and drive about six miles to the eastern terminus of the road. Here it "T's" with Rye Road. Turn left and drive .2 mile to the park entrance. Proceed to the park center, .8 mile. The Sheriff Youth Camp signs lead you to the park.

Bone Valley Museum
Bradley/Polk County
Highlights: nature study, natural history museum
Fee(s): entrance donation

Surrounded by miles and miles of phosphate mining pits, there is the village of Bradley and the Bone Valley Museum. This small but unique and informative museum interprets the role of phosphate in our daily lives. In fact, Polk County contains the richest known deposits in the world. In the course of digging for the precious mineral, prehistoric fossil evidence of what Florida was like millions of years ago was discovered, preserved and now displayed at the Bone.Valley Museum.

"Bone Valley" refers to the underground geological formation found in Polk and surrounding counties, created 5 to 6 million years ago. The appropriately-named museum contains an amazing quantity of quality fossil remains from the Pleistocene and Pliocene epochs, two to 12 million years ago. Ancient sharks, ground sloths, rhinoceros, peccaries, whales, saber-toothed tigers, camels, jaguars, lions, mastodons, giant armadillos, wolves, bear, giant beavers, and manatee fossils are exhibited. Petrified wood was also uncovered in the digging for phosphate. Palm, oak, pine, cypress, cedar, ash, and other stone-like woods comprise the collection of flora from this distant time. Additional exhibits include paintings and murals, animated dioramas and life-sized sculptures of prehistoric mastodons, saber-toothed tigers, three-toed ground sloths, and the giant armadillo. Collections of minerals, Indian artifacts and curios are also displayed. The majority of the collections were found by Joe Larned when he was employed in the phosphate industry.

The Bone Valley Museum is on S.R. 37 at Bradley about 20 miles south of Lakeland and I-4. The museum is open Tuesday-Saturday, 10 a.m. to 4 p.m. from October 1 to May 1. During the summer months it is closed to the public, except for group appointments.

Paynes Creek State Historic Site
Bowling Green/Hardee County
Area: 340.5 acres
Trail Distance: 4 trails total 2.75 miles
Highlights: nature study, nature trails, historic interpretive sites, visitor center & museum, picnicking, shelters, fishing, canoe launch
Fee(s): entrance, shelter reservations

The confluence of Paynes Creek and the Peace River is where the day visitor to Paynes Creek Historic Site travels backwards through time to over a century ago when the United States was at war with the Seminole Indians in 1849-50. This site was near the third and final campaign in the Seminole Wars, the longest and costliest Indian wars in American history. The Seminoles never officially surrendered. They finally signed a peace treaty with U.S. officials in 1936.

Your journey through the past begins at the visitor center and museum where exhibits and slides will visually help to bring the historic events alive. After your tour inside, step outside behind the center to the trailhead of the **Fort Chokonikla Trail**. The quarter-mile, 10-minute trail walk leads to the site of the former blockhouse fort, erected in 1849 but abandoned in 1850 due to sickness. Interpretive markers line the short loop trail.

Three additional trails are near the picnic shelter area by Paynes Creek: Peace River Trail, Monument Trail and the Store Trail. The **Peace River Trail** is a 40-minute, one-mile loop trail that follows Paynes Creek downstream to the junction with the Peace River, a popular canoe stream. The Monument Trail and Store Trail are just upstream on Paynes Creek from the Peace River trailhead. The **Monument Trail** is a 20-minute, half-mile loop trail that forks off from the Store Trail, crosses a suspension bridge over Paynes Creek and leads to a monument marking the burial place of George Payne and Dempsey Whiddon, who were killed by renegade Seminoles. The longest trail is the 60-minute, 1.5-mile **Store Trail.** This woodland path leads to the overlook of the Kennedy-Darling Store, a trading post on the frontier between the Seminoles and the settlers. The loop trail is lined with interpretive markers detailing the history and local flora and fauna.

Paynes Creek Historic Site is in north Hardee County. Take U.S. 17 to Bowling Green and follow the brown information signs east on S.R. 664-A about two miles to the state park entrance. The park opens at 8 a.m. and closes at sunset year round.

While in Hardee County, you may want to visit Pioneer Park at the junction of U.S. 17 and S.R. 64 in Zolfo Springs, about 10 miles south of Bowling Green. The county park features user-made trails along the Peace River, camping, a small zoo, and historic sites.

Morgan Park
Arcadia/De Soto County
Area: 200 acres
Trail Distance: 3 miles
Highlights: nature study, nature trails, picnicking, shelters, restrooms

Morgan Park is a prime example of preserved parkland that every community should emulate and set aside for posterity. Due to the foresight of the former owner, Louie R. Morgan, the land was transferred to the charitable Morgan Foundation and the County of DeSoto assists in its maintainence. Four road-wide trails penetrate the dense native vegetation; rustic wooden bridges and benches are scattered throughout: North Trail (.6 mile), River Loop (.6 mile), Main Trail (.5 mile) and the South Trail (1.25 mile).

The **North Trail** begins at the picnic grounds and heads into a thick, oak-sabal palm hammock and joins the River Loop Trail. Five-foot-high saw palmettos testify that this land has not been cleared for awhile. Both pond and bald cypress trees are found, as well as water oak and a dense growth of myrtle oak. Although the trail skirts the Peace River, it nevers descends into the floodplain.

Rest bench on the Peace River

Evidence of wild hog and armadillo "rooting" can be seen along the trail. Fire-charred trunks of sabal palms indicate a recent burning. The **River Loop Trail** joins the Main Trail that leads over bridges and blackwater tributary streams. Cardinals and woodpeckers are common along this portion of the trail. The **Main Trail** connects to the South Trail, or you may continue back to the picnic grounds.

The longest walk, **South Trail** passes by the Peace River, the western boundary of Morgan Park. Bass, brim, catfish, perch, mullet and an occasional snook can be found in the river, but there is no fishing allowed. Alligators can be seen sunning along the river bank. During the dry season, shark teeth and bones are found along the sandy river banks. The Peace River marked the boundary between the Americans and the Seminole Indians for a few years. The Seminoles referred to the river as "Peas," for the cowpeas and other legumes that grew abundantly along the riverbanks.

Morgan Park and Arcadia are located near the center of De Soto County. Morgan Park is 1.1 mile west of the intersection of U.S. 17 and S.R. 70 on the Old Bradenton Road, also known as Hickory Street. The one main entrance can be reached by travelling west on Hickory Street from the center of Arcadia. No motor vehicles are allowed past the park entrance. A caretaker lives on the park premises. The park is open sunrise to sundown.

De Soto Environmental Learning Laboratory
Arcadia/De Soto County
Area: 40 acres
Trail Distance: 4 miles
Highlights: nature study, nature trails, zoo, alternative energy displays

Dedicated to environmental education, this De Soto County "school without walls" is open to area students as well as the general public. Except for major holidays, the "lab" is open year round from 9 a.m. to 4:30 p.m. A facility and trail map guide is available at the parking entrance.

Immediately north of the parking area is a working alternative energy display focussing on wind, solar, and methane. To the west of the parking lot is the small zoo, with rabbits, birds, goats, and sheep. Adjacent to the zoo is a 60-yard-long boardwalk that penetrates a water pop ash swamp, looping back to the alternative energy display and main classroom.

Just north across Pomeroy Creek is a white-tailed deer pen, a railroad-tie-lined trail, and a large animal zoo that includes such inhabitants as bobcats, foxes, raccoons, opposums, skunks, squirrels, snakes, and a pig-tail macaque monkey. The four miles of grassy walking trails that weave about the property pass through and around wet lowland swamp, cypress bayhead, hammock and live oak hammock. Red maple, coastal plain willow, American elm, bald cypress, and sabal palms are the common trees. Labeled red signs identify the plants by their common names.

To reach De Soto Environmental Learning Laboratory from I-75 near Port Charlotte, exit north on C.R. 769/761 and drive 10-11 miles north to Environmental Lab Road, then west a quarter-mile, north of C.R. 760. (An identification or directional sign is posted at the road entrance). The lab is two miles west at the dead end of Environmental Lab Road from C.R. 761.

Myakka River State Park
Trip 1: Interpretive Center, nature trail, birdwalk
Sarasota and Manatee Counties
Area: 28,875 acres
Trail Distance: .6 mile total
Highlights: nature study, nature walks, picnicking, shelters, fishing, boat ramp, canoeing, bicycling, airboat and tram tours, ranger-guided walks, interpretive center, cabins, camping, rentals, concessions
Fee(s): entrance, tours, bicycle & canoe rentals, cabins, camping

The visitor to Myakka River State Park will discover a multitude of outdoor recreational opportunities at Florida's largest state park. If your visit is time-limited, you may consider at least three stops that will give an idea of what exists in the surrounding vastness: the interpretive nature center, nature trail, and the bird boardwalk.

After paying the entrance fee and acquiring all of the available literature about the wildlife and ecology of the park, turn at the first left about 100 yards from the gatehouse to the interpretive center. The small rustic building houses dioramas and exhibits on the flora and fauna of Myakka. A daily slide program is conducted at 3 p.m. by the park naturalist.

As you continue the drive on the main park road over the Myakka River past the cabins, you will come to the parking trailhead for the half-mile nature trail. This walk encircles a mature live oak and sabal palm hammock and penetrates marshlands. Sixteeen interpretive markers line the sandy trail at scattered intervals. Hammocks, summer floods, feral pigs, epiphytes, fire's role, and marshlands are some of the topics dealt with on the markers. Guided ranger walks are conducted at 9 a.m. on Sundays and meet at the parking area.

Further on, where the main park road forks to the left, is a lakeview picnic area with concessions, canoe and bicycle rentals, the world's largest airboat, and tram train tours. After lunch you may want to cruise the lake on the *Gator Gal* or board the 70-passenger tram train into the back country.

If you return to the road fork, then take the main park road to the right past the main campground and lake shore, you will arrive at the birdwalk on the upper side of the lake. Equipped with plenty of benches, this elevated boardwalk provides scenic vistas of Upper Myakka Lake. Morning or dusk is a good time to observe the feeding birdlife in this shallow part of the lake. Over 227 bird species have been observed in the park. There is a good possibility that you will see black feral pigs that come down to the lake edge to root and wallow.

To reach Myakka River State Park from I-75, take S.R. 72 exit 38 east 17 miles to the park entrance. The park opens at 8 a.m. and closes at sunset year round. There is a north entrance to the park on S.R. 780 (from I-75 exit 39) that is open only on weekends and holidays from 8 a.m. to 5 p.m.

Myakka River State Park
Trip 2: Backpacking
Sarasota and Manatee Counties
Area: 28,875 acres
USGS Maps: Old Myakka, Myakka City 1:24,000
Trail Distance: 38.9 miles
Highlights: nature study, hiking, primitive camping
Fee(s): entrance, primitive camping

Myakka River

Thanks to the Florida Trail Association volunteers and the Florida Park Service, day hikers and overnight backpackers can enjoy the nearly 40 miles of developed trail through hammocks of live oaks and sabal palms, open pine flatwoods, and along dry and wet prairies, streams, ponds, sloughs and marshes where wildlife is plentiful. Four loop trails, located in the remote eastern section of the park, offer several days of rigorous hiking and primitive camping: Bee Island, Honore, Deer Prairie and East Loops. At the entrance station, report to the ranger that you will be either day hiking or overnight camping. He or she will give you the gate number for parking and the necessary overnight camping permit.

The trailhead begins 6.2 miles from the entrance stations at the Bee Island Loop trail parking area. The main routes have white blazes painted on tree trunks. All cross trails and campsite trail spurs have blue blazes and trail junctions are marked with signposts.

The shortest route to Bee Island campground, an oak hammock, is just over five miles on the western section of the loop trail and seven miles on the rough, unfinished eastern section. Begin your hike early in the day in order to reach the site and set up camp if you are on an overnight. Water is not available, but a privy toilet has been provided. The other four campsites (Honore, Panther Point, Prairie, and Oak Grove) do have purified pump water, but do not have privy toilets. Campfires are permitted. A maximum of 12 people are allowed at each campsite. Be prepared for muddy and wet feet at certain times of the year. Be advised wild hogs have rooted up several sections of the trail, especially where it has been built up to an elevated narrow walkway in sections of Honore and Deer Prairie Loops. The old railroad grade is high and dry and intersects all the loop trails except for Bee Island.

To reach Myakka River State Park from I-75, take the S.R. 72 exit 38 east 17 miles to the park entrance. A trail map is available at the entrance station to the park.

Myakka River State Park
Trip 3: Wilderness Preserve
Sarasota County
Area: 7,500 acres
USGS Map: Lower Myakka Lake 1:24,000
Trail Distance: 3 miles
Highlights: nature study, nature walk, fishing

Lower Myakka Lake and its watershed form this vast wilderness preserve of 7,500 acres. A very small area is accessible by foot in this undisturbed natural tract. Before venturing off down the only firelane trail to the lake, you will have to register at the park entrance with the park ranger. Daily access is limited to 30 persons.

The preserve's entrance and parking area are one mile west of the Myakka River State Park entrance station on S.R. 72. The 1.5-mile one-way trail cuts throuph the pine flatwoods of mostly saw palmetto and views are limited. About halfway to Deep Hole, a major limestone sinkhole, is a spur trail that leads to the lake shore. You will have to retrace your steps back to the main trail road and continue on to trail's end at the lake.

Once you reach the lake, there is a wildlife path along the lakeshore and through the sabal palm hammock. Fishing is popular at Lower Myakka Lake. Plans are to establish a nature trail around the lake in the future. Canoeists can also enjoy the preserve.

To reach Myakka River State Park from I-75, take the S.R. 72 exit 38 east 17 miles to the park entrance. Be advised to visit the preserve early in the day before the quota is filled.

Koreshan State Historic Site
Estero/Lee County
Area: 305 acres
Trail Distance: .75 mile
Highlights: nature study, nature trail, Koreshan Settlement tour, picnicking, fishing, boat ramp, interpretive programs, camping
Fee(s): entrance, settlement tour, camping

Those fascinated by the social and natural history of southwest Florida will find Koreshan State Historic Site of special interest. The park's 305 acres are divided into parcels of land: the "home area" or former headquarters of the Koreshan United and the main park, the 70 acres of mangrove swamp embracing the entrance or "mouth" of Estero River at Estero Bay, and 100-acre Mound Key.

In 1894, a religious visionary named Dr. Cyrus R. Teed brought his followers from Chicago to establish a settlement of people who "lived inside the world." Dr. Teed's grandiose plan of a "New Jerusalem" did not come to pass. Nonetheless, the commune flourished during the years from 1894 to 1911. In the process, many cultural activities were introduced to the wilderness of southwestern Florida. A guided tour by the park ranger will explain the lifestyle of the Koreshans, who advocated "Cellular Cosmogony" and practiced celibacy, communal living, and group ownership of property. The 45-minute tour includes identification of the numerous plants the Koreshans introduced and a tour of the well-preserved buildings. Planned for the future is a "living history" of life as it once was at Koreshan during the turn of the century. The present day Koreshan Headquarters and World College of Life is just outside the park at the northeast corner of Tamiami Trail/U.S. 41 and Corkscrew Road.

West of the Koreshan Settlement, by the Estero River, is the campground, picnic area, boat ramp, and nature trail. The self-guiding trail features interpretive markers that describe the vegetation associated with the scrub and pine flatwoods. Saw palmetto, cabbage palm, slash pine and established exotics such as Brazilian pepper and melaleuca or "cajeput" comprise the major plants of the habitat. Amateur botanists may also recognize live oak, wax myrtle, Spanish bayonet, coontie, prickly pear cactus, and leather ferns.

Canoeists on the Estero

Near the mouth of Estero Bay (Estero is Spanish for estuary) is **Mound Key**, accessible only by canoe or boat, three miles down the river from the boat ramp. Boat access is provided on the north side of the island, where a small lagoon offers shelter. A one-mile trail begins here and traverses the Indian mounds to the other side of the island. The man-made island became the site of a religious ceremonial mound of the Calusa Indians, who controlled all of south Florida before the arrival of the Spanish. With the gradual deposition of shells by several generations, Mound Key became the highest elevation in the region (31 feet) and remains the highest geographical point in Lee County, The Calusa constructed canals, a temple mound, domiciliary mounds, burial mounds and other features. There is botanical evidence of plants being introduced from Mexico and the American Southwest for food and medicine.

Today the mounds are still intact. Excavation has been minimal. Mound Key is listed in the National Register of Historic Places. An interpretive boat tour of the Estero River and an interpretive center on Mound Key is being considered for future development. Koreshan State Historic Site is easily reached from I-75 just south of the community of Estero at Corkscrew Road exit 19. Turn west and drive directly across the Tamiami Trail/U.S. 41 to the park entrance.

Corkscrew Swamp Sanctuary
Collier County
Area: 11,000 acres
Trail Distance: 2 miles
Highlights: nature study, nature trail, picnicking, shelters, gift shop, Audubon Society membership
Fee(s): entrance

Once threatened by logging and development, 11,000 acres of Corkscrew Swamp became a sanctuary through the tireless efforts of the National Audubon Society in the early 1950's. This oasis exists on the north edge of the Big Cypress Swamp and is nationally known for 500-year-old virgin bald cypress trees and the largest colony of woodstorks in the United States.

Along the paved and boardwalk trail, day visitors can learn about the abundance of life within the tranquil sanctuary as the walk traverses pine flatwoods, wet prairie, pond cypress borders, bald cypress forest strands (unique formations of trees in slowly mov-

Nesting wood storks

ing water), willow borders, marsh, "lettuce" lakes, and custard apple ponds. All life is dependent on the water flow and level. An illustrated guided tour book describes the flora and fauna. Audubon naturalists are available along the trail to answer your questions.

All seasons bring their special treasures. Spring and summer is the time to see wildflowers in abundance, particularly orchids and bromeliads. The dry winter months are when the endangered wood storks build their nests. The name "Corkscrew" was given to the twisting, winding Imperial River by coastal pioneers who made inland journeys in pursuit of freshwater.

The Sanctuary entrance is 30 miles northeast of Naples and 14 miles west of Immokalee on Collier County Road 849, 1.5 miles from Collier County Road 846. From I-75 exit Naples-Immokalee Highway/C.R. 846 and drive east to the sanctuary. Groups may request a naturalist-guided tour in advance by writing or telephoning the sanctuary. The hours are 7 a.m. to 5 p.m., December to May and 8 to 5, May througb November. The address and telephone number are:

Corkscrew Swamp Sanctuary
National Audubon Society
Route 6, Box 1875-A
Naples, Florida
(813) 657-3771

Stephen F. Briggs Nature Center
Naples/Collier County
Area: 8,000 acres
Trail Distance: 3 trails total 1 mile
Highlights: nature study, nature trail, nature center, naturalist canoe & boat trips, birding excursions
Fees: entrance, guide books, field trips/excursions

Red mangrove prop roots, Stephen F. Briggs Nature Center

National estuarine sanctuaries are rare, but the 2,500 members of the Conservancy, Inc. have been successful in helping to establish an 8,000-acre preserve in Rookery Bay that is now managed by The Conservancy, National Audubon Society, and the Florida Department of Natural Resources. Shallow bays, tidal creeks, and mangrove forests compose the bulk of Rookery Bay's estuarine habitat, which is accessible only by boat. But a boardwalk loop of 500 feet winds its way through 10 acres of scrub oak, pinelands, salt marsh and mangrove, allowing the day visitor to stay high and dry. The wooden trail begins at the nature center where a self-guiding booklet on the plant and animal life of southern Florida can be obtained. There are nature displays and a full-time naturalist is on duty to answer any question you may have.

More than 100 species of birds reside here, including pelicans, ospreys, roseate spoonbills, screech owls, egrets, herons, towhees, woodpeckers, Carolina wrens, and southern bald eagles. The observation deck overlooking a shallow lake is a good place to observe water birds. Raccoons, bobcats, deer, dolphins, and rare mammals such as the manatee, Florida panther and Florida black bear add to the rich variety of wildlife. Marine research laboratories are operated by both The Conservancy and the Florida Department of Natural Resources.

A section of the walk, Stephen F. Briggs Nature Center

The Briggs Nature Center is south of Naples on Shell Island Road. Take the Tamiami Trail/U.S. 41 south to S.R. 951, turn west towards Marco Island and drive three miles on S.R. 951 to Shell Island Road, where you turn right. The Nature Center is about a mile northwest of S.R. 951.

Naturalist-guided tours of the boardwalk are available for groups that request them in advance. The Nature Center and boardwalk are accessible to the handicapped. Canoe trips and boat rides to other parts of the sanctuary are scheduled on a regular basis from November through April. Please make reservations.

The Briggs Nature Center is open from 9 to 5 daily, November 1 through May 1. It is closed on holidays and weekends May through October. For information and schedules call (813) 262-0304.

Two additional walking trails are found at the end of Sbell Island Road to the left of the boat ramp. The quarter-mile **Catclaw Trail** leads through mangrove forest, where several plants are labelled by their common and scientific names. The linear shell and sand path ends after an eighth of a mile and you must retrace your steps. The **Monument Trail** leads out to an open vista point overlooking

Rookery Bay and a vertical rock monument dedicated to conservationists Henry and Katherine Boyd. Retrace your steps.

Collier Seminole State Park
Naples/Collier County
Area: 6,423 acres
Trail Distance: 7.5 miles total
Highlights: nature study, nature trails, interpretive center, picnicking, shelters, fishing, boat ramp, canoe rental, wilderness canoe trips, camping
Fee(s): entrance, camping, canoe rental

Nearly two-thirds of the vast acreage of Collier-Seminole State Park is wilderness preserve and more accessible by boat than walking. Mangrove forests lined with tidal creeks and bays predominate and are a major part of the estuarine system of southwest Florida. Land areas of the park are available to the visitor on foot, however. The one-mile, self-guiding **Hammock Trail** begins in the northwest of the park near the boat basin and picnic area parking lot. The loop walk passes through tropical hammock forest, mangrove forest, and the borders of a salt marsh. The boardwalk section of the trail penetrates the mangrove forest. The mid-point overlook platform provides a sweeping view of a salt marsh composed primarily of salt-tolerant grasses and succulents. Benches have been provided here and elsewhere along the trail.

One of the interesting botanical features along the trail is the rare Florida royal palm. Although a commonly planted and desireable landscape palm, the tree is found growing naturally in the wild only in two other south Florida locations: the nearby Fakahatchee Strand and the Everglades National Park. The royal palm was so admired by town dwellers in the early part of the century, they were transplanted in large numbers from the wild to grace streetsides, yards and parks.

Slightly higher in elevation than the surrounding area, the second growth hammock has characteristics of a Caribbean-West Indian, coastal forest with a significant number of diverse plant species. The trail marker points out that there are a greater variety of plant species in tropical forests than in northern temperate forests, but there are fewer individual specimens of each species. Typical trees and shrubs of the tropical hammock include gumbo limbo, sabal palm, Jamaica dogwood, white stopper, mastic, strangler fig, inkwood, pigeon plum, cat's claw, live oak, lancewood, and red mulberry (a temperate zone tree mingling with tropical ones). Climbing vines such as devil's claw and hippocrata adorn the trees. Ferns are common on the hammock floor as are stumps and fallen logs.

Animal life is common also along the Hammock Trail. Rare inhabitants include wood storks, bald eagles, red-cockaded woodpeckers, black bear, and manatees, along with alligators, marsh rabbits, hawks, and wading birds. Mosquitoes are also abundant, so be prepared.

The 6.5-mile **Collier-Seminole Hiking Trail** loop was recently established in cooperation with the Florida Trail Association. The trailhead and parking area are half a mile southeast of the main park entrance on U.S. 41, just after crossing the second canal bridge on the left/north side of the highway. Register at the main park gatehouse before you begin your hike.

After unlocking the gate, enter and park in the designated area. The main route is blazed with eye-level white rectangles appearing at regular intervals on trees. Both directions are blazed. The overnight camping area is 3.1 miles from the trailhead parking area. The .4-mile campground spur is blazed with blue rectangles. Overnight campers must register at the main park gatehouse and pay a small fee. It is an additional 3.4 miles from the campground back to the parking area following the loop. The trail traverses sabal palm hammocks, slash pinelands, and a 100-yard section of bald cypress slough that will require some knee-deep wading, though for the most part the trail is high and dry. The trail can easily be hiked in one day, or even a half-day. Tennis shoes are adequate but the trail surface is sometimes rough oolitic limestone and narrow in places. A trail map is available from the main park gatehouse where you register.

Collier-Seminole State Park entrance is 15 miles southeast of Naples on the Tamiami Trail/U.S. 41. From I-75 exit south on Isle of Capri Road/C.R. 951, the last exit before or the first exit after the Alligator Alley toll booth at Naples. Go south on C.R. 951 to the junction with U.S. 41/Tamiami Trail, turn left/south and proceed to the park entrance, just south of the junction with S.R. 92 to Marco Island.

Fakahatchee Strand State Preserve
Copeland/Collier County
Area: 60,000 acres
USGS Maps: Ochopee, Weavers Station, Deep Lake, Deep Lake SW
1:24,000
Trail Distance: 4,000-ft. boardwalk one-way, forest roads at Gates 2, 7, 12, 16
Highlights: nature study, nature walks, picnicking

Pristine landscapes untouched by civilization are a rarity in southern Florida and the Fakahatchee Strand is no exception. The place name "Fakahatchee" is a Seminole Indian word meaning muddy river. The word "Strand" has a unique meaning in the Big Cypress Swamp. Roughly defined, a strand is a tree-filled narrow channel or slough. Rainfall is the primary source of water in the Big Cypress Swamp. Surface water then moves slowly southward towards the Gulf of Mexico. In the process, the moving water cuts a channel in the soft limestone that gradually fills in with water-loving vegetation. The Fakahatchee Strand is over 20 miles long and three to five miles across, making it one of the largest strands in the Big Cypress Swamp.

The only section of the strand saved from logging crews is at Big Cypress Bend. A 4,000-foot linear boardwalk penetrates the primeval jungle-like world of virgin mixed bald cypress, laurel oaks, sabal palms, willow, red maple, lancewood, wild coffee, marlberry – the dominant trees and shrubs that also harbor an abundance of epiphytic plants such as rare orchids and bromeliads. Additional plant life includes outstanding strangler fig specimens, an assortment of vines, 20 species of ferns, coco plum, pop ash, pond apple, alligator flag, pickerel weed, and arrowhead.

Birdlife is plentiful with white ibis, wood duck, green heron, barred owls, migratory warblers, pileated woodpeckers, and wood storks in evidence. Deer, squirrel, raccoon, opposum, otter, bobcat, and othor mammals frequent the preserve, including the endangered mangrove fox squirrel, Everglades mink, Florida black bear, and Florida panther (this is the feline's most important site).

The Big Cypress Bend Boardwalk is a National Natural Landmark of the U.S. Park Service. The boardwalk is located at Big Cypress Bend on Tamiami Trail/U.S. 41, seven miles west of the junction of

S.R. 29 and about five miles east of the Collier-Seminole State Park entrance. A large light-blue and white lettered sign identifies the trail's entrance on the north side of the highway adjacent to an Indian village, where limited parking is available. The boardwalk trailhead is about 100 yards north along a service road. Numbered stations of interpretation are spaced along the boardwalk, which ends at an overlook of Lake Surprise. You must retrace your steps.

Just east of the boardwalk along the Tamiami Trail are canoe access points where park rangers lead guided day-long canoe tours through five miles of mangrove-lined passageways to Fakahatchee Bay and Daniels Point. You can enjoy this free outing by making advance reservations with the park rangers at Collier-Seminole State Park.

The northern section of the Fakahatchee Strand can also be explored, either by car or on foot along Janes Scenic Drive, which begins at the Copeland Ranger Station and Firetower, three miles north of the Tamiami Trail on S.R. 29. A popular day hike into this area is the West Main Trail, an old logging road. Located west of Janes Scenic Drive at Gate 7, the second bend after the ranger station, West Main goes due west while the drive curves north. The old road is a straight route, but does penetrate the strand. Several overgrown side roads venture off south from West Main. You will need to retrace your way back to Janes Scenic Drive.

About six miles north of the Copeland ranger station is Royal Palm Hammock Picnic Area and Gate 12, the trailhead for the southern terminus of the abandoned and overgrown East Main logging trambed or road. East Main runs nearly 10 miles due north to Alligator Alley/I-75, the north terminus located about 3.2 miles west of S.R. 29 at the intersection of Alligator Alley. This trail is recommended for experienced hikers only. The trail becomes very wet in the north portion of the property. Palms Hammock is located about mid-point on Janes Scenic Drive, where royal palms can be seen. Fakahatchee Strand contains the largest concentration of these palms in the wild.

Perhaps the most remote unmarked nature walk is north of Palms Hammock at Gate 16 or Mud Tram, situated at the third bend or curve of the drive from the ranger station. The old road goes straight north to Guzmania Gardens or Area 15. Orchids are commonly seen in this area. The Fakahatchee Strand is noted for over 40 species of orchids and as many as 10 are found only here, including the rat-tail orchid, Acuna's Epidendrum and dwarf Epidendrum. You must retrace your steps. A compass is advisable when exploring the strand, as are maps. Return south to the ranger station and Copeland along Janes Scenic Drive, a distance of eleven miles one-way.

There are plans to expand the Strand's acreage and to create a Panther Wildlife Refuge administered by the U.S. Fish and Wildlife Service.

"Wet hikes" with the preserve rangers are usually conducted every two weeks during the dry winter season. For further information please contact Fakahatcbee Strand State Preserve, P.O. Box 548, Copeland, Florida 33926; (813)695-4593.

Big Cypress National Preserve
Loop Road To Alligator Alley Section 1/Florida Trail
Collier and Monroe Counties
Area: 580,000 acres
USGS Maps: Monroe Station, Monroe Station NE, Immokalee 4 NE,
Trail Distance: 38 miles
Fee(s): Florida Trail Association membership for private property crossing north of the Big Cypress National Preserve boundary

Big Cypress National Preserve is currently the southern terminus of the Florida Trail. From Alligator Alley/Everglades Parkway S.R. 84/I-75 (different names for the same road) south to Loop Road/S.R. 94 is a total of 38 hiking miles through cypress strands, cypress prairies, pinelands, and some oak-sabal palm hammocks. Big Cypress is home to a mix of wildlife such as the Florida panther, black bear, bald eagle, mangrove fox squirrel, wood stork, feral hog, mink, wild turkey, swallow-tail kite, and the Cape Sable sparrow.

Be advised that if you are not a Florida Trail Association member hike only within the boundary of the National Preserve. Portions of the trail in the north section cross private property. Plan on getting your feet wet even during the normally dry winter season since sections of the trail remain underwater year round, particularly in the north. Also the trail surface is rough limestone in most places, which can make hiking one mile seem like two, especially with gear. Park rangers report the best month to hike is March, but anytime between December and April can be good.

Trail access begins at the Oasis Ranger Station in the heart of the preserve on the Tamiami Trail/U.S. 41. Vehicle day or overnight parking is allowed in the Oasis Ranger Station parking lot at the west end near the trailhead registration box. The Tamiami Trail/U.S. 41 actually divides the Florida Trail into two sections of north and south.

The north section (29.7 miles one-way), begins at the Oasis Ranger Station and ends at Alligator Alley/Interstate 75. The last six miles cross private property and are outside of the preserve. Please register at the posted box at the trailhead. Follow the F.T.A. orange blazes that appear on the trunks and branches of trees. After 2.9 miles of hiking, a blue blazed return loop joins from the west. There are two campgrounds in this section. One is Seven-Mile Camp, a pine-palmetto island located 6.8 miles from the Oasis Ranger Station. The second camp is 16.7 miles from Oasis in a sabal palm hammock. Both campsites have pump well water, but no privy toilets. After 14 miles the return loop begins and follows a blue-blazed route south, back to the ranger station. You may continue northward to the Alligator Alley northern terminus if you are a card-carrying member of the Florida Trail Association.

Although overgrown and not recommended, the south section of the Big Cypress Florida Trail begins at the Oasis Ranger Station and continues southward 8.3 miles one-way to Loop Road/S.R. 94. The first 2.4 miles are marked by a large orange blaze that indicates a direct southerly course. The trail then heads east in Roberts Strand (usually wet) on a tram road where trail blazes begin. Two campsites are located in the south section. One is at an abandoned cabin site on the tramway (three miles) and the second camp is in a sabal palm hammock (3.3 miles). After 5.3 miles you arrive at Sawmill Road where trail blazes end. Follow the trail south on Sawmill Road to Loop Road for three miles. Retrace your steps back 8.3 miles from this southern terminus of the Big Cypress Florida Trail to the Oasis Ranger Station.

Primitive offroad campsites near U.S. 41 are located at Burns Lake (five miles east of Ochopee), Monument (12 miles east of Ochopee), Midway (2.5 miles east of Oasis Ranger Station), and

Fifty Mile Bend (six miles east of Oasis Ranger Station). The Oasis
Ranger Station is 55 miles west from downtown Miami or 52 miles
east of Naples on the Tamiami Trail/U.S. 41.

Loop Road Interpretive Center
Pinecrest/Collier County
Trail Distance: .5 mile
Highlights: nature study, nature trail, interpretive environmental educ-
tion center

Since 1977, school children of south Florida have visited the Loop
Road Interpretive Center to gain an awareness of the Big Cypress
web of life. By learning through sensory awareness, the students
become more attuned to the natural world around them. Adults
can also enjoy the Center's short, but informative loop trail into
Tree Snail Hammock – a tropical hardwood tree island surrounded
by the Big Cypress National Preserve. The Interpretive Center is
administered by the National Park Service.

The nature trail begins at the gate just across the loop road from the
Interpretive Center, where you can park. The trail signs identify
the more common plants of the hammock such as cocoplum,
gumbo limbo, white stopper, sabal palm, lancewood, live oak,
marlberry, leather fern, coastal plain willow, wild coffee, poison
ivy, pigeon plum and wild tamarind, a host tree of the liguus tree
snail for whom the hammock was named. Tropical tree snails are
very colorful, with patterns that vary widely. One variety may
adorn a particular hammock and no other. During the dry winter
months the snail becomes dormant, sealing itself tight to the tree
bark. In summer they become active and are observed eating
lichens and algae that grow on the tree bark. Collection and habitat
destruction has severely curtailed the tree snail population.

The trail is hard to follow in places as it snakes through the
hammock, so keep an eye open for identifying markers. Watch
your step, for the floor of the hammock is mostly potholed limestone rock. There is a clearing where the remains of a late 1920's
moonshine still operated.

The Loop Road Interpretive Center and Tree Snail Hammock Trail
is on C.R. 94/Loop Road, approximately eight paved miles west
from the Tamiami Trail/U.S. 41 at the west edge of the Miccosukee

Indian Village. The scenic but unpaved Loop Road continues west from the Interpretive Center and trail and is recommended for short road walks. Loop Road runs 15 miles from the Interpretive Center to the Tamiami Trail at Monroe Station. Primitive campgrounds can be found enroute.

The Loop Road Interpretive Center is open during the week from 8 to 5 and is closed weekends. The hammock trail is open daily.

Everglades National Park

Unique to North America and the world, the 2,200 square miles of Everglades National Park are a subtropical wilderness that depends on the combination of flowing fresh water, a nearly frost-free climate, fire, and slight changes in elevation for its existence. Established in 1947 as a national park, Everglades is the third largest U.S. National Park after Yellowstone and Denali. The semi-aquatic, prairie-like landscape has been designated a World Heritage Site and an International Biosphere Reserve by the United Nations.

Several plants and animals are unique and exist nowhere else in the nation. Over 300 varieties of birds are found and 700 native plants. The park is also the home of many rare species such as the American saltwater crocodile, West Indian manatee, and the southern bald eagle.

The origin of the "Pa-hay-okee" or "grassy waters," as it was known to the Seminole Indians who arrived in the uninhabited land after 1842, is Lake Okeechobee, 110 miles north of the park. This "river of grass" was originally a seasonally flooded sawgrass prairie and swamp that sloped gently in a broad arc 40 miles wide and 100 miles long, flowing less than half a mile daily towards Florida Bay and the Gulf of Mexico, where nearly half of the park is under salt water. Before man's intervention with canals, levees, dikes and ditches, Lake Okeechobee overflowed its banks annually during the rainy months of summer, sending its waters southward. Legislation now determines how much water flows through the park and how much goes to thirsty urban areas and farmlands of southern Florida.

For the nature walker, the 5,000-year-old Everglades ecosystem is a watery domain where high land is scarce. The 1.5 million acres are comprised of freshwater sloughs and marl prairies, ponds, lakes, creeks, estuaries, channel passages, bights, coves, sounds, and bays. The grassy prairies are dotted with vegetated hammocks or "tree islands" and cypress domes. Sawgrass may grow as tall as 12 feet on the fertile vast expanses of watery prairie. This biological

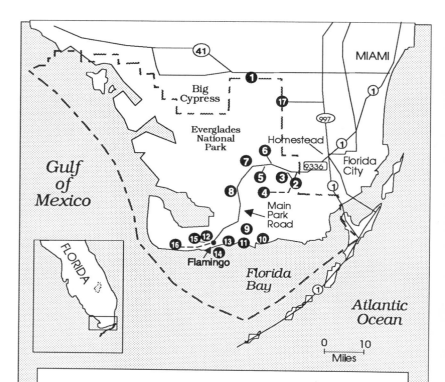

Everglades National Park

1. Shark Valley
2. Anhinga Trail
3. Gumbo Limbo Trail
4. Old Ingraham Highway
5. Long Pine Key Nature Trails
6. Pinelands Trail
7. Pa-hay-okee Overlook
8. Mahogany Hammock
9. West Lake
   Mangrove Nature Trail

10. Snake Bight Trail
11. Rowdy Bend Trail
12. Bear Lake Trail
13. Christian Point Trail
14. Guy Bradley Trail
15. Eco Pond
16. Coastal Prairie Trail
    and Bayshore Loop
17. Chekika

reserve is an aquatic paradise ideal for canoeists, but hikers also can share the terrain now that roads, canals, dikes and boardwalks have been built. Each ecological habitat of the Everglades can be seen on the trails.

Winter is normally the ideal season for hiking, when insects are minimal and the wildlife concentrates around the remaining sloughs and waterholes. Although the boardwalks and short paved trails are in excellent condition and accessible to the handicapped, the foot path conditions vary considerably. Most land trails are all but impassable during the summer, when it rains almost daily and the insects are unbearable.

Though winter is the dry season, some years are wet and warm, as if summer never ended. The gray marl, black muck and peat soils make an excellent walking surface when dry, but will be hazardous and slippery when wet. Tennis or canvas shoes that grip and dry quickly are recommended for the terrain, but hiking boots are best in areas where the surface is limestone rock. Long pants and shirt, hat and sunscreen are also recommended, along witb insect repellent and a snake bite kit. Be sure to bring drinking water on your hikes.

Except for Clubhouse Beach at the western terminus of the Coastal Prairie Trail and the two established campsites along the Old Ingraham Highway, primitive camps are limited. Canoeists will find plenty in the backcountry on a first-come, first-served basis. All campsites require a permit available at the ranger stations. Developed campgrounds at Long Pine Key and Flamingo are open for fee camping on a first-come basis, but the stay is limited to 14 days from November 1 to April 30. Camping is free from May 1 to October 31 due to the heat, humidity, and insects. Cooler weather and reduction of the insect population does not normally begin until late December or January.

The main park entrance is 12 miles west from Homestead on S.R. 27. It is best to stop at the main visitor center and become oriented to the park. Rangers are on duty to assist you. Films, books, and other park literature are available. Thirty-four common plants of the Everglades National Park are labeled along the sidewalk between the visitor center and parking area. Be sure to bring all your

Morning feeding in the Everglades

supplies with you. Trails are non-existent at Everglades City Ranger Station. Only boat tours are available.

The north portion of the park between Shark Valley and Pa-hay-okee Boardwalk was drastically changed by the 164 m.p.h winds of Hurricane Andrew on August 24, 1992. However all boardwalks and trails have been restored to their near-original design.

Shark Valley
Trail Distance: 2.75 miles
Highlights: nature study, nature trails, bicycling, tram, ranger hikes, park office, concession, observation tower, restrooms
Fee(s): entrance, tram, bicycle rentals

Shark Valley lies on the western edge of the Shark River Slough, a wide shallow waterway that is regarded as crucial to sustaining life in the Everglades National Park ecosystem. This freshwater sawgrass and marl prairie is punctuated with bayheads, cypress domes, and hardwood hammocks, some of which were once farmed by the Seminole Indians. Unique animal life to be seen includes numerous alligators, otters, the smaller Everglades variety of white-tailed deer, the wood stork and the rare snail kite – a specialized hawk that dines only on the algae-feeding apple snails.

Plant life is also abundant everywhere in this watery world, including poisonwood. Be aware.

The 15-mile loop road allows visitors to walk, bicycle, or take the tram the entire route, which is off-limits to motorized traffic. Nature walks near the park office and concessions area beyond the east and west loop road gates include **Bobcat Hammock Boardwalk** (.25 mile), **Otter Creek Trail** (one mile) and **Heron View Trail** (one mile). The trails are well-maintained, marked, and have interpretive stations and brochures. The half-mile **Observation Tower Trail** begins eight miles south of the park entrance near the 65-foot observation and fire tower. Large alligators can be seen from the observation tower in the adjacent canals. Please inquire at the visitor center for trail guide booklets and other information.

Shark Valley park entrance lies just off S.R. 41/Tamiami Trail at the east edge of the Miccosukee Indian Village, 30 miles from Miami and 70 miles from Naples. Shark Valley is open from 8:30 to 5 daily. A walk-in gate is open for off-hour access to the park. Ranger-led day outings are also worthwhile.

Anhinga Trail
Trail Distance: .5 mile
Highlights: nature study, nature walk, visitor center, museum ranger walks, gift shop

One of the most popular trails in Everglades National Park, the Anhinga Trail is noted for its abundant wildlife, seemingly oblivious to human observers. The winding boardwalk loop provides access to Taylor Slough, a slow-moving, marshy river that forms a deep depression in the oolitic rock, where water remains year-round, supplying life to plants and animals.

Wildlife congregates here during the winter dry season and scatters when the life-giving summer rains arrive. The fauna includes many creatures such as garfish, large mouth bass, southern bullfrogs, leopard frogs, snapping turtles, soft-shelled turtles, banded watersnakes, cottonmouths, alligators, otters, marsh rabbits, grebes, gallinules, coots, herons, egrets, grackles, limpkins and, of course, anhingas. Plants the visitor will see include bladderwort, cattails, water hyacinth, arrowheads, yellow water lily, pickerelweed, coastal plain willow, coco plum, wax myrtle, buttonbush, saltbush, pond apple, white swamp lily and sawgrass. Please take your time and enjoy the close-up view of all the wildlife. Park rangers lead scheduled hikes to enhance your visit.

Anhinga Trail begins near Royal Palm Visitor Center, located two miles wast of the main entrance station, and west of Homestead.

Gumbo Limbo Trail
Trail Distance: .5 mile
Highlights: nature study, nature walk, visitor center, museum, ranger walks

Adjacent to the Royal Palm Visitor Center, the paved Gumbo Limbo Trail loops through a 70-acre lush tropical hammock. At times called Paradise Key, this island-in-the-Everglades is where plants grow upon plants, creating an aerial forest. Before a devastating fire in 1945, the hammock was considered by many to be the most beautiful in southern Florida. The hammock has recovered over the past 40 years, and the visitor is introduced to a jungle-like floral world of giant vines, elegant royal palms, ferns, orchids, pigeon plums, lancewood, poisonwood, strangler figs, and numerous gumbo limbo trees, also known as "tourist tree" or "naked Indian" because of its conspicuous peeling red bark. Avian life includes white-eyed vireos, blue-gray gnatcatchers, redstarts, palm warblers, yellow-rumped warblers, woodpeckers, catbirds, cardinals, barred owls, and red-shouldered hawks. This forest is a truly precious natural resource.

Royal Palm Visitor Center is two miles from the main park entrance, west of Homestead. The Anhinga Trail is on the east side of the visitor center and the Gumbo Limbo Trail. Ranger-led hikes are scheduled. Paradise Key and the Anhinga Trail boardwalk were greatly altered by Hurricane Andrew. Although many of the gumbo limbo trees survived, they were severely "pruned" by the high winds.

Old Ingraham Highway
Trail Distance: 10.8 miles one-way
Highlights: nature study, nature walk, primitive camping

The Old Ingraham Highway was replaced by the main park road to Flamingo during the 1940's. Today walkers, bicyclists, and some

The Anhinga Trail

motorized traffic move along this normally dry and paved stretch of narrow highway that traverses open miles of Everglades and scattered cypress stands. Some of the best wildlife viewing is available to those who venture forth along this extension of roadway built up from earthfill of the adjacent Homestead Canal. Views of Taylor Slough are seen through the occasional breaks in the green roadside facade of ficus trees, coco plum, and reedgrass. Two backcountry campsites have been established along the route. A backcountry permit must be obtained from the main visitor center at the park entrance.

This ribbon of roadway is straight as an arrow with only one big bend four miles southwest of the Long Pine Key metal barrier gate. Once past the bend, the trail heads due west seven miles to the main park road at Sweet Bay Pond, but the Ingraham Highway terminates about two miles from the main park road, where the park service has bulldozed the roadbed, making the remainder of the. walk very wet. It is advised that you begin your walk at the northeast end, starting at Long Pine Key metal gate where trail parking is available.

The road trailhead is at the end of Long Pine Key Road, two miles south of the turnoff for the Research Center from the Royal Palm

Visitor Center entrance road, or four miles southwest of the main park entrance.

Long Pine Key Nature Trails

Trail Distance: 22 miles total
Highlights: nature study, nature trails, picnicking, shelters, bicycling, amphitheatre, camping, ranger station, restrooms
Fee(s): camping

Swamp lily, Long Pine Key

Walking though the slash pine forest along the fire roads of Long Pine Key is an especially unique and diverse woodland experience. The forest floor is composed of exposed ancient limestone called pinnacle rock that is filled with solution holes, giving it a "swiss cheese" effect and making it rather treacherous to venture off the trail. Two hundred different understory plants are growing here and 30 of these are found nowhere else on earth. Outside the park, pineland communities are highly valued by realtors, thus making remaining stands the most endangered pinelands in the United States.

There are three marked trails at Long Pine Key, and all three begin and end at the campground area. **Loop Trail A** begins at gate 3 and heads east and south to gate 2A, then west on Research Center Road to gate 2B. It then goes north to gate 3A and the campground, for a total of three miles. **Loop Trail B** is a continuation of the shorter Loop Trail A, beginning at gate 3, then heading east and south to gate 2 and the Research Center Road. It then veers west to gate 2B and north to 3A, for a total of five miles. The **Long Pine Key Nature Trail** runs seven miles one-way west from the campground to Pine Glades Lake along fire roads. Bicyclists are often seen along the route.

Long Pine Key campground and visitor area is four miles from the park entrance. Pine Glades Lake can be accessed from the main park road 9.5 miles from the park entrance. You may hike from either direction.

Pinelands Trail
Trail Distance: .5 mile
Highlights: nature study, nature walk

Pinelands Trail is a paved short loop through a section of slash pine forest on Long Pine Key. The visitor is introduced to the flora and fauna of this disappearing forest: saw palmetto, coontie, poison-wood, wild grape, ferns, moon flower vine, gallberry, raccoon, opossum, box turtle, screech owl, pine warbler, liguus tree snail, pygmy rattlesnake, white-tailed deer, and the endangered Florida panther–to name a few residents of the evergreen habitat.

The visitor also learns that pinelands cannot survive without periodic natural or induced fires. A pine tree is adapted to fire with its thick corky outer bark that insulates the woody plant from the hottest blaze. Without fire, hardwood trees would replace the softwood pines, which are unable to survive in the deep shade of the hardwood trees' foliage.

Pinelands Trail

Pinelands is 6.5 miles from the main park entrance.

Pa-hay-okee Overlook
Trail Distance: .4 mile
Highlights: nature study, nature walk, overlook tower

The Seminole Indians called the Everglades "Pa-hay-okee," meaning "grassy waters" – a name truly descriptive of this vast prairie-like land. Scientifically, the sawgrass is not really a grass, but a sedge with saw-like teeth.

The boardwalk is lined with quotations from famous naturalists as well as school children who have come to philosophical grips with the watery environment. The boardwalk leads to the observation tower overlook and surveys the largest expanse of sawgrass in the world. At the tower one can observe the wide, shallow river and learn how water flow is now controlled by man's dams and canals. Wildfire also has its role of maintaining the grassy world. The wet and dry seasons have their impact. Patient observers may see red-shouldered hawks, red-winged blackbirds, common yellow-throats, vultures, pygmy rattlesnakes, indigo and king snakes, and an occasional alligator.

The Pa-hay-okee Overlook and Tower are 12.5 miles from the entrance station of the park just beyond Rock Reef Pass.

Mahogany Hammock
Trail Distance: .5 mile
Highlights: nature study, nature walk

Mahogany Hammock is literally a green island of tropical hard-woods surrounded by a sea of sawgrass. This high ground hammock is characterized by a rich variety of plant and animal life. Mahogany Hammock is aptly named since several large mahogany trees are found growing here, including the largest one in the United States – 11 feet in circumference.

The elevated boardwalk zigzags across the heavily-shaded understory and is broken by sunlight only where some of the huge trees were downed by Hurricanes Donna and Andrew. The rare paurotis palm inhabits the margin of the hammock. The boardwalk trail penetrates a small thicket of these exquisite palms. Other plants include a variety of orchids, mosses, ferns, bromeliads, strangler figs, gumbo limbos, poisonwood, wild coffee, paradise trees, tamarinds, white stoppers, and sabal palms. The dense forest canopy traps the heat from decaying vegetation and keeps the temperature relatively frost-free during the winter months, but shady and cooler in summer. Animal life includes the colorful tree snail, spring migratory birds such as warblers, small mammals, reptiles and insects, like the gold and black zebra butterfly. Mosquitoes are also among the fauna and are a severe nuisance in summer.

Enroute to Flamingo, be sure to stop and stroll the boardwalk and learn about life in Mahogany Hammock. The hammock is 19.5 miles from the park's main entrance.

West Lake Mangrove Nature Trail
Trail Distance: .25 mile
Highlights: nature study, nature walk, fishing, boat launch ramp, interpretive displays, restrooms, canoe trail

The West Lake boardwalk helps you explore the role the mangrove communities play in the coastal ecology of southern Florida. This brief but well-marked boardwalk weaves through three separate mangrove habitats, extending over the waters of West Lake, where benches have been provided for observation. Exhibits are housed in the nearby interpretive center and restroom building. West Lake is a perfect example of a pristine mangrove estuary. Information listed below is found along the boardwalk and the center.

The Three Species of Mangroves:
White Mangrove
Black Mangrove
Red Mangrove

Wildlife of the Mangroves:
Mangrove water snake
Barred owl
Florida panther
Swallow-tail kite
Raccoon
Crab spider
Walking stick
Mangrove skipper
Bobcat
Diamond-back rattlesnake
Marsh rabbit
Blue-tailed skink

Birds of the Mangroves:
Wood stork
Louisiana heron
Lesser scaup duck
Baldpate
Pintail
Ring-neck duck
Blue-wing teal
Double-crested cormorant
Common egret
American-coot
White ibis
Chucks-wills widow

West Lake mangroves

West Lake is about eight miles north of the Flamingo Nature and Visitor Center.

Snake Bight Trail

Trail Distance: 2 miles one-way
Highlights: nature study, nature trail, tram tour

The Snake Bight Trail follows an old canal spur of the main Homestead Canal that originated during the drainage efforts of the 1920's. The trail road is maintained for the concession tram tours originating from Flamingo. The pathway is firm, dry, and fairly smooth over the entire four-mile round-trip. The spoil banks which form the foundation provide an environment in which hardwood trees such as gumbo limbo, strangler fig, cinnamon bark, and poisonwood flourish. This artificial hammock makes for a shady path.

There has been a long history of human occupation in the area. A short distance from the trail are several Calusa Indian shell mounds, now largely hidden by mangroves, that may be over 1,000 years old. The canal builders intentionally avoided the mounds. Of more recent vintage are the remains of settlers' shacks.

The trail ends with a view of Snake Bight; a bay within Florida Bay. The boardwalk at the bight enables the walker to view shore and wading birds without obstruction. Along the shore of the lake are numerous skeletons of mangrove trees destroyed in the 1960 Hurricane Donna. Crocodiles are a saltwater species which periodically venture into brackish waters of the bight. You must retrace your steps to return.

To reach Snake Bight Trail, drive six miles from the Flamingo Visitor Center north and park in the turnouts alongside the road. The trail and trailhead are marked.

Rowdy Bend Trail

Trail Distance: 2.5 miles one-way
Highlights: nature study, nature trail,

The Rowdy Bend Trail is a former road constructed during the 1930's for access to eradicate the native cotton plants that harbored pink boll worms. These worms were spreading to the cultivated commercial cotton crops at the time. Today, this grass-stubbled trail is perhaps the only evidence the cotton pickers were here.

On the Snake Bight Trail

The linear trail spur road begins three miles north of the Flamingo Visitor Center. Park your car in the marked roadside turnout and continue walking up the road north about 100 yards to the trailhead sign. Head southeast through this inland "ridge" country of buttonwood and sabal palm forest. In about half a mile, the trail enters an open coastal prairie of salt-tolerant plants such as cordgrass, pickle weed, and glasswort. Numerous dead trees are scattered about, having been destroyed by past hurricanes. Ospreys have built nests in some of these dead trees. After 2.5 miles, the Rowdy Bend Trail will join with Snake Bight Trail. At this point, you have the option to extend the hike by heading south to Snake Bight or north to Snake Bight Trailhead. Or retrace your steps.

Bear Lake Trail

Trail Distance: 2 miles one-way
Highlights: nature study, nature trail, canoe launch ramp, canoe trail

The Bear Lake Trail is a short section of an old abandoned automobile road to Cape Sable that was built using fill from the Bear Lake Canal, which parallels the trail. The canal and the adjacent road were part of a plan to drain and develop the area during the earlier part of the 20th century. Instead of draining fresh water out to the sea, the canal allowed salt water to back up inland. The old roadbed is high and dry, however, and allows hikers the opportunity to explore this section of the park.

The canal provides a habitat for the many wading birds that feed here during the winter season. White ibis, Louisiana herons, snowy and great egrets, wood storks, and roseate spoonbills are often seen near the end of the trail where mangroves line the banks. The first mile and a half supports a buttonwood plant community while the slightly higher roadbed fosters a growth of tropical hardwoods. Be alert for poison ivy and poisonwood. The shady, tree-lined path ends at the shores of Bear Lake, where you can rest and enjoy the scenery before heading back to the parking area. Allow an hour and a half to three hours to complete the walk.

Bear Lake Trail

To reach Bear Lake, drive north from the Flamingo Visitor Center about a mile and turn left onto a dirt road just before the Buttonwood Canal. Drive about two miles to the road end where limited parking is available. The trail begins just west of the parking and canoe launch area.

Christian Point Trail
Trail Distance: 2 miles one-way
Highlights: nature study, nature trail

Located just across the Buttonwood Canal, nearly 1.5 miles north from Flamingo Visitor Center, the Christian Point Trail winds through buttonwood forest and open coastal prairie enroute to Snake Bight and Florida Bay. The first quarter-mile of the trail is narrow and curving, somewhat hard to follow, with sign and paint blazes on tree branches. The trail enters a coastal prairie opening, dotted with numerous tree skeletons, the result of 200-m.p.h. hurricane force winds. During the 19th century, the dense pieces of buttonwood or mangrove were piled in heaps, covered with marl sand, and were burned slowly to form coal. This was then shipped to Key West for cooking fuel.

After another section of buttonwood forest, the trail emerges from the trees to join an old road that has been mowed for easy walking. This road, like many in the Flamingo area, was constructed by the wild cottonpickers in the 1930s. From here, the road leads through a fairly dense stand of trees that support clumps of epiphytic plants.

The last mile of the trail is open coastal prairie. Here there are salt-tolerant plants usually associated with deserts: cactus, agave and yucca. The trail ends at the mangrove-lined shores of Snake Bight Bay. If you arrive when the tide is part way out and the mud flats are exposed, numerous wading and shore birds can be seen feeding, indluding the southern bald eagle. It may be difficult to keep from getting muddy feet.

Guy Bradley Trail
Trail Distance: 1 mile one-way
Highlights: nature study, nature walk, museum, amphitheater, picnicking, shelters, ranger station, fishing, launch ramp, marina, grocery, fuel station, post office, restaurant, gift shop, bar lounge, camping, tours, boat rentals, motel, cottages
Fee(s): camping, tours, boat rentals, motel, cottages

Flamingo is in the southern portion of Everglades National Park, 38 paved road miles from the main entrance. The commercial center appears to be an unlikely location for a nature trail, but the Guy Bradley Trail links the commercial and lodging areas to the amphitheater and campgrounds. Guy Bradley was an Audubon game warden wbo died in the line of duty protecting the egret rookeries from plume poachers at the turn of the 19th century.

The one-mile paved path begins and ends at the visitors center, leading west alongside the parking lot and motel/cottage area. The all-weather path skirts Florida Bay, where vistas break the mangrove-lined shore revealing the watery world. Various wading birds may be seen feeding, especially at low tide. Interpretive stops are interspersed along the trail. Retrace your steps back along the linear route to the visitors center.

Be sure to visit the Flamingo Museum on the second floor of the visitors center for a greater understanding of the ecology of Florida Bay. Scheduled ranger tours begin at the visitors center.

Eco Pond
Trail Distance: .2 mile
Highlights: nature study, nature walk, ranger walks

Encircling Eco Pond is a short loop trail with benches and board-walk observation points where you can see migratory and resident birds and other wildlife through breaks in the cattail-lined shore, particularly during the dry winter months. Although the pond itself is man-made, the island near the center has natural vegetation that serves as a roost and refuge for the snowy egret, anhinga, roseate spoonbill, purple gallinule, great and little blue heron, green heron, grebe, cormorant, bittern, and ibis. Join in with ranger-led groups to gain a fuller understanding of the pond life.

Eco Pond was created as an evaporation pond and has no outlet. Since evaporation depends on area rather than depth, this pond has a surface area of eight acres, but an average depth of only two feet. The pond receives treated water from the Flamingo sewage plant in the final stage of sewage treatment, where evaporation takes place, before it returns to the Everglades water cycle.

Eco Pond is enroute to Flamingo campground from Flamingo Visitor Center. Similar pond walks are located alongside the main park road from the main entrance gate to Flamingo at Sisal Pond, Ficus Pond, Coot Bay Pond ,and Mrazek Pond.

Coastal Prairie Trail and Bayshore Loop
Trail Distance: 14 total miles
Highlights: nature study, nature walk, bicycling, primitive camp

The sandy shell beaches of Cape Sable and their sweeping views of Florida Bay await the hiker at the end of the six-mile (one-way) **Coastal Prairie Trail** or Main Trail. The well-marked path is actu-ally an old road that was constructed in the early 1930's for the "cottonpickers," who unsuccessfully attempted to control the northward movement of the pink cotton boll larvae and the wild cotton tree. Presently, cotton bollworms continue to pose a serious threat to the domestic cotton crops of the southern United States. You may encounter firsthand tree cotton and the bollworm along the trail. In recent years, the U.S.D.A. has attempted to control bollworm by releasing sterile male moths over the region, so no future generations will reproduce. To evaluate this approach, conspicuous white paper moth traps have been placed on shrubs and trees along the trail and throughout south Florida.

After three to four hours of walking through windswept coastal prairie and shady buttonwood hammocks, you will reach the sandy shores of Clubhouse Beach, the only designated primitive campsite on the trail. Clubhouse Beach is so named because of the accommodations that were built in 1912 by the Model Land Company for prospective land buyers who were lodged here. The building was not maintained and, after several devastating hurricanes,

Alligator, Coastal Prairie

the once-substantial lodgings were no longer. Today, only the old concrete foundation can be found on the beach. Overnight camping with ground fires is permitted only after obtaining a backcountry permit from the Flamingo Ranger Station at the campground entrance. The open higher ground of the marl flats directly in back of the beach provide better camping than the beach. You will need to bring your own drinking water. Depending on the seasonal rainfall, the trail may be muddy, slippery and mosquito infested, particularly in the buttonwood hammocks. The coastal prairie natural community invites observation. Wildlife is abundant here and the hiker may see such rarities as a southern bald eagle or phantom Florida panther.

The **Bayshore Loop Trail** shoots off from the Coastal Prairie Trail near the Flamingo camground trailhead. To take the Bayshore Loop, follow the trail west from the campground for a quarter-mile. There you will come to a junction where the loop trail forks to the left or south and the Coastal Prairie Trail continues 5.8 miles to Clubhouse Beach.

After a short walk along the Bayshore Loop, Florida Bay comes into view through the numerous openings between the black and red mangroves. Viewing the shore wildlife is the main attraction of this brief walk. The trail may vary between mowed roads and a narrow footpath along the half-mile of shoreline before it turns inland and rejoins the Coastal Prairie Trail. Go east back to the Flamingo campground. The Bayshore Loop and the Coastal Prairie Trail begin near site C-54 in Loop C of the Flamingo Campground.

Chekika
Trail Distance: 0.5 mile
Highlights: nature study, nature walk, museum, picnicking, shelters, swimming, fishing, camping, primitive youth camp
Fee(s): camping

This former state recreational area was transferred to the National Park Service in 1991. The site was hard hit by Hurricane Andrew but most of the facility was operational again in 1994. Like Shark Valley to the northwest, Chekika is isolated from the main visiting areas to the south. The upland area is actually a "tree island" or hammock oasis consisting of a tropical hardwood forest and a small lake surrounded by Everglades, willow heads, and other scattered tree islands.

Within the green "island" is an artesian spring that was unintentionally tapped by oil bunters in 1949. Each day for the last four decades, three million gallons of mineral sulpbur water has flowed from the spring into Lake Chekika. Chekika was a Spanish-Seminole Chieftain, who was active in the Second Seminole War (1835-1842). He was killed by American soldiers in a surprise raid at his encampment, 10 miles north of the present site.

The **Hammock Trail** begins and ends on the backside of the small museum that features exhibits and literature on the natural and social history of the Everglades. The hammock ecology is described, as is the geology of Rock Reef that overlays the hammock floor.

Chekika is 11 miles northwest of Homestead, Florida. From S.R. 997/Krome Avenue, go west on 168th Street/Richmond Drive and follow the directional signs for over six miles to the site. Ranger-guided walks and campfire programs are provided. This is a popular camping site during the cooler nearly bug-free dry season.

Southern Florida Environmental Organizations

Florida Trail Association

For those seeking accessible hiking trails to the "real" Florida, the Florida Trail Association is the hiker's best friend. The Association was founded in 1966 by 24 volunteers who had a vision of creating a hiking trail from the south end of the state to its north borders. Today over 5,000 members enjoy participating in the more than 100 outdoor activities sponsored annually by the FTA and its 13 local chapters throughout the state. Their present goal remains what it was when the Association was founded: to complete a 1,300-mile Florida National Scenic Trail.

In southern Florida, the Florida Trail System is not only the linear south-to-north pathway, but also numerous loop trails, several in state parks, forests, preserves and wildlife management areas. Nearly all the clearing, blazing, and maintainence of the trails is done by volunteers giving freely of their time. The Florida Trails described in this book are areas open to the general public. Many of the hikes herein appear in *Florida Hiking Trails: The Official Guide to the Florida Trail on Public Lands*, available at bookstores or from the central office in Gainesville, Florida.

Membership in the Florida Trail Association bas several benefits including hiking access to private lands restricted only to FTA members. A *Hiking Guide to the Florida Trail* is for sale to members only. Your membership is an important step towards completion of the Florida Trail. For further information please write:

The Florida Trail Association
P.O. Box 13708
Gainesville, FL 32604
(904) 378-8823 or 1-800-343-1882

The Nature Conservancy (Florida Chapter)

The Nature Conservancy is a non-profit conservation organization that works quietly to preserve natural lands and waters. The Conservancy concentrates on selecting jeopardized areas of the highest ecological value. Since its founding in 1951, the organization has won protection for over three million acres in the United States, Canada, and the Caribbean.

The Florida Chapter and its members have completed some 70 preservation projects, containing over 200,000 acres. Blowing Rocks, one of the Chapter's oldest projects, is the most visited area the Conservancy owns. Areas of biological sensitivity are usually not open to the public, but those properties that are open are accessible to non-members as well. The task of the Conservancy and its Florida members is to outrace the state's rapidly growing population and the accompanying development. For membership and information about publicly accessible lands write:

The Nature Conservancy
Florida Chapter
2699 Lee Road, Suite 500
Winter Park, FL 32789

Florida Audubon Society

Founded in 1900, the Florida Audubon Society is the oldest and largest conservation organization in the state. There are nearly 50 chapters throughout the state, totalling over 40,000 persons. Many activities are sponsored by local chapters for members and the general public. Some of the Society's affiliates include Possum Long, Babson Park, and Street Nature Centers, as well as the National Audubon Society's Corkscrew Swamp Sanctuary.

The Society is an established leader in conservation issues, natural resource protection, and environmental education. They want cooperative, positive relationships with industry, developers, and businesses involved in environmental issues and seek their financial help. But they do not hesitate to oppose activites which are contrary to the Audubon Society's philosophy and goals. For membership and additional information write:

Florida Audubon Society
1101 Audubon Way
Maitiand, Florida 32751

Helpful Books

Abbott, R. Tucker. *American Seashells*. Melbourne, FL: American Malacologists, Inc., 1972.

Abbott, R. Tucker. *Kingdom of the Seashell*. New York: Bonanza Books, 1982.

Abbott, R. Tucker. *Shells of Southeastern U.S., Bahamas & Caribbean*. Melbourne, FL: American Malecologists, Inc., 1984.

Allyn, Rube. *Saltwater Florida Fishes*. St. Petersburg: Great Outdoors Publishing, 1982.

Anderson, Robert. *Guide to Florida Mammals*. Winner Enterprises, 1985.

Anderson, Robert. *Guide to Florida Poisonous Snakes*. Winner Enterprises, 1985.

Anderson, Robert. *Guide to Florida Sea and Shorebirds*. Winner Enterprises, 1985.

Anderson, Robert. *Guide to Florida Seashells*. Winner Enterprises, 1985.

Anderson, Robert. *Guide to Florida Seashore Life*. Winner Enterprises, 1985.

Anderson, Robert. *Guide to Florida Turtles*. Winner Enterprises, 1985.

Anderson, Robert. *Guide to Florida Wading Birds*. Winner Enterprises, 1985.

Bell, C. Ritchie and Taylor, Bryan J. *Florida Wildflower and Roadside Plants*. Chapel Hill, North Carolina. Laurel Hill Press, 1982.

Boschung, Herbert, et al. *The Audubon Society Field Guide to North American Fishes, Whales and Dolphins*. New York: Alfred A. Knopf, 1987.

Brown, Robin C. *Florida's Fossils*. Sarasota, Florida. Pineapple Press, 1988.

Cafiero, L. ed. *Florida Annual Outdoor Guide*. Miami, Florida: Miami Herald Publishing Company, 1989.

Campbell, George R. *An Illustrated Guide to Some Poisonous Plants and Animals of Florida*. Sarasota, FL: Pineapple Press, 1983.

Carr, Archie, et al. *The Everglades*. New York: Time-Life Inc., 1973.

Carter, Luther J. *The Florida Experience: Land and Water Policy in a Growth State*. Baltimore, MD: The Johns Hopkins University Press, 1976.

Cooper, Harry. *1,001 Things to Do in Florida for Free*. Fox Lake, IL: Leatherstocking Press, 1982.

Dasmann, Raymond F. *No Further Retreat*. New York: Macmillan Company, 1971.

Delorme. *Florida Atlas and Gazetteer*. Freeport, ME: Delorme Mapping Company, 1987.

Douglas, Marjory Stoneman. *The Everglades – River of Grass*. New York: Rinehart and Company, 1947.

Doyle, Larry J., et. al. *Living With the West Florida Shore*. Durham, NC: Duke University Press, 1984.

Fernald, Edward A., ed. *Atlas of Florida*. Tallahasee, FL: Florida State University Foundation, 1981.

Fernald, Edward A. and Patton, Donald J., eds. *Water Resources Atlas of Florida*. Tallahasee, FL: Florida State University Foundation, 1984.

Fletcher, Colin. *The Complete Walker*. New York: Alfred A. Knopf, 1974.

Fleming, Glenn, Genalle, Pierre and Long, Robert W. *Wildflowers of Florida.* Miami, FL: Banyan Books, 1976.

Francis, Phil. *Florida Fish and Fishing.* New York: Macmillan Company, 1966.

Franz, Richard. *Volume 6: Invertebrates – Rare and Endangered Biota of Florida.* Gainesville, FL: University Presses of Florida, 1982.

Gantz, Charlotte Orr. *A Naturalist in Southern Florida.* Coral Gables, FL: University of Miami Press, 1977.

Gifford, John Clayton. *On Preserving Tropical Florida.* Coral Gables, FL: University of Miami Press, 1972.

Gilbert, Carter R. *Volume 4: Fishes – Rare and Endangered Biota of Florida.* Gainesville, FL: University Presses of Florida, 1978.

Glaros, Lou and Sphar, Doug. *A Canoeing and Kayaking Guide to the Streams of Florida. Volume II: Central and South Florida.* Durham, NC: Menasha Ridge Press, 1987.

Gleasner, Diana and Gleasner, Bill. *Off the Beaten Path, A Guide to Unique Places,* Chester, CT: Globe Pequot Press, 1986.

Grow, Gerald. *Florida Parks: A Guide to Camping in Nature.* Tallahasee, FL: Longleaf Publications, 1987.

Haast, William E. and Anderson, Robert. *Complete Guide to Snakes of Florida.* Miami, FL: Phoenix Publishing Company, 1981.

Hoffmeister, John Edward. *Land From the Sea.* Coral Gables, FL: University of Miami Press, 1974.

Hrdlicka, Ales. *The Anthropology of Florida.* New York: AMS Press, 1980.

Kale, Herbert W. *Volume 2: Birds – Rare and Endangered Biota of Florida.* Gainesville, FL: University Presses of Florida, 1978.

Kaplan, Eugene. *A Field Guide to Coral Reefs of the Caribbean and Florida.* Boston, MA: Houghton Mifflin Company, Peterson Field Guide Series, 1984.

Knox, Nancy and MeSwiney, Ethel. *Botany Handbook for Florida.* Tallahassee, FL: Florida Department of Agriculture, 1965.

Lakela, Olga and Long, Robert W. *A Flora of Tropical Florida.* Miami, FL: Banyan Books, 1978.

Lakela, Olga and Lono, Robert W. *Ferns of Florida.* Miami, FL: Banyan Books, 1976.

Lane, James. *A Birder's Guide to Florida.* Privately Printed: Distributed by L & P Press, Denver, Colorado, 1984.

Layne, James N. *Volume 1: Mammals – Rare and Endangered Biota of Florida.* Gainesville, FL: University Presses of Florida, 1978.

Lewis, Gordon. *Florida Fishing: Fresh and Saltwater.* St. Petersburg, FL: Great Outdoors Publishing, 1957.

Little, Elbert L. Jr. *Rare Tropical Trees of South Florida.* Washington, D.C.: U.S.D. A Forest Service Conservation Research, 1976.

Longstreet, R.J., ed. *Birds in Florida.* Tampa, FL: Trend House, 1969.

Marcus, Robert. *The Encyclopedia of Florida.* New York: Somerset Publishers, 1985.

Maxwell, Lewis S. *Florida's Poisonous Plants, Snakes, Insects.* Privately Printed: 1963.

McDiarmid, Roy W. *Volume 3: Amphibians and Reptiles – Rare and Endangered Biota of Florida.* Gainesville, FL: University Presses of Florida, 1978.

McMullen, James P. *Cry of the Panther.* New York: McGraw-Hill, 1985.

Milanich, Jerald T. and Fairbanks, Charles H. *Florida Archaeology.* New York: Academic Press, 1980.

Morris, Allen Covington. *Florida Place Names.* Coral Gables, FL: University of Miami Press, 1974.

Morrison, Ken. *Mountain Lake Almanac.* Sarasota, FL: Pineapple Press, 1984.

Morton, Julia F. *Plants Poisonous to People in Florida.* Stuart, FL: Privately Printed, 1982.

Morton, Julia P. *Wild Plants for Survival in South Florida.* Stuart, FL: Privately Printed, 1982.

Murray, Marion. *Florida Fossils.* Tampa, FL: Trend House, 1975.

Office of Coastal Studies, University of West Florida. *Florida's Sandy Beaches: An Access Guide.* Pensacola, FL: University of West Florida, 1984.

Pilkey, Orrin H. Jr., et. al. *Living With the East Florida Shore.* Durham, NC: Duke University Press, 1984.

Pisces Book Staff and Johnston, Grea. *Diving and Snorkeling Guide to Florida's East Coast.* New York: PBC International, Inc., 1987.

Pope, Patricia E. *Seashore and Wading Birds of Florida.* St. Petersburg, FL: Great Outdoors Publishing Company, 1974.

Pyle, Robert Michael. *Audubon Society Field Guide to North American Butterflies.* New York: Alfred A. Knopf, 1981.

Rabkin, Richard and Rabkin, Jacob. *Nature Guide to Florida.* Miami, FL: Banyan Books, 1978.

Rawlings, Marjorie Kinnan. *Cross Creek.* New York: Macmillan Publishing Company, 1961.

Read, W.A. *Florida Place Names of Indian Origin and Seminole Personal Names.* New York: Gordon Press, 1977.

Render, Harold A. *The Audubon Society Field Guide to North American Seashells.* New York: Alfred A. Knopf, 1987.

Scalpone, Joan Lundquist. *Lets Go Somewhere.* Privately Printed: 1986.

Shomon, J.J. *Open Land for Urban America.* Baltimore, MD: The Johns Hopkins University Press, 1971.

Silver, Vicki. *Back to the Water: Discovering Florida Urban Waterfronts.* Tallahassee, FL: Florida Department of Community Affairs, 1986.

Simpson, Charles Torrey. *Out of Doors in Florida: The Adventures of a Naturalist.* Darby, PA: Arden Library, n.d.

Stachowicz, Jim. *Guide to Florida Campgrounds.* Miami, FL: Windward Publishing, Inc., 1987.

Stevenson, Henry M. *Vertebrates of Florida.* Gainesville, FL: University Presses of Florida 1977.

Swartz, Maurice L. ed. *The Encyclopedia of Beaches and Coastal Environments.* Stroudsburg, PA: Hutchinson Ross Publishing Company, 1982.

Tolf, Robert W. *Discover Florida: A Guide to Unique Sites.* Fort Lauderdale, FL: Manatee Books, 1982.

Toner, Mike and Tonor, Pat. *Florida by Paddle and Pack.* Chester, CT: Globe Pequot Press, l984.

Truitt, John 0. and Ober, Louis D. *A Guide to Lizards of South Florida.* Miami, FL: Hurricane House Publishers, Inc. 1971.

Voegelin, Byron. *South Florida's Vanished People.* Ft. Myers Beach, FL: Island Press, 1977.

Voss, Gilbert L. *Seashore Life of Florida and the Caribbean.* Miami, FL: Banyan Books, 1976.

Ward, Daniel B. *Volume 5: Plants – Rare and Endangered Biota of Florida.* Gainesville, FL: University Presses of Florida, 1978.

Workman, Richard. *Growing Native.* Sanibel, FL: Sanibel-Captiva Conservation Foundation, Inc., 1980.

Williams, Joy. *The Florida Keys: A History and Guide.* New York: Random House, 1997.

Zak, Bill. *Florida Critters.* Dallas, TX: Taylor Publishing Company, 1986.

Additional Resources

INSIDER'S GUIDE TO FLORIDA
Packed with spectacular photographs and maps in full color, this extraordinary guide combines special sections on the history of each region in the state with practical detail: what to see, where to stay, where to eat in each area. 6 x 9 paperback with large fold-out map/224 pp/$15.95/1-55650-452-7

THE FLORIDA WHERE TO STAY BOOK
The best guide ever published on where to bed down for a night, a week, or more in Florida. Accommodations information on thousands of places to stay in literally every town and city in the state – hotels, motels, resorts, bed & breakfasts, even rental apartments and country inns... from $20 rooms to $1,000-a-day hotel suites. Each listing details the facilities and special features offered, plus the address, phone, and prices. Also included for each area are names and phone numbers of rental sources that can provide anything from a high-rise condo on the beach to a private home rental. Over 1,000 fax and toll-free numbers you can call for free literature, information, and reservations. 5 1/2 x 8 paperback/450 pp/$12.95/1-55650-539-6

Adventure Guide To The EVERGLADES & FLORIDA KEYS
South Florida's national parks and natural wonders. Includes diving and snorkeling tours, self-guided cycling and hiking trails, canoe and kayak expeditions, deep-sea and mangrove fishing, parasailing, shelling, Key West's historic Pelican Path, sightseeing flights, sunset cruises and boat tours. Where to spot alligators, dolphins, exotic wading birds, manatees, and much more. Accommodations, campgrounds, dining, and attractions as well.

"The Everglades will always be mysterious, but finding them? – It doesn't have to be! This book makes it easy to discover the whole region, even the secret places like Corkscrew Swamp." Ed Carlson, National Audubon Society
"Vastly informative, absolutely user-friendly, and chock full of the kind of interesting information that makes me want to put the book under my arm, pack my gear and leave immediately to investigate those places so well described... from trails to historic sites to underwater adventure, it is all there." Dr. Susan Cropper, Society of Aquatic Veterinarians

"A great book – practical and easy to use. Ther perfect traveler's guide to these two beautiful and ecologically sensitive areas." Ted Wesemann, Wilderness Southeast

5 1/2 x 8 paperback/192 pp/maps & color photos/$14.95/1-55650-494-2

BEST DIVES OF THE WESTERN HEMISPHERE

"A scuba enthusiast's encyclopedia – every coral reed, ship wreck and exotic fish has been identified for the edification of expert and novice divers alike." H.V. Pat Reilly, Travel Journalist

"Make sure you consult this little gem of a book. Its contributors from the world's scuba diving community will guide you to and through some of the best dives of the Western Hemisphere. Concise and informative... one of the few bargains of the 90s." Wendy Canning Church, Divers Exchange International

The ultimate scuba and snorkeling guide to the best dive sites as recommended by top divemasters in Florida, the Caribbean, Belize, Cozumel, Hawaii, California, and Latin America. Maps of each site; 100-plus color photos. 320 pp/$17.95/1-55650-250-8

Adventure Guide to COSTA RICA (2nd Edition)

"This extensive up-to-date guide for Costa Rica is a welcome sight. Selected accommodations and restaurants span the scale from luxury to low budget, while the author's respectful, ecologically aware perspective contributes a progressive view of the mountains and lowlands, rain forests and beaches." American Library Association Booklist

"May be the best-balanced, most comprehensive guide of the entire Tico bunch. Excellent sections on the national parks, flora and fauna, and Costa Rica's history. This is the one to take with you on your next trip." Lan Sluder, Great Expeditions and Compuserve

"Straightforward, easy to use... valuable practical tips... beautiful color photos." Tico Times

"A good combination of practical travel information, background, and descriptions of sights and activities. Travelers will find all the information they need to prepare for a trip.... For its mix of practical information and the range of travel activities described, the book is difficult to beat." Travel Library

The definitive guide to Costa Rica, now completely updated. Filled with maps & color photos. 480 pp/$15.95/1-55650-598-1

Adventure Guide to BELIZE (2nd Edition)
Indisputably the best companion on a trip to Belize, this guide will introduce you to its vibrant history, culture and wildlife. All types of accommodations, from camping to top resorts. Dining for gourmets, vegetarians and lovers of Creole cooking. The best hiking trails, tips on birdwatching spots, and horseback riding. Travel to and from the outlying islands, parks, reserves, and archaeological sites. Car rental, taxi, bus & air flight information, plus island hopping by ferry. Maps & color photos. 288 pp/$14.95/1-55650-493-4

Other books in the Adventure Guide Series:

BARBADOS 224 pp/$16.95/1-55650-277-X
DOMINICAN REPUBLIC 256 pp/$13.95/1-55650-537-X
JAMAICA 288 pp/$17.95/1-55650-499-3
PUERTO RICO 320 pp/$15.95/1-55650-628-7
VIRGIN ISLANDS 288 pp/$14.95/1-55650-597-3

THE GREAT AMERICAN WILDERNESS:
TOURING AMERICA'S NATIONAL PARKS
Other guides offer pretty pictures, but information too sketchy to be useful. The Great American Wilderness thoroughly describes the sights and the facilities of each park, but then explains in detail how to tour them: how much time to allow, what to see and do if you have only a few hours (or if you have several days to spend), how to avoid the crowds, what each place is really like, what you can safely skip, and what you must not miss.

Complete directions on getting to and from the park are included, as well as how to get around once you're there, where to eat, and where to bed down for the night. Maps show each park's features, along with all surrounding access routes. Are you wondering about the best time to visit a particular park? The author tells what conditions are like during each season and recommends the ideal times to go.

A unique section – Suggested Trips – contains special itineraries, describing ways to combine visits to one or more parks with tours of other nearby attractions, complete with driving routes and recommended places to stay each night.

From *Acadia* to *Bryce Canyon, Mammoth Cave* to *Zion National Park,* this is the one indispensable guide to exploring their riches. 300 pp/$11.95/1-55650-567-1

Write Hunter Publishing, 300 Raritan Center Parkway, Edison NJ 08818 or call (908) 225 1900 for our free color catalog describing these and hundreds of other unusual travel guides and maps to all parts of the world. Find them in the best bookstores or you can order direct from the address above (add $2.50 to cover shipping/handling).